THE RAGING TORRENT

THE RAGING TORRENT

Historical Inscriptions from Assyria and Babylonia Relating to Ancient Israel

SECOND UPDATED & EXPANDED EDITION

Translated and Annotated
by
Mordechai Cogan

A CARTA HANDBOOK

Second updated and expanded edition 2015

First published in 2008 by
CARTA Jerusalem

Frontispiece: Soldiers swimming across river, from the Northwest Palace of Ashurnasirpal at Calah (*Courtesy of the Trustees of the British Museum*).

ISBN: 978-965-220-868-2

Printed in Israel

Table of Contents

Preface

The seasonal flooding of the Tigris and the Euphrates rivers, fed by the melting snows of the high mountains of central and eastern Anatolia, posed a logistic difficulty to wayfarers of every sort down to modern times, even more so to advancing armies on campaign that sought to cross the raging torrents with men, animals and equipment. In the face of nature's challenge, it comes as no surprise that Assyria's kings included among their heroic feats such claims as: "I crossed the Tigris and the Euphrates in full flood, the high waters of spring, as if it were dry land" (Sargon II); "They (the troops) safely crossed the Tigris and the Euphrates in high flood" (Ashurbanipal).

The raging torrents of Mesopotamia's mighty rivers also found a place in the rhetoric of the prophets of Ancient Israel. But here the image was always threatening. For example, one finds Isaiah, in the late 8th century BCE, warning his audience: "The mighty, massive waters of the Euphrates, the king of Assyria and his multitude—it shall rise above its channels, and flow over its beds, and swirl through Judah like a flash flood reaching up to the neck" (Isa 8:7–8). A hundred years later, Jeremiah referred to the impending Babylonian advance in similar terms: "See, waters are rising from the North, they shall become a raging torrent, they shall flood the land and its creatures, the towns and their inhabitants" (Jer 47:2).

To be sure, the very real dangers thrown up by the Tigris and the Euphrates are behind these contrasting images, each one reflecting in its own way the perspectives of different authors and their intended audiences. The rivers' raging torrents could not arrest the advance of the kings of Assyria and Babylonia who were set on conquering the four quarters of the world; nor could the inhabitants of the Land of Israel hold back the conquering flood that would overwhelm them time and again. In what follows, the heroic view of the Mesopotamians takes stage center.

The present volume brings together all the cuneiform historical texts composed during the 9th to 6th centuries BCE that relate to Ancient Israel. This is the period during which Assyria and Babylonia cast their imperial shadow over the Near East and brought the kingdoms of Israel and Judah under their control. Some of the texts have direct bearing on biblical accounts (e.g., the fall of Samaria; Sennacherib's attack on Judah), while many others inform on events that the ancient Israelite historians chose not to include in their works (e.g., the tribute payments of Jehu, king of Israel, and Manasseh, king of Judah). But the net has been cast wide, beyond the borders of Ancient Israel, to include texts dealing with Tyre, Damascus, Ashdod and others among its neighbors. The time span, too, has been stretched a bit, to include two texts from the beginning of the Persian Period that are, as it turns out, propagandistic Babylonian compositions (e.g., the Cyrus cylinder). For in this International Age ruled over by great empires, no kingdom lived in splendid isolation; all lived under the watchful eye of the Great King and the affairs in the Land of Israel were no exception.

All the texts have been newly translated from the latest scholarly editions of the original documents; each is accompanied by an introduction and a commentary, i.e., explanatory and interpretative notes that enable the reader to follow the course of events. In most cases, the full document is presented, so that the relevant passage may be seen in its context. This also permits a better appreciation of the various styles and rhetoric used in cuneiform historical writing.

Though a continuous history of Ancient Israel is not offered here, the critical treatment of the individual documents goes a long way towards clarifying the nature of these building blocks of history, a task that is the prerequisite for erecting the historical edifice.

ACKNOWLEDGMENTS

I have had the privilege of reading the texts gathered together in this handbook with a generation of students at Ben-Gurion University of the Negev and The Hebrew University of Jerusalem; together we probed the intricacies of Mesopotamian historical traditions. This teaching experience ultimately led to the publication of a collection of historical texts in Hebrew translation in the Biblical Encyclopedia Library, vol. 19 (Jerusalem 2003). For the present volume, prepared for a wider readership, I have thoroughly revised and expanded that work.

The careful reading of the manuscript by my colleague Prof. Israel Eph^{c}al prompted the clarification of a number of authorial lapses for which I am most grateful.

The copyediting and layout of this book were skillfully realized by Barbara Laurel Ball of the Carta staff to whom much credit is due.

I acknowledge with thanks generous subventions by the Intramural Research Funds of The Hebrew University of Jerusalem and the Ben-Zion Dinur Center for Research in Jewish History, which helped make the publication of this book possible.

Finally, I dedicate this work to the memory of Prof. Hayim Tadmor, eminent historian of the ancient Near East, whose inspired guidance and friendship are enduring.

Mordechai Cogan

Supplement to the Second Edition

The warm critical reception of *The Raging Torrent* (2008), as well as the remarks of colleagues who have used it in the classroom, encouraged me to update and expand the first edition of this book. Consequently, in numerous instances, I have added to the discussions and bibliographies and have augmented the original presentation with a considerable number of texts (e.g., king lists). As in the past, Carta Jerusalem and its efficient staff continue to encourage this enterprise, for which I am most grateful.

In all, the guiding principle of this work has been the mutual elucidation of the interactions between Ancient Israel and the Mesopotamian empires.

M. C.
Omer and Jerusalem
June 2015

LIST OF ABBREVIATIONS

ÄAT	Ägypten und Altes Testament
ABD	*Anchor Bible Dictionary*. Edited by D. N. Freedman, 6 vols. New York, 1992
ADAJ	*Annual of the Department of Antiquities of Jordan*
AfO	*Archiv für Orientforschung*
ANEP	*The Ancient Near East in Pictures*. Edited by James B. Pritchard. 2nd ed. Princeton 1969
ANET	*Ancient Near Eastern Texts Relating to the Old Testament*. Edited by James B. Pritchard. 3rd ed. Princeton 1969
AOAT	*Alter Orient und Altes Testament*
ARAB	*Ancient Records of Assyria and Babylonia*. Daniel David Luckenbill. 2 vols. Chicago 1926–1927
ARRIM	*Annual Review of the Royal Inscriptions of Mesopotamia Project*
AS	Assyriological Studies
BA	*The Biblical Archaeologist*
BAR	*Biblical Archaeology Review*
BASOR	*Bulletin of the American Schools of Oriental Research*
Bib	*Biblica*
BJPES	*Bulletin of the Jewish Palestine Exploration Society*
CBQ	*Catholic Biblical Quarterly*
CHANE	Culture and History of the Ancient Near East
COS	*The Context of Scripture*. Edited by W. W. Hallo and K. L. Younger. 3 vols. Leiden 1997–2002
CUSAS	Cornell University Studies in Assyriology and Sumerology
DOTT	*Documents from Old Testament Times*. Edited by D. Winton Thomas. London 1958
ErIsr	*Eretz-Israel*
HSM	Harvard Semitic Monographs
HTAT	*Historisches Textbuch zum Alten Testament*. Edited by Manfred Weippert, Grundrisse zum Alten Testament 10, Göttingen 2010
IEJ	*Israel Exploration Journal*
JANESCU	*Journal of the Ancient Near Eastern Society of Columbia University*
JAOS	*Journal of the American Oriental Society*
JARCE	*Journal of the American Research Center in Egypt*
JBL	*Journal of Biblical Literature*
JJS	*Journal of Jewish Studies*
JCS	*Journal of Cuneiform Studies*

JEH	*Journal of Egyptian History*
JNES	*Journal of Near Eastern Studies*
JSOT	*Journal for the Study of the Old Testament*
JSOTSup	Journal for the Study of the Old Testament: Supplement Series
JSSEA	*Journal of the Society for the Study of Egyptian Antiquities*
KAI	*Kanaanäische und aramäische Inschriften.* Edited by H. Donner and W. Röllig. 3 vols. 2nd ed. Wiesbaden 1966–1969
N.A.B.U.	*Notes assyriologiques brèves et utiles*
NEA	*Near Eastern Archaeology*
NEAEHL	*The New Encyclopedia of Archaeological Excavations in the Holy Land.* Edited by E. Stern, 4 vols. Jerusalem 1993
OIP	Oriental Institute Publications
Or	*Orientalia* (NS)
PEQ	*Palestine Exploration Quarterly*
RA	*Revue d'assyrilogie et d'archéologie orientale*
RlA	*Reallexikon der Assyriologie*
RIMA	The Royal Inscriptions of Mesopotamia. Assyrian Periods
RINAP	The Royal Inscriptions of the Neo-Assyrian Period
SAA	State Archives of Assyria
SAAB	*State Archives of Assyria Bulletin*
SAAS	State Archives of Assyria Studies
ScrHier	*Scripta Hierosolymitana*
SBLMS	Society of Biblical Literature Monograph Series
TGI	*Textbuch zur Geschichte Israels.* Edited by Kurt Galling, 2nd ed. Tübingen 1968
TPOA	*Textes du Proche-Orient Ancien et histoire d'Israël.* Edited by J. Briend and M-J Seux. Paris 1977
TUAT	*Texte aus der Umwelt des Alten Testaments.* Edited by R. Borger, W. Hinz, W. H. P. Römer. 1/4, Gütersloh 1984 NF II. Edited by Bernd Janowski and Gernot Wilhelm, 2005
UF	*Ugarit-Forschungen*
VAB	Vorderasiatische Bibliothek
VT	*Vetus Testamentum*
VTSup	Vetus Testamentum, Supplements
WO	*Die Welt des Orients*
ZA	*Zeitschrift für Assyriologie*
ZAW	*Zeitschrift für die alttestamentliche Wissenschaft*
ZDPV	*Zeitschrift des deutschen Palästina-Vereins*

NOTE ON TRANSLATIONS

1) Transcriptions of names of persons and toponyms mostly follow the standard English translation of the Hebrew Bible. In other cases, they reflect the cuneiform, with vowel length being omitted.

2) Individual and / or unreadable cuneiform signs are indicated by *x*.

3) Italicized words in translations indicate doubt about the interpretation or the suggested reconstruction.

4) In a number of instances, the configuration of the original document is represented, e.g., the column arrangement of the Eponym Chronicle (Text no. 10.1); the line arrangement of the Babylonian Chronicles (Text nos. 11.01–11.06); the fragmentary state of the Summary Inscriptions of Tiglath-pileser III (Text nos. 4.05–4.08). Translations have suffered accordingly.

LIST OF MAPS AND FIGURES

Maps

Figures

Fig. 1. Two Assyrian scribes listing the fallen during battle. Detail of relief from the palace of Sennacherib at Nineveh (*Courtesy of the Trustees of the British Museum*).

Introduction

The cuneiform inscriptions of Assyria and Babylonia serve as key witnesses to the course of events upon which they report, a role assigned to them by modern historians. Most students of ancient history acknowledge that history *per se* was not always, if ever, the purpose for the composition of these inscriptions, yet they return again and again to cross-examine these texts in search of the "facts of history," that is, after getting over the rhetorical hurdle, they hope to meet up with the events themselves.[1]

The formal categories of the inscriptions, which comprise the bulk of the texts treated in the following study, are Assyrian royal inscriptions—annals and summary texts—and Babylonian chronicles.

ASSYRIAN ROYAL INSCRIPTIONS

The royal inscriptions were, first and foremost, ideological compositions, designed to memorialize the achievements of the reigning monarch. Their authors were scribes in the employ of the monarch, charged with extolling their lord, whose valorous deeds in the service of the gods were rewarded with "length of days" and "everlasting kingship." The texts they composed were emblazoned on the walls of palaces and temples, inscribed on large clay tablets and prisms, appeared on statues of the king and giant mythological figures that stood as guardians at thresholds and gates, and were displayed on stelae erected in conquered territories. Even the sides of high mountain passes in distant lands served as broadsides for these royal communications.

1 In his discussion of the "objectivity and accuracy" of Mesopotamian chronicles, Glassner cogently puts forward the case for crediting the ancient author's subjectivity, because "he himself is imbued with the idea that he is writing 'reality'" (2004:48–51).

All in the name of publicizing the royal personage and his achievements, now and forever more.

A first reading of the royal inscriptions leaves one with the impression that the style of writing—the imagery and figures of speech, as well as the word stock—was altogether uniform and formulaic. But while this is in good part true,[2] upon closer study, the presence of unique elements hidden under the cover of unity reveals itself. It is in them that the individual personality of each king found its expression; for the king was not only the patron, he was also the final arbiter when it came to choosing the events surveyed in the inscriptions and their manner of presentation. This is not to diminish the contribution of the scribes to the process of creating a royal inscription, for in the end, it was they who were responsible for the final product. The evidence shows that they could produce descriptions of the same event in a whole variety of versions, long and short, and in innumerable combinations. It is for this reason that one often finds more than a single description of a particular event, which at times contradict one another. It is at this juncture that historical criticism steps in, in an attempt to recover history "as it actually happened."[3]

Among the Assyrian royal inscriptions, two types stand out: the annals and the summary texts.

1. ANNALS

DEFINITION. Annalistic writing is undoubtedly the hallmark of the Assyrian empire. For over five hundred years, beginning in the reign of Tiglath-pileser I (1115–1076 BCE), dozens upon dozens of so-called "annals" were composed. From a formal point of view, the annals appear to be an inner-Assyrian development.[4] They share several features with inscriptions

2 The utilization by the scribes of a given set of words and phrases and its manipulation in accord with an accepted "literary code" were shown to be operative in the texts of Ashurbanipal by Fales 1981 and in those of Sargon II by Renger 1986.

3 For a useful classification of the Assyrian and Babylonian historical literature, see Grayson 1980; see, too, the earlier remarks of Oppenheim 1964:143–153. Tadmor (1997) surveyed the advances in literary and historiographic study of the corpus of Assyrian royal inscriptions during the last quarter of the twentieth century. For a programmatic agenda for future study, see Fales 1999–2001.

4 Güterbock's suggestion (1938:98) of a Hittite influence on the development of the Assyrian annals was never shown. See, too, Speiser 1955:65, n. 79 and Tadmor 1997:325.

of the dedicatory type[5] that were the predominant form of commemoration in Mesopotamia.

Dedicatory inscriptions were already in use at the end of the third millennium BCE among the Sumerian city rulers and are in evidence as late as the days of the Neo-Babylonian kings in the sixth century. The dedicatory form was relatively prosaic: on an object dedicated to the temple, the donor inscribed his name and invoked his god for blessing. Thus one finds utensils and various cult objects (e.g., tables, altars), as well as whole buildings (temples and palaces) and public works (city gates, walls, bridges, aqueducts), whether repaired or built from scratch—all seen as gifts to the gods—accompanied by dedicatory inscriptions. For example, Shalmaneser III (858–824 BCE) inscribed on several stone mace heads (found at Tarbiṣu): "To the god Nergal, who dwells in the city of Tarbiṣu, his lord: Shalmaneser, great king, strong king, king of the universe, king of Assyria. He dedicated for his life, that his days may be long, his years many, for the well-being of his offspring and his land" (Grayson 1996:154, no. 96); Esarhaddon incised on a stone door socket in a temple at Ashur: "To the god Ashur, his lord: Esarhaddon, king of the world, king of Assyria, governor of Babylon, king of all of Karduniash, king of the kings of Egypt, Pathros and Cush, king of the four quarters of the world, for his life, the prolongation of his days, and the well-being of his offspring, he placed and presented (this socket)" (Leichty 2011:145, no. 68).

Already at its first appearance, annalistic writing introduced several stylistic innovations. During the last two centuries of the second millennium BCE, the scribes sought to create compositions in which the triumphs of the king in battle and his building enterprises were the central themes, acknowledging, at the same time, that these were achieved with the help of the gods.[6] Thus an inscription of the new type opened with an invocation of the gods, as did the dedicatory inscriptions, followed by a passage that introduced the king and his titles, stressing his bravery and his selection by the gods. Next

5 This was pointed out by Mowinckel 1923:313–316; Grayson's criticism (1980:143) of Mowinckel is excessive.

6 Tadmor (1997:327–328) suggested that two known genres, the heroic epic and the chronicle, influenced the scribes as they created the new genre. Speiser (1955:67) took the theme of royal heroism, which is so prominent in the Assyrian annals, as deriving "not so much from the conceit of the ruler as from his excessive piety." The king's victories were, in the end, those of the gods.

comes the heart of the annal inscription. In order to exemplify the king's claim to greatness, many paragraphs laid out in full the king's victories on the battlefield. Towards the end, a description of the construction project, whose dedication was the formal excuse for composing the inscription, was given, and of course, the blessing of the god by his royal servant. As a rule, the annal inscription was written in the first-person, though one does find here and there that the third-person voice has slipped in, likely a sign of the source from which the description was taken before being introduced into the annalistic text.

In the inscriptions of Tiglath-pileser I, a division between the various campaigns was clearly marked. The scribe drew a horizontal line on the tablet between the campaigns, and began each new campaign with a short praise of the king in elevated style. The campaigns were not dated. Dating was introduced in the inscriptions of his successors, indicated either by the eponym year or the year of the king's reign. Thus the genre "annals" was fully born.

SOURCES. Information on the course of a campaign and the outcome of the battles was in all probability supplied by journals kept by the scribes who had accompanied the army on its march. A wall relief from the palace of Sennacherib at Nineveh shows such military scribes at work (see Fig. 1). Two scribes are seen writing down the items of spoil being carried out of the conquered city, as well as the number of captives who passed before them.[7] One of the scribes holds a writing board on which he wrote in Assyrian cuneiform;[8] the other scribe holds a scroll that served for writing Aramaic, the second language of the Assyrian bureaucracy.[9] Registers of these sorts have not survived, but the lists of booty that appear now and then in the annals must have been taken from such first-hand records. It is also likely

7 See Fig. 1 and *ANEP*, no. 236.

8 Writing boards were wax-covered and allowed for continuous writing over an extended period of time without concern for the drying out of the writing medium, as was the case with clay. For a permanent record, the information on the writing board was transferred to clay. See discussions of Wiseman 1955; MacGinnis 2002; and illustration in *ANEP*, no. 803.

9 By the end of the 8th century BCE, the vast number of Arameans in the Assyrian empire required the adoption of Aramaic as a diplomatic and administrative *lingua franca*; for the evidence, see Tadmor 1982. Note the repartee between the head of the Assyrian delegation and Hezekiah's representatives described in 2 Kgs 18:26–28 over the choice of the language in which to hold their negotiations

that the camp scribes kept other records; for example, the itinerary of the king and the army. Whole sections of the annals of Ashurnasirpal II point to existence of such a genre; thus, e.g., "On the fifteenth day of the month Tishri, I moved on from the city Kalzi (and) entered the pass of the city Babitu. Moving on from the city Babitu, I approached Mount Niṣir, which the Lullu call Mount Kiniba. I conquered the city Bunasi, their fortified city which was ruled by Muṣaṣina (and) 30 cities in its environs.... Moving on from this camp, I marched to the cities in the plain of Mount Niṣir which no one had ever seen. I conquered the city Larbusa ... (Grayson 1991:204, ii 33b–35, 39).

EDITIONS OF THE ANNALS. It became the practice to edit and update the annal inscriptions every number of years, especially after a major victory; at first this may have been done on a five- or ten-year cycle.[10] In the new edition of the annals, a summary of the events, based on the previous edition, was followed by extensive descriptions of the latest successes. But if the king's reign turned out to be exceptionally long, it became necessary to make room for the new reports by cutting back on the old ones, sometimes quite drastically. For example, in the late editions of the inscriptions of Shalmaneser III, which survey over thirty years of military activity, the abridgment reaches as much as ninety percent. It is, therefore, advisable for historical reconstructions to be based on the early editions of the annals when available, not only because of the tendency to shorten the report in the later editions, but also because the later editions are not always reliable, e.g., the number of enemy dead sometimes grows from edition to edition.[11] At the same time, the late editions should not be entirely disregarded. Careful comparison of the various editions reveals that reliable information that was not included in the first editions at times found its way into later editions.[12]

ORDER OF CAMPAIGNS AND CHRONOLOGY. During the final century of the Assyrian empire, from the reign of Sargon II until Ashurbanipal, new ways of ordering and numbering the king's campaigns were introduced into the annals. No longer was a sequential year-by-year order followed. In the inscriptions of Sargon II, though the "year of reign" (*palû*) formula is used

10 See Tadmor 1977:210.

11 This point was stressed by Olmstead in his pioneering study on Assyrian historiography, 1916:8.

12 For some examples of this phenomenon, see Cogan 1991:121–123

in the annal texts, descriptions were moved up from later years to earlier ones in order to fill in the empty space, as it were, in those years in which the king did not take the field. In the case of Sennacherib, his scribes hid similar gaps by counting the campaigns with ordinal numbers, e.g., "my first campaign," "my second campaign," etc., though they did preserve the actual chronological order of the activities. Still later, the scribes of Ashurbanipal created an entirely new system: the descriptions of the campaigns were organized according to geographical regions, as was the practice in the Summary Texts (on which see below), and each of these campaigns was given an ordinal number that had no relation to actual chronology. In addition, in the late editions of the annals of Ashurbanipal there are instances in which the description of an entire campaign that had appeared in the early editions was deleted. Surely the conventional term "annals" applied to these compositions looks like a misnomer.[13]

2. SUMMARY TEXTS

DEFINITION. In early studies, the designation "Display Inscriptions" (*Prunkinschriften*) was popularly applied to the Summary Texts, but this label is not at all appropriate. For in addition to examples of summary texts (and annals!) engraved on walls—prominently displayed for all to gaze upon—many summary texts were written on stone slabs or clay tablets, some of which were buried in the foundations of buildings.[14]

The typical summary text includes: the name of the king and his titles; a summary of his military activities; report on building project(s); prayer and blessing of the god. In some summary texts, the military aspect is handled in a few lines and is restricted to a single geographic area; in others, the description extends to dozens of lines and includes a full coverage of the battle, which may parallel the annal of the same event. The choice between these two options seems to have been dictated by the space available for the entire inscription. The order of presentation of the summaries is generally geographic, with the chronological considerations set aside.

13 Renger uses the general term "*Kommemorativinschriften*" for the entire corpus of Assyrian royal inscriptions, seemingly avoiding the pitfalls of genre analysis (1980–83:73–75).

14 From the practice of depositing texts in foundation boxes or leaving them in inaccessible places, Oppenheim concluded that the addressee of the royal inscriptions was the gods to whom "they report the king's victories and his piety and demand blessings in return" (1964:148).

BABYLONIAN CHRONICLES

This genre was most prominent in Babylonia, and though it was known in Assyria as well, it did not take root there.[15]

DEFINITION. The most prominent characteristic of the Babylonian Chronicles, which distinguishes them from other chronographic texts, such as king lists (Chapter 12, ahead) and the eponym chronicles (Chapter 10, ahead), is the recital of discrete, unrelated events arranged according to the years of the king's reign. These accounts are concise; they lack polemics and express neither praise nor disparagement, traits that suggest their non-royal genesis. The most-frequently treated topics in the Babylonian Chronicles are: military campaigns, changes in the regime, and sundry governmental matters. Other affairs of state are sometimes noted, e.g., the death of the queen or the queen mother. In the chronicle covering the reign of Nabonidus, alongside affairs of state, the interruption of the *Akitu* festival is noted for each of the ten years that the king was absent from Babylon (Text no. 11.06). The years of the non-celebration of the *Akitu* festival during the seventh century BCE is the subject of a separate chronicle (Grayson 1975:131–132, no. 16). There is even a chronicle in which the market prices in specific years were collected (Grayson 1975:178–179, no. 23). This variety of subjects does seem to suggest that these texts were drawn up in different scribal circles, for different purposes, in Babylon and in other cities as well.[16]

The style of the Babylonian Chronicles, which survey the history of Babylon for almost five hundred years—from the middle of the eighth century BCE to the Seleucid Period in the second century BCE—is surprisingly uniform. Though there are significant gaps in the extant texts, one can observe a consistent use over the centuries of a number of formulaic expressions that describe the mobilization of the army, the battles, the victories, as well as the defeats and retreats. Consistency of this sort surely points to a chronistic tradition, which was firmly established in Babylonian literary circles, and which survived the frequent upheavals in rule brought about by frequent foreign conquests.

15 See the discussion of Tadmor 1977 for the evidence on chronicles in Assyria in the late second millennium BCE.

16 Most of the chronicle texts are unprovenanced; Waerzeggers (2012) has argued that a fairly large number of them were written in Borsippa by scribes whose interests included "calendrical, metrological, and astronomical matters besides history."

The chronistic compositions of the Neo-Babylonian period are often credited with reporting events in a "reliable and objective manner" (Grayson 1975:8). As an example of this objectivity, the entry for 601 BCE is hailed: the failure of the Babylonian army in its attempt to invade Egypt (Text no. 11.05, rev. lines 5–7). According to this estimation, the Babylonian Chronicles are the sole example of history for history's sake in Mesopotamian tradition, and for that matter in all of the ancient Near East (Grayson 1980:175). Yet such excessive evaluations might be overstating the case. Selective reporting and/or editing can be detected in some chronicles. For example, the author of the "Esarhaddon Chronicle" (Grayson 1975:125–128, no. 14) chose not to include reference to the Elamite attack on Sippar in Esarhaddon's fifth year and to the Assyrian defeat in Egypt in his seventh year, both events known from another chronicle (cf. Text no. 11.01).[17] Moreover, the chronicle text that reports on the third year of Neriglissar (Grayson 1975:103–104, no. 6) is an example of divergent composition that was hardly part of the same series that surveyed the early years of the Neo-Babylonian empire. This text presents, in twenty-seven lines, the story of a campaign to Anatolia that in its sometimes broad, descriptive style—the march through "difficult mountains, where men must walk in single file"—reminds one of the narrative style of the Assyrian annals. This singular chronicle text allows us to appreciate better the conciseness of the Babylonian Chronicles, which was obviously achieved by trimming facts and details from a fuller report that its author used as his source. Therefore, the three or four "objective" lines for each year in the Chronicles should be seen as an abstract of a longer report, and what is given in the Chronicles represents the "historical" interests of its author.[18]

SOURCES. The sources of the Babylonian Chronicles are not known. Many hold that the historical information derived from astronomical diaries. These diaries were essentially records of astronomical observations and weather reports, with occasional historical notes concerning a battle, the king's

17 Given the lack of confirming data from other sources and the historical anomaly of the strike on Sippar, Brinkman (1990:92–94) observes that a pro-Assyrian bias in the "Esarhaddon Chronicle" is far from obvious.

18 One wonders whether it is correct to ascribe the title "historian" to this author, as his reports are more like a chronological table; they lack narrative, i.e., any suggestion of causal relationships between the reported events, which is the sign of historical thinking. On this point, see the incisive remarks of Drews 1975:95–97; Van de Mieroop 1999:76–85.

whereabouts or a cultic activity (Sachs and Hunger 1988, 1989). But these historical notes are wholly random and incidental, and they comprise a very small percentage of the diary reports. They certainly could not have supplied the information for the consecutive reporting given in the Babylonian Chronicles. Moreover, in the one instance where there is an overlapping report of a historical event in an astronomical diary and the Babylonian Chronicles, it turns out that they do not agree on details, which makes it hard to see the diary as having been the source of the chronicle (Brinkman 1990).[19] So for the present, there is no compelling solution to the question of the sources of the chronicles.

19 The incident is the battle between the armies of Assyria and Babylonia at Ḫiritu in 652 BCE reported in Chronicle 16 (Grayson 1975:132, lines 13–16) and Sachs and Hunger 1988:44–45, lines 18′–19′.

References

Brinkman, John A.

1990 The Babylonian Chronicle Revisited. Pp. 73–104 in T. Abusch, J. Huehnegard, P. Steinkeller (eds.), *Lingering Over Words, Studies in Ancient Near Eastern Literature in Honor of William L. Moran*, Atlanta.

Cogan, Mordechai

1991 A Plaidoyer on behalf of the Royal Scribes. Pp. 121–128 in Mordechai Cogan and Israel Eph^{c}al (eds.), *Ah Assyria... Studies Tadmor, ScrHier* 33.

Drews, Robert

1975 The Babylonian Chronicles and Berossus, *Iraq* 37:39–55.

Fales, Frederick Mario

1981 A Literary Code in Assyrian Royal Inscriptions: The Case of Ashurbanipal's Egyptian Campaigns. Pp. 169–202 in F. M. Fales (ed.), *Assyrian Royal Inscriptions: New Horizons*, Rome.

1999–2001 Assyrian Royal Inscriptions: Newer Horizons, *SAAB* 13:115–144.

Glassner, Jean-Jacques

2004 *Mesopotamian Chronicles*, Atlanta.

Grayson, A. Kirk

1975 *Assyrian and Babylonian Chronicles*, Locust Valley.

1980 Histories and Historians of the Ancient Near East: Assyria and Babylonia, *Or* 49:140–194.

1991 *Assyrian Rulers of the First Millennium BC. I (1154–859 BC)*, RIMA 2, Toronto.

1996 *Assyrian Rulers of the Early First Millennium BC. II (858–745 BC)*, RIMA 3, Toronto.

Güterbock, Hans G.

1938 Die historische Tradition und ihre literarische Gestaltung bei Babyloniern und Hethitern bis 1200, *ZA* 44:45–149.

Leichty, Erle

2011 *The Royal Inscriptions of Esarhaddon, King of Assyria (680–669 BC)*, RINAP 4, Winona Lake, IL.

MacGinnis, John

2002 The Use of Writing Boards in the Neo-Babylonian Temple Administration at Sippar, *Iraq* 64:217–236.

Mowinckel, Sigmund

1923 Die vorderasiatischen Königs- und Fürsteninschriften. Pp. 278–322 in H. Schmidt (ed.), *Eucharisterion I* (Festschrift H. Gunkel), Forschungen zur Religion und Literatur des Alten und Neuen Testament NF 19; Göttingen.

Olmstead, A. T.

1916 *Assyrian Historiography*, Columbia, Missouri.

Oppenheim, A. Leo

1964 *Ancient Mesopotamia*, Chicago.

Renger, Johannes

1980–83 Königsinschriften. Pp. 65–77 in vol. 6 of *RlA*.

1986 Neuassyrische Königsinschriften als Genre der Keilschriftliteratur. Zum Stil und zur Kompositionstechnik der Inschriften Sargons II. von Assyrien. Pp. 109–128 in K. Hecker and W. Sommerfeld (eds.), *Keilschriftliche Literaturen*, Berlin.

Sachs, Abraham J. and Hermann Hunger

1988 *Astronomical Diaries and Related Texts from Babylonia*. Volume I. Diaries from 652 B.C. to 262 B.C., Wien.

1989 *Astronomical Diaries and Related Texts from Babylonia*. Volume II. Diaries from 261 B.C. to 165 B.C., Wien.

Speiser, Ephraim A.

1955 Ancient Mesopotamia. Pp. 35–76 in R. C. Dentan (ed.), *The Idea of History in the Ancient Near East*, New Haven.

Tadmor, Hayim

1977 Observations on Assyrian Historiography. Pp. 209–213 in M. de Jong Ellis (ed.), *Essays on the Ancient Near East in Memory of Jacob Joel Finkelstein*, Memoirs of The Connecticut Academy of Arts and Sciences, Hamden (= pp. 47–56 in H. Tadmor, *"With my many chariots I have gone up the heights of mountains": Historical and Literary Studies on Ancient Mesopotamia and Israel*, M. Cogan [ed.], Jerusalem 2011).

1982 The Aramaization of Assyria: Aspects of Western Imperialism. Pp. 449–470 in H. J. Nissen and J. Renger (eds.), *Mesoptamien und seine Nachbarn* (RAI 25), Berlin.

1997 Propaganda, Literature, and Historiography: Cracking the Code of the Assyrian Royal Inscriptions. Pp. 325–338 in S. Parpola and R. M. Whiting (eds.), *ASSYRIA* 1995. *Proceedings of the 10th Anniversary Symposium of the Neo-Assyrian Text Corpus Project Helsinki, September 7–11, 1995*, Helsinki (= pp. 3–24 in H. Tadmor, *"With my many chariots I have gone up the heights of mountains": Historical and Literary Studies on Ancient Mesopotamia and Israel*, M. Cogan [ed.], Jerusalem 2011).

Van de Mieroop, Marc

1999 *Cuneiform Texts and the Writing of History*, New York.

Waerzeggers, Caroline

2012 The Babylonian Chronicles: Classification and Provenance, *JNES* 71:285–298.

Wiseman, Donald J.

1955 Assyrian Writing Boards, *Iraq* 17:3–13.

Fig. 2. The Black Obelisk of Shalmaneser III (*Courtesy of the Trustees of the British Museum*).

CHAPTER 1

Shalmaneser III

During his thirty-five-year reign, Shalmaneser III (858–824 BCE) vigorously pursued the military policies of his father, Ashurnasirpal II, on two main fronts: in the north against Urartu and in the west against the Aramean kingdoms on the opposite side of the Euphrates. The inscriptions of Shalmaneser, unlike those of his predecessors, are mostly numbered according to the years of the king's reign (Akkadian *palû*), which has made the reconstruction of his era relatively secure. The selections that follow deal with his campaigns to the West where he sought to gain the predominant position on the Phoenician coast and southern Syria.

1.01—THE BATTLE AT QARQAR—THE KURKH MONOLITH

The inscription on the Kurkh Monolith (see Fig. 3) is one of the most widely known Assyrian inscriptions, principally because of its reference to Ahab, king of Israel. It is also the earliest extra-biblical source to testify to the Kingdom of Israel at its height. The inscription tells of Ahab's participation in an alliance with Syrian and Phoenician states against Assyria, an affair that is not mentioned in the Bible. This absence is likely due to the critical stance taken by the author of the Book of Kings towards the dynasty of Omri, and in particular, King Ahab: "Ahab did what was displeasing to the Lord, more than all who preceded him" (1 Kgs 16:30).

The limestone monolith, measuring 2.20 m, was discovered near the village of Kurkh on the upper Euphrates, about 20 km south of Diyabakir; it is on display today in the British Museum. In the extant text of over 150 lines, the first six years of the reign of Shalmaneser III, excluding his fifth year, are surveyed. The early years of the king's reign are quite detailed and they are dated according to eponym-years (for eponym dating, see Text no. 10.01). The stela may have been erected in 852 BCE, during the Assyrian campaign in the vicinity of Kurkh (ancient Tidu), though a report on that campaign is not given on the stela as is expected. The appearance of the stone lacks the grand style of other royal stelae, and in fact, the inscription's engraver erred dozens of times in executing the cuneiform signs. Therefore the Kurkh monolith is best classified as an example of a provincial stela.

The events of Shalmaneser's sixth year, 853 BCE, follow.

Text edition: Grayson 1996:11–24, no. 2.
Translations: *ARAB* 1, §§610–611; *DOTT* 46–47; *TGI* 49–50; *ANET* 278–279; *TPOA* 85–87; *TUAT* 1/4, 360–362; *COS* 2, 261–264; *HTAT* 254–259.
Photograph: *ANEP*, no. 443.

Col.ii,
78–81 In the eponymate of Dayan-Ashur, on the 14th of Iyyar, I set out from Nineveh, crossed the Tigris (and) approached the cities of Giammu on the River Baliḫ. They (i.e., the inhabitants of these cities) were afraid of the fearsomeness of my lordship and the splendor of my furious weapons, and with their own weapons, they killed Giammu, their lord. I entered the cities Saḫlala and Til-sha-turaḫi. I took (the images of) my gods into his palaces and held a feast in his palaces. I opened his storehouses and saw his treasures. I carried off as booty his possessions (and) his property (and) brought (them) to my city, Ashur.

81–87 I set out from Saḫlala and approached Kar-Shalmaneser. I crossed the Euphrates in its flood for the second time on rafts of goatskins. I received tribute of the kings from the opposite side of the Euphrates in the city Ana-Ashur-utir-aṣbat, which is on the other side of the Euphrates, on the River Sagur and which the people of Ḫatti call Pitru, from Sangara of Carchemish, Kundashpi of Kummuḫ, Arame, son of Gush, Lalli of Melid, Ḫayani, son of Gabbari, Qalpurada of Patina, Qalparuda of Gurgum: silver, gold, tin, bronze (and) bronze bowls. I set out from the Euphrates and approached Aleppo. They (i.e., the inhabitants of Aleppo) were afraid of battle and seized my feet. I received their tribute, silver and gold, and offered sacrifices to the god Adad of Aleppo.

87–96 I set out from Aleppo and approached the cities of Irḫuleni of Hamath. I captured the cities Adennu, Parga (and) Argana, his royal citi(es); I took his booty, his property, the possessions in his palaces, and set fire to his palaces. I set out from Argana and approached Qarqar. Qarqar, his royal city, I

Fig. 3. The Kurkh Monolith (*Courtesy of the Trustees of the British Museum*).

demolished, tore down and burned. He took as his allies these twelve kings: 1,200 chariots, 1,200 horsemen, 20,000 soldiers of Hadad-ezer of Damascus; 700 chariots, 700 horsemen, 10,000 soldiers of Irḫuleni of Hamath; 2,000 chariots, 10,000 soldiers of Ahab of Israel; 500 soldiers of Byblos; 1,000 soldiers of Egypt; 10 chariots, 10,000 soldiers of Irqatu; 200 soldiers of Matinu-Baʾal of Arvad; 200 soldiers of Usanatu; 30 chariots, [ ],000 soldiers of Adunu-Baʾal of Siannu; 1,000 camels of Gindibu, the Arab; [ ]00 soldiers of Ba'asha, son of Rehob from Mount Amana. They attacked me, waging battle and war.

96–102 I fought with them with the exalted strength that Ashur, my lord, had granted me, and with the mighty weapons of Nergal, who goes before me, had granted me. I defeated them from Qarqar up to Gilzau. I felled with the sword 14,000 of his fighting men, and like the god Adad, I rained down on them a flood. I scattered their corpses and filled the plain (with them). ‹I struck down› with the sword their numerous troops and let their blood flow into the wadis of *x x*. The plain was too small for all their bodies and the broad field vanished in burying them. I blocked the River Orontes with their bodies like a bridge. In the midst of this battle, I took from them their chariots, their horsemen, (and) their horse-teams.

---

col. ii,

78–81 **In the eponymate of Dayan-Ashur**—One of the most influential persons at the court of Shalmaneser III, he served as *turtānu*, "commander-in-chief" in 853 and again in 826. In the later editions of the inscriptions of Shalmaneser, the year is dated: "the sixth year of the king." For the appearance of *turtānu* (Hebrew תַּרְתָּן) in the Bible, cf. 2 Kgs 18:17; Isa 20:1.

On the 14th of Iyyar—Early spring, as reflected in the ensuing description of the high waters of the Euphrates. The month Iyyar is the second month of the Assyrian year.

I entered the cities Saḫlala and Til-sha-turaḫi. I took (the images of) my gods into his palaces and held a feast in his palaces—These cities were located on the River Baliḫ, south of Harran. The introduction of the king's gods points to their becoming Assyrian outposts.

81–87 **I set out from Saḫlala and approached Kar-Shalmaneser**—The city Kar-Shalmaneser (literally "quay or customs house of Shalmaneser") is the Assyrian name given to Til-Barsip (Tell Aḥmar), on the Euphrates, some 20 km south of Carchemish. It had been the royal city of Aḫuni of Bit-Adini,

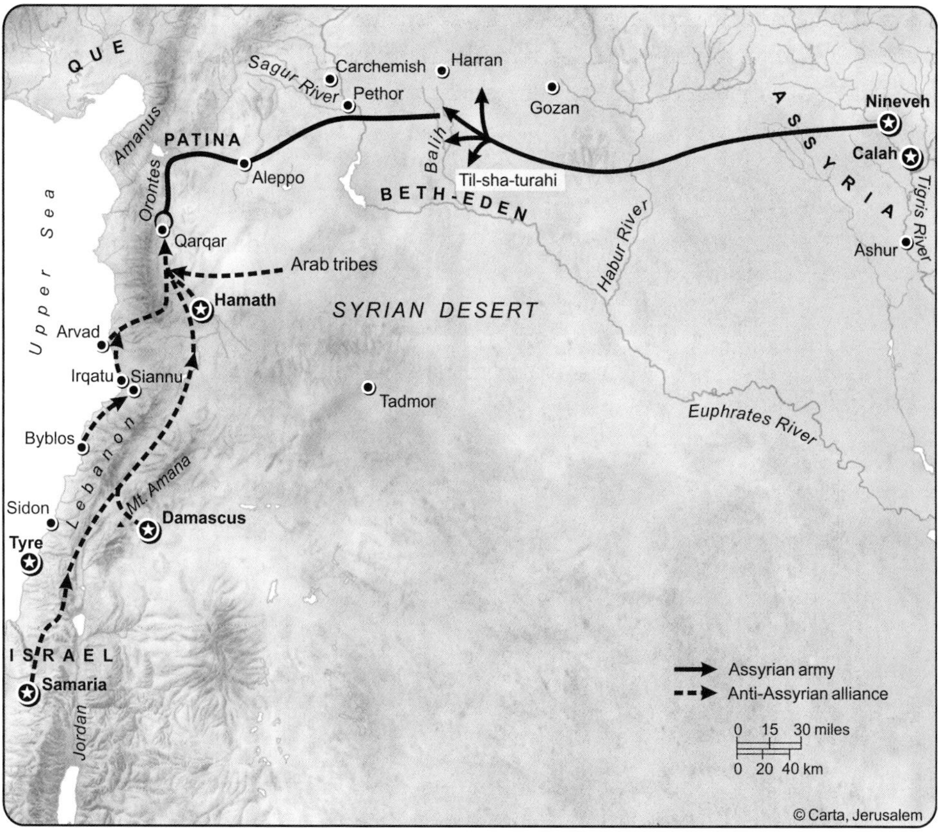

Shalmaneser III—The Battle of Qarqar, 853 bce

where, in 856, Shalmaneser established an Assyrian settlement.

I crossed the Euphrates in its flood for the second time on rafts of goatskins—Royal boasting often includes the ability to overcome the difficult crossing of the river at flood stage. Heavy equipment was transferred on rafts; soldiers forded the waters by swimming, supported by inflated skins. For scenes of river crossings, see frontispiece and Yadin 1963:388–389.

I received tribute of the kings from the opposite side of the Euphrates—In his earlier campaigns to northern Syria, Shalmaneser had subdued these monarchs; they now appear before him as loyal vassals, presenting tribute. The kingdoms are referred to either by the name of the royal city, territory, or the founder of the ruling dynasty.

In the city Ana-Ashur-utir-aṣbat, which is on the other side of the

Fig. 4. Assyrian troops crossing a river on campaign (Balawat Gates; *Courtesy of the Trustees of the British Museum*).

Euphrates, on the River Sagur and which the people of Ḫatti call Pitru—The city Pitru is situated on the eastern bank of the Euphrates, about 20 km south of Carchemish, at the confluence of the River Sagur. After its conquest in the earlier campaign, it was renamed *Ana-Aššur-utīr-aṣbat*, "I returned (it) to Ashur." The biblical seer Balaam son of Beor hailed from Pitru (Num 22:5).

Sangara of Carchemish—Jerablus on the Euphrates, 100 km northeast of Aleppo. For the Battle of Carchemish in 605, see Text no. 11.05. Biblical references to the city include Isa 10:9; Jer 6:2; 2 Chr 35:20.

Kundashpi of Kummuḫ—This Anatolian territory is south of Malatya; in classical sources it is referred to as Commagene.

Arame, son of Gush—The kingdom of Bit-Agusi, whose capital was Arpad (Tell Rif^{c}at), about 30 km north of Aleppo. Affiliations within tribal units are noted in Assyrian inscriptions as "son of (*mār*) X"; the tribe is called "house of (*bīt*) X" after the eponymous ancestor; see further examples ahead and in text no. 1.02 with reference to Jehu.

Lalli of Melid—Located at Arslantepe, near Malatya.

Ḫayani, son of Gabbari—King of the kingdom of Samʾal, located at the foot of Mount Amanus; its capital, also named Samʾal, is to be found at Zenjirli.

Qalpurada of Patina—Also referred to as Unqi, i.e., the Antiochian plain. The king's name is known from Luwian hieroglyphic inscriptions from Tell Ta^{c}yinat in the form Halparuntiya (Hawkins 2009:167).

Qalparuda of Gurgum—In the vicinity of Maraş in southeastern Turkey.

I received their tribute, silver and gold, and offered sacrifices to the god Adad of Aleppo—Shalmaneser offered sacrifice to the storm god Adad at the sanctuary in Aleppo. Assyrian recognition of local deities is not unusual; they held that the non-Assyrian gods granted victory to Assyria and so were duly honored. Adad of Aleppo was worshipped in other cities of north Syria (e.g., Til-Barsip) and is referred to in the Aramaic Sefire inscription as הדד חלב (*KAI* 222 A, 10).

87–96 **I set out from Aleppo and approached the cities of Irḫuleni of Hamath**—Hamath, modern Ḥamā, on the left bank of the Orontes, was the royal city of Irḫuleni.

I took his booty, his property, the possessions in his palaces—Remnants of booty from Hamath were discovered at Calah (Nimrud). On an ivory plaque, the name Hamath (חמת) was inscribed (Millard 1962:42, Plate XXIIIa) and a few shell fragments were engraved with the inscription in hieroglyphic Luwian: "Urḫilana, the king" (Barnett 1963).

Qarqar, his royal city, I demolished, tore down and burned—The attack and destruction of Qarqar as well as the other cities were engraved on the bronze strips affixed to the gates of the palace at the town of Imgur-Enlil (the mound of Balawat, c. 28 km southeast of Mosul); see King 1915: plates xlviii–liii (lower register). Qarqar is identified with Tell al-Qarqur, 7 km south of Jisr esh-Shughur on the east bank of the River Orontes, northeast of Latakia; see Lipiński 2000:264–266.

He took as his allies these twelve kings—The alliance that had been organized against Assyria comprised the kingdoms of central and southern Syria, the Phoenician cities and the other small kingdoms in their vicinity, all of which had escaped the earlier ravages of Shalmaneser. Their common interest was the struggle to maintain control of the local trade routes. The leaders of the alliance were the kings of Hamath and Damascus whose names always appear in the short reports of the battle together with "the 12 kings of the coast."

these twelve kings—The number "twelve" is not verified by the following list, which has only 11 names. All later texts that report the battles between Shalmaneser and the western allies also speak of Irḫuleni and "the twelve kings" at the battle of Qarqar and in the subsequent engagements in later years. If not a "scribal error" (Yamada 2000:160), then the "twelve" kings is likely a "literary expedient," a round number, used here and in the inscriptions of other Assyrian kings as well; see De Odorico 1995:133–136.

Hadad-ezer of Damascus—Hadad-ezer (Akkadian *Adad-idri*) might be Ben-hadad (II), the foe of King Ahab, referred to in 1 Kgs 20 and 22; following Mazar 1986. The name בֶּן־הֲדַד is the Hebrew form of Aramaic בר הדד, "son of (the god) Hadad," and three kings bore this name (1 Kgs 15:18; 20:1; 2 Kgs 13:3). See Cogan 2001:472–473 for controversy over this identification. The city Damascus is referred to in the text by the appellation "city of its asses" (Akkadian *ša māt imērišu*), that is, "land of ass drivers," descriptive of the position of Damascus as the central station on the north-south route that connected northern Syria and southern Transjordan; see Pitard 1987:14–17.

Irḫuleni of Hamath—His leadership was remembered a century later in an inscription of Sargon, see discussion in Text no. 5.06.

Ahab of Israel—Akkadian *Aḫabu Sirʾilāya*. The identification of Ahab as from Israel is unique in Assyrian inscriptions, in which the rulers of Israel are regularly referred to as "the house of Omri." See, further, Text no. 1.02.

Comparing the numbers shows that Ahab had assembled the largest contingent of chariots of all the participants in the alliance, a fact that has been the subject of much debate ever since the first decipherment of the text. Some have suggested that the figure should not be credited, being nothing more than an example of scribal exaggeration used to enhance the victory of the Assyrian king. Others have opined that the 2,000 chariots assigned to Ahab is the sum total of vehicles that were mobilized in the Land of Israel and Transjordan, that is, it included contingents from Judah (that was dependent on Israel at this period) and other small regional kingdoms (Malamat 1973:144). But the large number is more likely an engraver's error, one of many on this monolith. Thus, for example, it is hardly credible that the small city of Irqata could have assembled 10,000 fighting men and its contingent must have been much smaller; cf. the contingent of 200 fighters from Arvad, a neighboring city of similar size. Thus the number of chariots brought to Qarqar by Ahab was much smaller. The error could have occurred due to the similarity between two cuneiform signs:  = 1,000 and 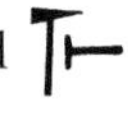 = 100.

The number of Israelite chariots at Qarqar was likely in the neighborhood of 200. Even this number is large for a mountainous kingdom like Israel that would have had little use for a large chariot force, not to mention the means to maintain it. Finally, consider that Assyria, at the height of its power, put 2,000 chariots on the field. (See further Elat 1975, Na'aman 1976; Yamada 2000b:161–162.)

Byblos—This major port is situated on the Lebanese coast between Beirut and Tripoli at Jubeil; cf. Ezek 27:9; 1 Kgs 5:32. (It should be noted that this reading of the cuneiform signs is a correction of one of the dozens of errors on the Kurkh monolith; see Tadmor 1961b:144–145.)

Egypt—This "long-distance" participation in the anti-Assyrian coalition can be understood as stemming from Egypt's commercial interests in Phoenicia that go back to the 3rd millennium BCE. Some years later, the delivery of tribute—diplomatic gifts(?)—from Egypt is depicted on the Black Obelisk; cf. *ANEP*, nos. 351–354, iii.

Irqatu—Tell ᶜArqā, located about 20 km northeast of Tripoli; the Arkites referred to in Gen 10:17 were from this town. (Note, here too, the scribe erred in his text and wrote *Irqa‹‹na››tu*.)

Matinu-Baᵓal of Arvad—This small island kingdom, renowned for its seamen (cf. Ezek 27:8, 11), is located about 3 km from the coast between Tripoli and Latakia.

Usanatu ... Adunu-Baᵓal of Siannu—Two small towns between Tripoli and Latakia; Usanatu is also known as Usnu. The Sinites in Gen 10:17 hail from Siannu. (The reading Siannu is a correction of the error *Si-ZA-nu*.)

Gindibu, the Arab—This is the earliest historical reference to the Arabs. Their base seems to have been the area of Wadi Sirhan, which traverses the Arabian Desert from south to east, from Amman to an-Nabk and then as far as Dumah, on the border between Jordan and Saudi Arabia. Gindibu's interest in joining the anti-Assyrian alliance was wholly commercial. See Ephᶜal 1982:75–77.

Ba'asha, son of Rehob, from Mount Amana—The small Aramean kingdom of Beth-rehob was located near Damascus (cf. Judg 18:28), and may have been related to Rehob mentioned in David's wars (2 Sam 8:3, 12).

Mount Amana—Located in the Anti-Lebanon mountain range (Jebel esh-Shaqif), from which the River Barada—the biblical Amana (2 Kgs 5:12)—flows down to water the Valley of Damascus (Cogan 1984). Some suggest rendering Mount Amana as "Land of Ammon" or "the Ammonite," thus restoring the missing twelfth kingdom (so Rendsburg 1991); but Ammon in Assyrian inscriptions is always Beth-Ammon; see Text nos. 4.04, 6.01, 8.02.

96–102 Several lines at the end of the text are damaged and their meaning is not clear.

I fought with them with the exalted strength that Ashur, my lord—the chief god of Assyria and the head of its pantheon—**had granted me, and with the mighty weapons of Nergal**—the god of war and battle—**who goes before me**—to protect me—**had granted me**.

I defeated them from Qarqar up to Gilzau—The claimed Assyrian victory is expressed in the very large number of enemy killed and the abundant booty taken. Yet this must be tempered by the fact that Shalmaneser did not continue his campaign onto other objectives. Indeed, during the next decade, he had to face this same alliance at least three more times, in 849, 848, and 845 BCE, before he could reach the gates of Damascus. Therefore, the entire description should be considered an example of boasting and literary exaggeration.

And like the god Adad, I rained down on them a flood—This image derives from the position held by Adad as the god of rain and storm.

I felled with the sword 14,000 of his fighting men—The number of casualties seems high, and its continued to grow in the reports of the Battle of Qarqar in the later inscriptions of the king: on the Black Obelisk, the number of slain is 20,500; on the stone tablet from the year 839, the number is 25,000; and on the king's statue erected in 829—29,000.

1.02—THE ARAMEAN WARS—THE BLACK OBELISK

This magnificent royal stela was discovered by Austin Layard at Calah (Tell Nimrud) in 1846, at the dawn of Assyriological investigation and is displayed today at the British Museum. The black diorite monument is carved as an obelisk, with its upper third in the shape of a stepped temple-tower (*ziqqurratu*). A text of 190 lines is inscribed around the tower and beneath the five bands of reliefs on the body of the obelisk; it presents in summary fashion the military activities of Shalmaneser III up until his thirty-third year (826 BCE). The years are numbered according to the king's *palû*, his "year of reign" (except for Year 4, which has an erroneous date). The following selections tell of Shalmaneser's campaigns against the West and Damascus, the tribute of Jehu of Israel, and include, as well, the caption under the second band in which Jehu is depicted on his knees, submitting to the Assyrian king (see Fig. 5).

Text edition: Grayson 1996:62–71, no. 14; 149, no. 88.
Translations: *ARAB* 1, §§553–593; *DOTT* 48; *ANET* 278–281; *TPOA* 89–90; *TUAT* 1/4, 362–363; *COS* 2, 269–270; *HTAT* 264.
Photographs: *ANEP*, nos. 351–355.

54–66 In the sixth year of my reign, I approached the cities on the banks of the River Baliḫ. They (i.e., the inhabitants of these cities) killed Giammu, their city ruler. I entered Til-turaḫi. I crossed the Euphrates in its flood and received the tribute of all the kings of Ḫatti. At that time, Hadad-ezer of Damascus and Irḫuleni of Hamath, together with the kings of Ḫatti and the seacoast, trusted in their own power and they attacked me, waging battle and war. By the word of Ashur, the great lord, my lord, I fought with them and defeated them. I took from them their chariots, their riding horses, (and)

Fig. 5. Jehu kneeling before the Assyrian king; scene from the Black Obelisk (*Courtesy of the Trustees of the British Museum*).

their weaponry. I slew with the sword 20,500 of their fighting men.

85–86 In the tenth year of my reign, I crossed the Euphrates for the eighth time. I captured the cities of Sangara of Carchemish. I approached the cities of Aramu and captured Arne, his royal city together with 100 cities.

87–89 In the eleventh year of my reign, I crossed the Euphrates for the ninth time. I captured cities without number. I went down to the cities of the people of Hamath; I captured 89 cities. Hadad-ezer of Damascus (and) twelve kings of Ḫatti stood together (trusting) their own power; I defeated them.

91–92 In the fourteenth year of my reign, I mustered my troops; I crossed the Euphrates. Twelve kings attacked me; I fought (with them) and defeated them.

97–99 In the eighteenth year of my reign, I crossed the Euphrates for the sixteenth time. Hazael of Damascus attacked for battle. I took 1,121 of his chariots, 470 of his riding horses, together with his camp.

102–104 In the twenty-first year of my reign, I crossed the Euphrates for the twenty-first time. I marched to the cities of Hazael of Damascus; I captured four of his centers. I received tribute from the people of Tyre, Sidon (and) Byblos.

Caption, Band 2

I received the tribute of Jehu, son of Omri: silver, gold, a gold bowl, a gold vase (?), gold goblets, gold buckets, tin, a royal scepter (and) javelins.

54–66 **In the sixth year of my reign**—853 BCE. The summary of the campaign that ended in the battle of Qarqar and reported in detail on the Kurkh monolith (Text no. 1.01). The two reports are decidedly different: Ahab is not listed among the leaders of the anti-Assyrian alliance despite his major contribution; the number of casualties—20,500—is larger than the 14,000 given in the earlier monument. On this point, it should be noted that there is a general tendency over the years to inflate the number of enemy soldiers killed and booty taken in order to aggrandize the king's achievements; see the study of De Odorico 1995.

85–86 **In the tenth year of my reign**—849 BCE. The conciseness of the report deletes all mention of the battle waged by Shalmaneser in this year against the alliance led by Hadad-ezer. The recension of the king's annals from the year 842, written on clay tablets from Ashur, supplies the following details:

At that time, Hadad-ezer of Damascus and Irḫuleni of Hamath, together with twelve kings of the seacoast, trusted in their own power, and they attacked me for war and battle. I fought with them and defeated them. I took from them their chariots, their riding horses, and their weaponry. They fled to save their lives. (Grayson 1996:37–38, ii 60–65)

87–89 **In the eleventh year of my reign**—848 BCE. The names of the leaders of the alliance are not given; the formulaic phrase "twelve kings" identifies the foe of this year. It is, therefore, unclear whether Jehoram, son of Ahab, king of Israel, who succeeded his father in 852, took part in this battle. In the annals of 842, Hamath is mentioned as the main area of confrontation, and Irḫuleni appears to have suffered a serious blow, though he did not submit to Shalmaneser at this juncture. He appears three years later, again as a leader of the anti-Assyrian kingdoms.

91–92 **In the fourteenth year of my reign**—845 BCE. The very short summary of the year's campaign given here is supplemented by the annal report of an encounter with Hadad-ezer, Irḫuleni and "twelve kings of the entire seacoast." They were defeated and scattered to save their lives. The arena for this battle was likely Hamath, which continued to resist despite the repeated Assyrian attacks.

97–99 **In the eighteenth year of my reign**—841 BCE. Hazael of Damascus is mentioned here for the first time in the inscriptions of Shalmaneser III. His predecessor, Hadad-ezer, was last referred to in 845, from which it is inferable that Hazael came to the throne between 845 and 841. Assyrian scribes dubbed Hazael "son of nobody," meaning, a person without pedigree; see further Text no. 1.04. Yet Hazael held the reins of power in Damascus for well over three decades, down to the end of the ninth century, when his son, Ben-hadad III, replaced him.

Alongside this view, there is that of Hazael himself, who on the Aramaic stela from Tel Dan, which he likely set up after a victory over Israel, he repeatedly refers to his predecessor as "my father." This suggests that Hazael may have been of royal blood, but from a side branch of the Damascene royal family. See Biran and Naveh 1993:90.

In contrast to the reports of the previous four occasions when Shalmaneser campaigned in Syria, in 841, he seems not to have encountered any organized military resistance on his march south to Damascus. The anti-Assyrian alliance of the last decade had disbanded, likely due to the violent usurpations in both Damascus and Samaria; Irḫuleni may have surrendered (without a battle?). Consequently, Hazael had to face Shalmaneser alone; see further Yamada 2000b:188–190.

102–104 **In the twenty-first year of my reign**—838 BCE.

I marched to the cities of Hazael of Damascus; I captured four of his centers—Damascus goes unmentioned in this summary; as in the previous campaign, its fortifications held against the Assyrian attack. Further details on this second campaign to southern Syria are given in Text no. 1.05.

I received tribute from the people of Tyre, Sidon (and) Byblos—According to an annalistic fragment (see Text no. 1.03), these Phoenician cities submitted to Shalmaneser III three years earlier; see further Text no. 1.05.

Caption, Band 2

I received the tribute of Jehu, son of Omri—Jehu, son of Jehoshaphat, son of Nimshi, or simply, son of Nimshi (cf. 2 Kgs 9:2, 20), came to the throne of Israel in an army-backed coup. It is unusual to find three generations enumerated in genealogies, so perhaps the reference to Nimshi was due to his grandfather's fame, or maybe it was the name of a particular branch of a clan to which Jehu belonged. Whatever the case, Jehu was certainly not a "son of Omri" (*Iaua mār Ḫumri*) as recorded in Assyrian inscriptions. This ascription was not due to any lack of knowledge concerning events in Israel; Jehu's having seized the throne was certainly known beyond Israel's borders. It was Assyrian scribal practice to refer to certain kingdoms by the names of their founders. Thus Arpad is "the house of Agusi"; Damascus is "the house of Hazael"; and Israel is "the house of Omri." This turn of phrase first appears with reference to Jehu and remained in use into the eighth century, even after the last of Jehu's descendants was gone. The history of Jehu's reign in 2 Kgs 9–10 makes no mention of his submission to Shalmaneser III or of his tribute payments. Indeed, Assyria goes unmentioned in the biblical record until the days of Tiglath-pileser III, some hundred years later. For the view that Jehu was indeed a descendant of Omri, but from a branch of the family shunted by Ahab, see Baruchi-Unna 2013.

There is no item for item correspondence between the relief on the obelisk and the accompanying inscription.

Silver, gold, a gold bowl, a gold vase (?), gold goblets, gold buckets, tin, a royal scepter (and) javelins—The unusual present of a royal scepter may have symbolized Jehu's submission to Shalmaneser, a turning over of his authority to the sovereign (so Elat 1975).

1.03—JEHU'S SUBMISSION—SHALMANESER III'S 18TH YEAR

The text on the large marble slab recovered from the wall of the city of Ashur summarizes the events of Shalmaneser III's reign down to the king's 20th year. The report on the battle of Qarqar in the king's sixth year is virtually identical with the one on the Black Obelisk, save for the larger number of slain (25,000). The description of his attack on Damascus and the surrender of Jehu of Israel in 841 BCE are among the most detailed and it augments the Black Obelisk (Text no. 1.02).

Text edition: Grayson 1996:54, no. 10; similar recension: 60, no. 12.
Translations: *TUAT* 1/4, 366–367; *COS* 2, 267–268; *HTAT* 263–264.
Photographs: Safar 1951, pls. 1–3.

Col. iii, 45–iv,15a

In the eighteenth year of my reign, I crossed the Euphrates for the sixteenth time. Hazael of Damascus put his trust in his vast army and called up his troops in great number. He made Mount Senir, a mountain peak facing the Lebanon, his fortress. I felled with the sword 16,020 of his fighting men; I took away 1,121 chariots, 470 riding horses, as well as his camp. He fled to save his life. I followed (and) locked him up in Damascus, his royal city. I cut down his orchards and burned his stocks of grain. I marched as far as the mountain(s) of Hauran. Cities without number, I destroyed, tore down, and burned and carried off their spoil. I marched to Mount Baʾali-rasi, at the head of the sea facing Tyre, and set up my royal stela there. I received the tribute of Baʾali-manzeri of Tyre (and) Jehu, son of Omri. On my return, I ascended Mount Lebanon and set up my royal stela alongside the stela of Tiglath-pileser, the great king, who preceded me.

Col. iii, 45–iv,15a

In the eighteenth year of my reign—841 BCE.

Hazael of Damascus put his trust in his vast army and called up his troops in great number—For the first time in over a decade, Damascus faced the Assyrian army alone; the alliance that had challenged the previous advances

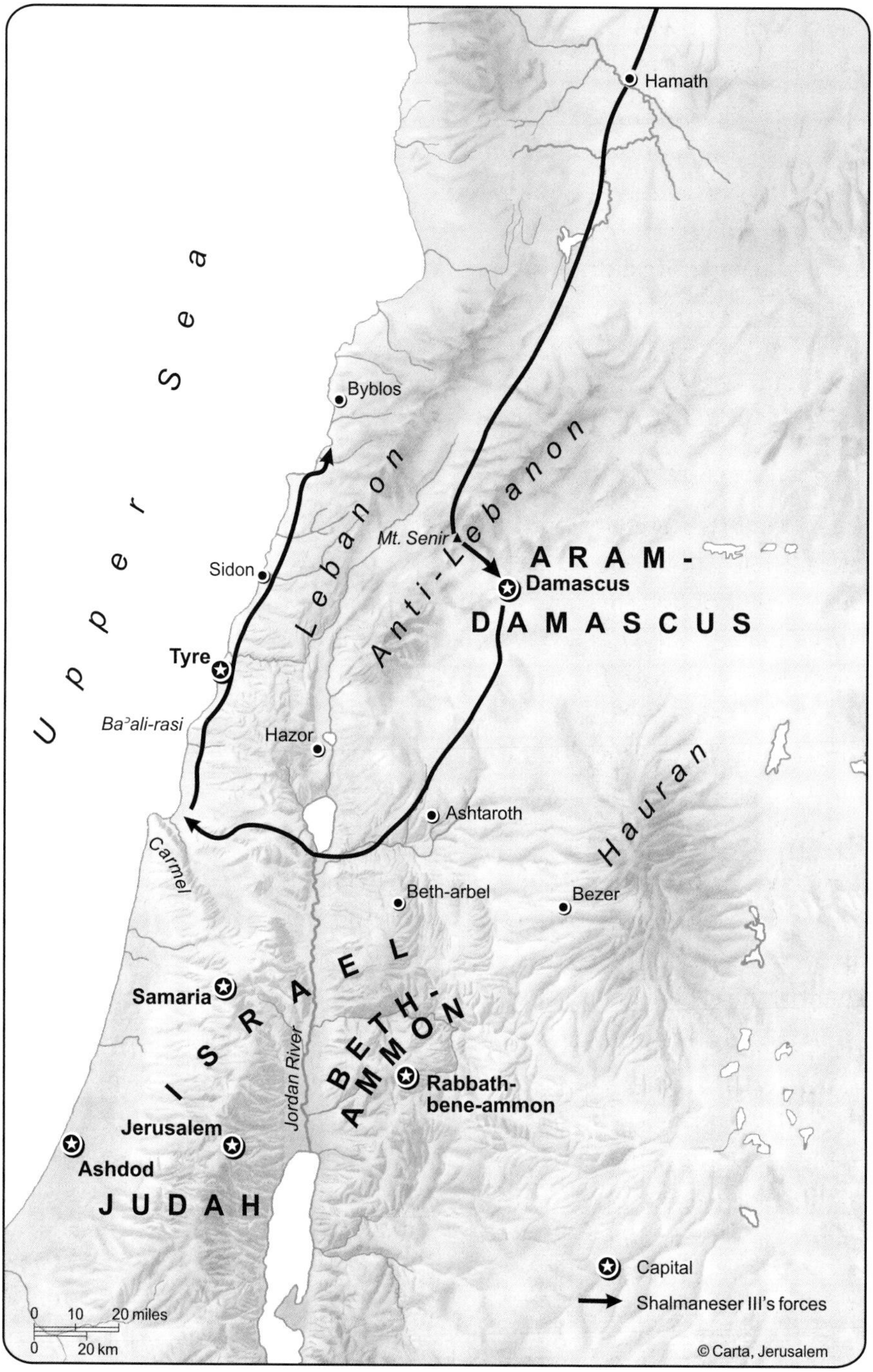

CAMPAIGN OF SHALMANESER III, 841 BCE

of Shalmaneser was not renewed under the new leaders that had come to power in Damascus and Samaria.

He made Mount Senir, a mountain peak facing the Lebanon, his fortress—One of the highest peaks in the Anti-Lebanon Range. In Babylonian and Hittite texts of the 2nd millennium BCE, the mountain is referred to as *Sariyana*, apparently a variant of *Saniru* in the present text. Biblical tradition does not seem to have made a distinction between the peaks of the Anti-Lebanon to the west of Damascus and the mountains to the south, Jebel esh-Sheikh, that is Mount Hermon; cf. Deut 3:9: "Sidonians call (Mount) Hermon Sirion and the Amorites call it Senir"; also Cant 4:8. See Ikeda 1978:36–37.

I followed (and) locked him up in Damascus, his royal city—Damascus came under siege, but its defenses were not breached.

I cut down his orchards and burned his stocks of grain—This wanton destruction of the economy of Damascus was not unique in Assyrian warfare; punishment of this sort was employed in other places and other times by Assyria in the hope of psychologically breaking the resistance of stubborn enemies. See, too, Tiglath-pileser III, Text no. 4.09; and the discussions of Cole 1997; Oded 1997. In the attempted re-conquest of Moab, the Israelite forces under Jehoram took similar action: "They threw stones in every fertile plot, filling it up, stopped up every spring, and cut down every good tree" (2 Kgs 3:25).

I marched as far as the mountain(s) of Hauran. Cities without number, I destroyed, tore down, and burned and carried off their spoil—Shalmaneser spread destruction throughout the territory of Damascus, including the area south of the capital known in the Bible as Bashan.

Hauran—Identified with Jebel ed-Druz. This area was the easternmost region of the biblical Land of Israel, according to the map of Ezekiel: "As the eastern limit: A line between Hauran and Damascus, and between Gilead and the land of Israel: with the Jordan as a boundary, you shall measure down to the Eastern Sea (i.e. the Dead Sea)" (Ezek 47:18). In classical texts, the area was known as *Aurana* and also *Auranitis*. The Mishnah tells of Mount Hauran as one in a chain of signal stations used for sending word of the new moon to distant communities (*Rosh Hashanah* 2:4). In Arab sources, *Hawran* is the entire area between Damascus and the River Yarmuk.

I marched to Mount Baʾali-rasi, at the head of the sea facing Tyre and set

Fig. 6. "I received tribute from the boats of Tyrians and Sidonians" (Balawat Gates, *Courtesy of the Trustees of the British Museum*).

up my royal stela there—Very likely to be identified with Rosh Haniqra, on the Israel-Lebanon border (so Malamat 1965:370; Lipiński 1971); from this height one can see Tyre. This is preferable to taking Baʾali-rasi as Mount Carmel (Aharoni 1970; Olmstead 1923:139) or even the outcrop overlooking the sea at Nahr el-Kalb near Beirut.

I received the tribute of Baʾali-manzeri of Tyre (and) Jehu, son of Omri—The tribute payments were exacted from the city of Sidon as well, as recorded in a parallel text. On the bronze engravings fixed to the gates of Imgur-Enlil (Balawat), the transfer of gifts from Tyre are depicted: boats loaded with goods are seen leaving the island kingdom, and upon reaching the coast, porters carry them into the presence of the Assyrian king; see Fig. 6 and *ANEP*, nos. 356–361 (upper register).

Baʾali-manzeri of Tyre—He is Baʿal-ʾazor (Balezoros), son of Ethbaal, king of Tyre, referred to by Josephus, *Against Apion* 1.124; cf. Katzenstein 1997:167–168.

Jehu, son of Omri—See comment in Text 1.02.

It is not clear which road the Assyrian army took to cross from Transjordan to the Phoenician coast. They may have traveled west on *via Maris*, from Beth-shean passing by Megiddo and then on to Mount Carmel (so Aharoni 1970). Or after crossing the Jordan, the army may have turned north, traversing the Upper Galilee and southern Lebanon towards Tyre (Oded 1971). In either case, it was at this point in time that Jehu paid tribute to Shalmaneser, thus avoiding military confrontation with the superior Assyrian forces (for a contrary view, see Astour 1971).

On my return, I ascended Mount Lebanon and set up my royal stela alongside the stela of Tiglath-pileser, the great king, who preceded me—The reference is most likely to Tiglath-pileser I (1115–1076 BCE) who campaigned in northern Mount Lebanon and reached the Mediterranean at Arvad (cf. *ANET* 274–275); the site of the royal stela is not known.

1.04—QARQAR AND DAMASCUS—STATUE OF SHALMANESER III FROM ASHUR

A statue of Shalmaneser III, broken in two large pieces and many small fragments and missing the head, was discovered at Ashur out of its original location. The inscription on the statue records seven campaigns, ordered geographically in the manner of the summary inscriptions. The campaigns are undated, but they can be identified by comparison to the reports in the king's annals. The latest event is apparently the campaign to Namri of 834 BCE. The following excerpt relates the campaign against the Syrian coalition at Qarqar (853 BCE) and the attack on Damascus (841 BCE).

Text edition: Grayson 1996:118 (no. 40).
Translations: *ARAB* 2, §§ 679–683; *ANET* 280; *TUAT*, 365; *COS* 2, 270; *HTAT* 262–263.

i 14–24 (front)

I defeated Hadad-ezer of Damascus together with twelve kings, his helpers. I laid down like reeds 29,000 of his brave fighters; the remainder of his troops I pushed into the Orontes River (and) they fled to save their lives.

i 25–ii 1 (left hip)

Hadad-ezer disappeared forever; Hazael, son of a nobody, seized the throne. He called up a large army and set out to engage me in battle. I fought against him, defeated him, and captured his camp. He fled to save his life. I marched as far as Damascus, his royal city [and cut down his] orchards.

---

i 14–24 **I defeated Hadad-ezer of Damascus together with twelve kings, his helpers**—The reference is to the initial encounter with the allied Syrian forces at Qarqar in 853; for details of this engagement, see Text no. 1.01.

29,000 of his brave fighters—The number of the defeated has grown from the "14,000 soldiers" reported lost in Text no. 1.01. This is an example of the inflation of the total number of enemy dead, cf., too, Text no. 1.02, line 66.

I laid down like reeds—The image of instability and inability to stand up under stress associated with reeds is also known from the threat of the prophet Ahijah against Israel: "The Lord will smite Israel, as a reed is shaken in the water" (1 Kgs 14:15).

i 25–ii 6

Hadad-ezer disappeared forever—That is, he died (cf. Text no. 6.03). The reported demise of Hadad-ezer leaves much unsaid, that is, whether he died a natural death or was eliminated by a rival. According to the biblical prophetic tale, Ben-hadad of Damascus (perhaps Hadad-ezer; see note on Text no. 1.01) met his end at the hand of Hazael. After consulting with the prophet Elisha concerning the king's health, Hazael returned to his master, who said to him, "What did Elisha say to you?" And he answered, "He told me that you would certainly recover. But the next day, he (Hazael) took the bed-cover and dipped it in water and spread it over his face, until he died. And Hazael succeeded him" (2 Kgs 8:7–15).

Hazael, son of a nobody, seized the throne—The epithet expresses the Assyrian view of the usurper: Hazael was not of the royal line and so was seen as unfit to rule. But in another instance, common origin did not prevent Assyria from recognizing ascent to the throne. Thus, for example, Tiglath-pileser III reported his having placed Ḫulli, "son of nobody," on the throne of Tabal (see Text no. 4.04, rev. 15′).

I fought against him, defeated him, and captured his camp. He fled to save his life—The closest parallel to this report is the one on the marble slab from Ashur (Text no. 1.03), which permits setting the date of these events to the king's eighteenth year, 838 BCE.

I marched as far as Damascus, his royal city [and cut down his] orchards—Compare the fuller description of the destruction in Text no. 1.03.

1.05—THE CITIES OF HAZAEL—SHALMANESER III'S 21ST YEAR

A fragmented statue of the king was discovered by the wall of the acropolis of Calah. The annal text engraved on the torso is quite similar to the one on the Black Obelisk (Text no. 1.02), yet there are several deviations and additions. Both texts cover military events down to the king's thirty-third year and were likely composed in the same year. The report for the twenty-first year (838 BCE) treats the second engagement with the kingdom of Aram-Damascus close to the capital. Shalmaneser attacked Hazael from the West; he marched down the Beqa^{c} Valley and crossed the Anti-Lebanon Range to descend against four fortified cities. Damascus itself is not reported as having been attacked; it may be that its defenses were strong enough to withstand the Assyrian assault, as they had three years earlier (see Text no. 1.02, lines 97–99).

The names of two of the cities captured during this campaign also appear in the Eponym Chronicle (see Text no. 10.01): Year 838: "To Malaḫu"; Year 837: "To Danabi." If the Eponym Chronicle is accurate, then the annal report on the Black Obelisk and the statue conflates the activities of two years into a single one (see Reade 1978).

Text edition: Grayson 1996:78–79, no. 16; Yamada 2000a:76–87.
Translation: *HTAT* 265.
Photograph: Læssøe 1959: Pls. XL–XLII.

152′–162′

In the twenty-first year of my reign, I crossed the Euphrates for the twenty-first time. I received the tribute of the kings of Ḫatti. From [*Ḫatti*] I departed; I took the route along Mount Lebanon. I crossed Mount Senir and went down to the cities [of] Hazael of Damascus. The (inhabitants of the) cities were frightened and sought refuge in the mountain. The city Ya-*x*-*x*, [the city . . .], the city Danabu, the city Malaḫa, fortified cities, I captured by means of [tunnels, battering] rams and siege towers. I defeated them and carried off their spoil. The towns, I destroyed and burnt down. Baal of [ ] took hold of my feet; I received his tribute. I placed my royal image in the temple of Laruba, his fortified city. I received the tribute of Tyre, Sidon and Byblos. I marched to Muḫuruna.

Danabu—Danabu may be the city Sedanaya, some 20 km north of Damascus; for an alternate identification with Danibu in the Bashan, 18 km east of Naveh, see Aḥituv 1984:89.

Malaḫa—Malaḫa is of uncertain identification; for a number of possible sites to the east and south of Damascus, see Sader 1987:266. For an item of booty taken from the city, see Text no. 1.06.

Baal of [ ] took hold of my feet—Considering that the name Baal is Phoenician, these lines refer to the second stage of the campaign, the movement of the army to the Mediterranean coast. In his previous campaign to the area, Shalmaneser received tribute from Baʾali-manzeri of Tyre (Text no. 1.03); but the surviving cuneiform signs do not support reading this name here. Perhaps it might read: Baʾal of Ṣ[imirra]; see Yamada 2000:80.

Laruba—An unknown toponym. Perhaps the first cuneiform sign *la* should be read *ma*, thus giving Maruba, a coastal city situated between Tyre and Sidon, known from an inscription of Esarhaddon (Text no. 8.02, col. iii, 1–19).

Muḫuruna—A city on the Phoenician coast, as yet unidentified; for a survey of suggestions, see Yamada 2000b:159, n. 282.

1.06—BOOTY FROM MALAḪA—SHALMANESER III'S 21ST YEAR

A small cylinder of black marble(?) with white veins, 1.5 cm in diameter by 4.1 cm in length, was found by the small ziggurat in the city of Ashur. The inscription shows that the cylinder was part of the booty taken from the city of Malaḫa after its capture by Shalmaneser III in 838 BCE; see Text no. 1.05.

Beads and cylinders of precious and semi-precious stones were used as jewelry and were often dedicated to the gods to enhance the adornment of their statues. In many cases, these small objects bear dedicatory inscriptions; see the study of these objects by Galter 1987.

The inscription is written in 8 short lines. There is no photograph of the object and its present whereabouts is unknown.

Text editions: Galter 1987:19, no. 8; Grayson 1996:155, no. 102.92.
Translations: *ANET*, 281; *COS* 2, 271; *TUAT* 1, 367; *HTAT* 265.

1 Booty of the temple of the god Sheri
of Malaḫa,
the royal city of Hazael
of Damascus,

which Shalmaneser,
son of Ashurnasirpal, king of Assyria,
brought inside the wall
of the city of Ashur.

---

the god Sheri—The god is likely to be identified as the deified "Dawn" or "Morning Star." The name of this deity is likely to be found in the formulation: "Day Star, son of Dawn" (Isa 14:12).

Malaḫa, the royal city of Hazael—Of unknown identification; see Text no. 1.05.

brought inside the wall of the city of Ashur—Literally, "the inner city"; that is, it was buried within the city wall, as a foundation deposit(?).

References

Aharoni, Yohanan
 1970 Mount Carmel as Border. Pp. 1–7 in A. Kutschke and E. Kutsch (eds.), *Archäologie und Altes Testament: Fs. K. Galling*, Tübingen.

Aḥituv, Shmuel
 1984 *Canaanite Toponyms in Ancient Egyptian Documents*, Jerusalem.

Astour, Michael C.
 1971 841 B.C.: The First Assyrian Invasion of Israel, *JAOS* 91:383–389.
 1979 The Kingdom of Siyannu-Usnatu, *UF* 11:11–28.

Barnett, Richard D.
 1963 Hamath and Nimrud: Shell Fragments from Hamath and the Provenance of the Nimrud Ivories, *Iraq* 25:81–85.

Baruchi-Unna, Amitai
 2013 The House of Omri, the House of Ahab and the House of Jehu: Blood Relationship and Bloody Battles, *Beit Mikra* 58:5–30 (Hebrew).

Biran, Avraham and Joseph Naveh
 1993 An Aramaic Stela Fragment from Tel Dan, *IEJ* 43:81–98.

Cogan, Mordechai
 1984 From the Peak of Amanah, *IEJ* 34:255–259.
 2001 *I Kings*, Anchor Bible 10, New York.
 2002 Locating *māt Ḫatti* in Neo-Assyrian Inscriptions, *Beer-Sheva* 15:86–92.

Cole, Steven
 1997 The Destruction of Orchards in Assyrian Warfare. Pp. 29–40 in *ASSYRIA 1995. Proceedings of the 10th Anniversary Symposium of the Neo-Assyrian Text Corpus Project Helsinki, September 7–11, 1995*, Helsinki.

DeOdorico, Marco

1995 *The Use of Numbers and Quantifications in the Assyrian Royal Inscriptions*, SAAS 3, Helsinki.

Elat, Moshe

1975 The Campaigns of Shalmaneser III against Aram and Israel, *IEJ* 25:25–35.

Eph^cal, Israel

1982 *The Ancient Arabs*, Jerusalem.

Galter, Hannes D.

1987 "On Beads and Curses," *ARRIM* 5:11–30.

Grayson, A. Kirk

1996 *Assyrian Rulers of the Early First Millennium BC. II (858–745 BC)*, RIMA 3, Toronto.

Hawkins, J. David

2009 Cilicia, The Amuq, and Aleppo: New Light in a Dark Age, *NEA* 72:163–173.

Ikeda, Yutaka

1978 Hermon, Sirion and Senir, *Annual of the Japanese Bible Institute* 4:32–44.

Katzenstein, H. Jacob

1997 *The History of Tyre*, 2nd ed., Beer-sheva.

King, L. W.

1915 *Bronze Reliefs from the Gates of Shalmaneser*, London.

Læssøe, J.

1959 A Statue of Shalmaneser III, from Nimrud, *Iraq* 21:147–157.

Lemaire, André

1991 Hazael de Damas, roi d'Aram. Pp. 91–108 in *Marchands, Diplomates et Empereurs* (Festschrift Garelli), Paris.

Lipiński, Edward

2000 *The Aramaeans. Their Ancient History, Culture, Religion*, Leuven.

2004 Mount Baᵓlu-Rasi, Rasu Qudshi, and Baᵓlu. Pp. 1–16 in *Itineraria Phoenicia*, Leuven.

Malamat, Abraham

1965 Campaigns to the Mediterranean by Iahdunlim and Other Early Mesopotamian Rulers. Pp. 365–373 in *Studies in Honor of Benno Landsberger on His Seventy-fifth Birthday*, Chicago.

1973 The Arameans. Pp. 134–155 in D. J. Wiseman (ed.), *Peoples of Old Testament Times*, Oxford.

Mazar, Benjamin

1986 The Aramean Empire and Its Relations with Israel. Pp. 151–172 in idem, *The Early Biblical Period. Historical Essays*, Jerusalem.

Michel, Ernst

1954–59 Die Assur-Texte Salmanassars III. (853–824), *WO* 2: 27–45.

1955 Die Assur-Texte Salmanassars III. (853–824), *WO* 2:137–157.

1956 Die Assur-Texte Salmanassars III. (853–824), *WO* 2:221–233.

Millard, Alan R.

1962 Alphabetic Inscriptions on Ivories from Nimrud, *Iraq* 24:41–51.

Na'aman, Nadav

1976 Two notes on the Monolith Inscription of Shalmaneser III from Kurkh, *Tel Aviv* 3:89–106.

Oded, Bustenay

1971 Darb el-Hawarneh, An Ancient Route, *ErIsr* 10:191–197 (Hebrew).

1997 Cutting Down Orchards in Assyrian Royal Inscriptions—The Historiographic Aspect, *Journal of Ancient Civilizations* 12:93–98.

Olmstead, A. T.

1923 *History of Assyria*, Chicago.

Pitard, Wayne T.

1987 *Ancient Damascus*, Winona Lake, IN.

Reade, Julian E.

1978 Assyrian Campaigns, 840–811 B.C., and the Babylonian Frontier, *ZA* 68:251–260.

Rendsburg, Gary

1991 Baasha of Ammon, *JANESCU* 20:57–61.

Sader, Helene S.

1987 *Les etats arameens de Syrie: depuis leur fondation jusqu'a leur transformation en provinces Assyriennes*, Wiesbaden.

Safar, Fuad

1951 A Further Text of Shalmaneser III from Aššur, *Sumer* 7:3–21 and pls. 1–3.

Tadmor, Hayim

1961a Azriyau of Yaudi, *ScrHier* 8:232–271.

1961b Que and Muṣri, *IEJ* 11:143–150.

Yadin, Yigael

1963 *The Art of Warfare in Biblical Lands in the Light of Archaeological Study.* Translated by M. Pearlman. 2 vols. New York.

Yamada, Shigeo

2000a Peter Hulin's Hand Copies of Shalmaneser III's Inscriptions, *Iraq* 62:65–87.

2000b *The Construction of the Assyrian Empire*, Leiden.

Fig.7. Royal stela of Adad-nerari III, from Tell al-Rimaḥ (*Baghdad Museum*).

CHAPTER 2

ADAD-NERARI III

Adad-nerari III (811–783 BCE) was the son of Shamshi-Adad V and Queen Sammuramat (the legendary Semiramis). In most unusual fashion, the queen mother is mentioned alongside her son in his military undertakings against Arpad. Late classical sources even credit her with an independent reign and extensive official activity, but there is no contemporary support for these views (see Schramm 1972). There is also no Assyrian evidence for the suggestion that Sammuramat served as regent during the minority of Adad-nerari III. It is true that during the reign of Adad-nerari III, a number of provincial governors and high officials rose in power, extolled their own competence, claiming for themselves victories that were as a rule accredited to the king. This led ultimately to the weakening of the monarchic authority.

Only fragmentary texts have survived from the reign of Adad-nerari III, most of them summary inscriptions, besides several dedicatory tablets. Recently, two stelae from his days were discovered; they had served as boundary markers between Arpad and Hamath (see Text no. 3.01). In the extant texts, activities in the West, and around Damascus in particular, are highlighted; these actions clearly marked a new departure—the return of Assyria to southern Syria after an absence of over 30 years. Assyria's presence relieved the local kingdoms—including Israel—of the dominance of Damascus, and they entered into the circle of Assyrian vassal states.

No. 2.01—DAMASCUS AND BABYLONIA—STONE TABLET FROM CALAH

The upper part of a large stone slab was discovered at Calah in 1854, and after a paper squeeze was made of the text, it was left at the site and lost. The inscription notes the achievements of Adad-nerari III, in particular, the surrender of Damascus and the vassalage of Babylonia. The date of the Calah

Slab can be determined by the dates of the campaigns to Babylonia, which according to the Eponym Chronicle, were directed against the Ituʾa tribe in 790 and 783–782 (Text no. 10.01). Although Adad-nerari did not take the title "king of Babylon," he was ceremoniously received in its major cities, an act usually reserved for the Babylonian king.

Text edition: Grayson 1996:212–213, no. 8.
Translations: *ARAB* 1, §§738–741; *DOTT* 51; *TGI* 53–54; *ANET* 281–282; *TPOA* 95; *TUAT* 1/4, 367–368; *COS* 2, 276–277, *HTAT* 274–275.

1–5a Palace of Adad-nerari, great king, strong king, king of the universe, king of Assyria, king, in whose youth, the god Ashur, king of the Igigi gods, chose him, granted him unrivaled kingship; (the gods) made his shepherdship pleasing to the people of Assyria like the plant of life, and (they) established his throne. Holy priest, who continually provides for the temple Esharra, who maintains the rites of Ekur, who sets out to battle with the support of Ashur, his lord, who makes the kings of the four quarters (of the earth) submit at his feet.

5b–15 Conqueror—from Mount Siluna in the east, the lands of Namri, Ellipi, Ḫarḫar, Araziash, Mesu, Media, Gizilbunda in its entirety, Munna, Parsua, Alabria, Abdadana, Nairi to its limit, Andiu, which is far away, Mount Badḫu to its limit, as far as the great sea in the east. From the bank of the Euphrates, Ḫatti, Amurru in its entirety, Tyre, Sidon, the Land of (the house of) Omri, Edom, Philistia as far as the great sea in the west—I made (them) submit to my feet and imposed tax (and) tribute on them.

15–21 I marched to Damascus. I locked up Mariʾ, king of Damascus, in Damascus, his royal city. The awesome splendor of the god Ashur, my lord, overwhelmed him and he seized my feet and became my servant. I received from him within his palace in Damascus, his royal city, 2,300 talents of silver, 20 talents of gold, 3,000 talents of bronze, 5,000 talents of iron, multicolored linen garments, a bed (inlaid) with ivory, a couch with ivory inlay and fittings, his property (and) possessions without number.

22–24 All the kings of Chaldea became my servants and I imposed tax (and) tribute on them in perpetuity. (The priests of) Babylon, Borsippa, (and) Cutha brought me the remnants (of the offerings) of the gods Bel, Nabu, (and) Nergal. [I offered (?)] pure sacrifices.

1–5 **The god Ashur, king of the Igigi gods**—This expression originates in the 3rd millennium BCE and refers to all the gods in heaven; the Igigi gods appear alongside the Anunnakki, and both groups are described as "the great gods."

Who continually provides for the temple Esharra, who maintains the rites of Ekur—It was the duty of Mesopotamian kings to provide for the main sanctuaries throughout their realm, and this act of piety is proudly broadcast in many inscriptions. Esharra was the sanctuary of Ashur in the city Ashur; Ekur (lit. "The Mountain House") was its sobriquet, taken from the name of the temple of Enlil in Nippur.

5–15 **Conqueror—from Mount Siluna in the east...Ḫatti, Amurru in its entirety, Tyre, Sidon, the Land of (the house of) Omri, Edom, Philistia as far as the great sea in the west**—The list surveys the countries that recognized the hegemony of Adad-nerari. It follows the standard pattern for such lists as they appear in summary inscriptions—a geographical order: the lands are enumerated beginning in the east, proceeding through northern Syria (Ḫatti) and then south along the Mediterranean seacoast (Philistia).

the great sea in the east . . . the great sea in the west—These two terms meant to indicate the extremes of the realm. In this period, the eastern sea (literally "of the sunrise") seems to refer to the Caspian Sea (in later times, the Persian Gulf); the western sea (literally "of the sunset") refers to the Mediterranean Sea. The changes in usage of these designations is studied by K. Yamada 2005.

Ḫatti—The standard term for North Syria. "The land of Ḫatti" originally signified the Hittite empire and the geographical sphere under Hittite rule; later it came to serve as the name for the states of Anatolia and Upper Syria that were the political and cultural heirs of the Hittite empire.

Amurru—The general term in Neo-Assyrian usage for "West," which retained its original meaning from the early 2nd millennium and long after the Amarna-Age kingdom of Amurru had disappeared.

The Land of (the house of) Omri—The conventional name for the kingdom of Israel; see note in Text no. 1.02. From this reference, there is no way of determining when Israel submitted to Adad-nerari; see further in Text no. 2.03.

Philistia—Adad-nerari III did not campaign as far south as Philistia (i.e., Ashdod, Ashkelon, Gaza), nor did he directly control this territory. Its mention indicates that the Philistine kingdoms rendered tribute in recognition of Assyria's renewed influence in southern Syria.

15–21 **I marched to Damascus**—The scribe used the two names of Damascus interchangeably; here it is "the city of ass drivers" (see Text no. 1.01), while in the next line it is the phonetic *Dimašqi*.

I locked up Mariʾ, king of Damascus, in Damascus—The king of Damascus, most likely Ben-hadad III, is referred to by the honorific Aramaic term מרא, "my lord." The Assyrian scribes used this term as if it was his personal name, and in fact, this appellation is documented in a number of Aramaic inscriptions. For example, on the ivory inscription recovered at Arslan-Tash: למראן חזאל בשנת, "to our lord Hazael in the year" (*KAI* 232; *COS* 2, 162); inscribed on a horse blinker found at Samos: זי נתן הדד למראן חזאל מן עמק בשנת עדה מראן נהר, "That which Hadad gave our lord Hazael from Umqi in the year that our lord crossed the river" (Eph^{c}al and Naveh 1989; *COS* 2, 162; see Fig. 8); and on an ivory fragment from Calah: מר]אן חזאל, "our lord Hazael" (that might have reached Calah as part of the booty taken from Damascus by one of Assyria's kings, the last of whom was Tiglath-pileser III; *COS* 2, 163).

Solid chronological data concerning the Aramean kings from the end of the 9th to the beginning of the 8th century BCE is not at hand, and so Mariʾ may be either Hazael or his son Ben-hadad III. Most suggested identifications of Mariʾ are made by comparing the dates of Jehoahaz (817–800 BCE) and Joash (800–784 BCE), kings of Israel. The statement in 2 Kgs 13:3–5 tells of Israel being sorely pressured by these two Aramean kings, and that already during the reign of Jehoahaz, the appearance of a "savior" partially freed Israel from Aramean domination. In the opinion of many, this unnamed savior is Adad-nerari III, whose campaigns to north Syria began in 805 BCE, during the last days of Jehoahaz. See further Text no. 2.02, and for the date of the surrender of Damascus to Assyria, see Text no. 2.03.

22–24 **(The priests of) Babylon, Borsippa, (and) Cutha brought me the remnants (of the offerings) of the gods**—At the completion of the ritual meal served

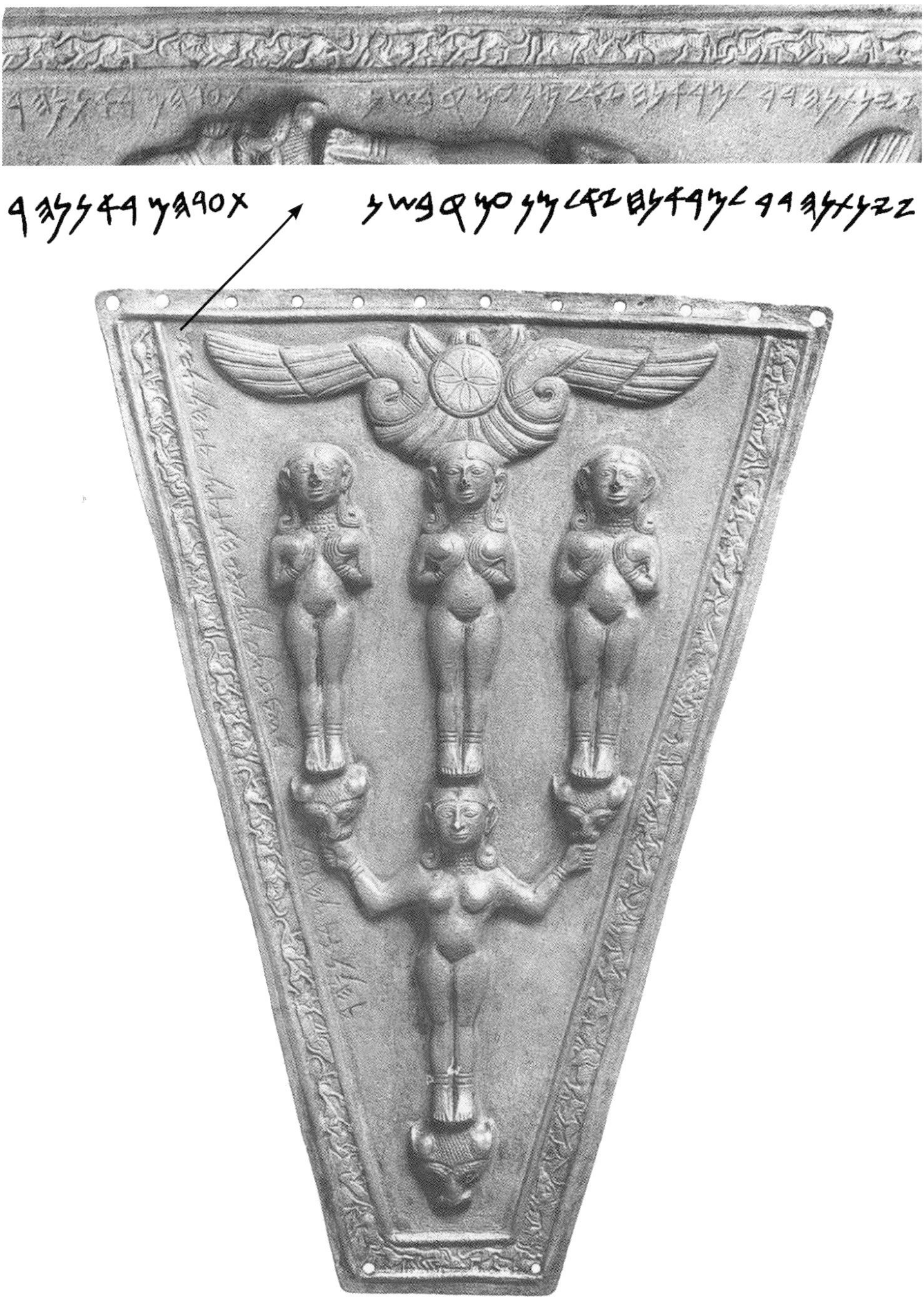

Fig. 8. Horse blinker, booty of Hazael; see Text no. 2.01, lines 15–21 (Eph^cal and Naveh 1989, Plate 24; drawing by Ada Yardeni).

before the images of the gods, the Babylonian king was honored with partaking in the "leftovers" of this meal. The presentation to Adad-nerari III of such remnants points to the appreciation of Babylonia's holy cities for the protection given them by the Assyrian king from Chaldean incursions. In the 8th century, Tiglath-pileser III and Sargon II were similarly honored.

Borsippa—Birs-Nimrud, south of Babylon.

Cutha—Tell Ibrāhīm, 25 km north of Babylon; cf. the reference to settlers brought from Cutha to Samaria in 2 Kgs 17:24.

No. 2.02—THE BATTLE FOR DAMASCUS—SABA'A INSCRIPTION

This Assyrian stela was discovered at Saba'a, south of Jebel Sinjar, west of the Iraqi-Syrian border. It bears a dedicatory inscription to the god Adad, which includes typical praise of the king and summarizes his military activity in the West. It is likely that the stela was erected by Nergal-eresh, an influential governor whose name appears in the last section of the text; it may be dated to 797 BCE (or shortly thereafter), the year in which, by royal decree, Ḫindanu was added to the territory under the control of Nergal-eresh. The section presented below complements two other reports on the western campaigns of Adad-nerari III (Text nos. 2.01 and 2.03), and all three should be compared in order to reconstruct the full picture.

Text edition: Grayson 1996:208–209, no. 6.
Translations: *ARAB* 1, §§734–737; *DOTT* 51–52; *ANET* 282; *TPOA* 93–94; *TUAT* 1/4, 369; *COS* 2, 274–275, *HTAT* 276.
Photograph: *ANEP*, no. 444.

11–20 In the fifth year of my sitting on the royal throne in majesty, I mustered the land and ordered the vast troops of Assyria to march to Ḫatti. I crossed the Euphrates in its flood. The kings of the wide [land of Ḫatti], who, in the days of Shamshi-Adad, my father, had become strong, withheld their [tribute?]. By the word of the gods Ashur, Marduk, Adad, Ishtar, the gods who support me, the awesome splendor overwhelmed them and they took hold of my feet. Tribute and ta[x] *x x x* [...] they brought to Assyria and I received [...] I ordered [*my troops to march to Damascus*]. Mari᾿ [I locked up] in Damascus. [...] 100 talents of gold, 1,000 talents of silver, as tax [... I received].

11–20 **In the fifth year of my sitting on the royal throne in majesty**—This declaration has often been interpreted to mean that only in his fifth year did Adad-nerari III become full sovereign in his own right; until that year, Sammuramat (Semiramis in Greek tradition), his mother, ruled Assyria as regent for her young son. Information on Sammuramat's reign comes from Ctesias (end of 5th–beginning of 4th centuries BCE), but his report is hardly reliable, as it contains mythical motifs along with historical traditions (see Weinfeld 1991). It is possible that Adad-nerari came to the throne at an early age, which might explain the extraordinary influence his mother seems to have had on him; a sign of this is the reference on a royal stela that Sammuramat accompanied her son on a battle against Atarshumki of Arpad (Grayson 1996:205). But there is no evidence to suggest that Adad-nerari III was not credited with all the years that he ruled. In any case, "the fifth year" notes his first campaign to the West, after which, a summary of later engagements in that area up until the submission of Damascus is given.

In the Assyrian Eponym Chronicle (Text no. 10.01), the first campaign to the West is recorded as "to Arpad" for the 805 BCE, which was the sixth year of Adad-nerari. This calculation is based on the understanding that the king held the position of eponym in his second regnal year. A number of suggestions have been put forward to account for this discrepancy; see Tadmor 1973:146; Hasegawa 2008.

This campaign and the others that followed sought to dislodge Ben-hadad from northern Syria and break the decades-long dominance of Damascus over the Aramean states in that area. An example of this may have been the rescue of Zakur, king of Hamath, whose Aramaic inscription tells of the siege laid to the city of Hadrach by a coalition of kingdoms led by Bar-hadad (=Ben-hadad) from which his god Ba᾿al-shamayin delivered him; see *ANET* 501–502; *COS* 2, 155; and discussion of Millard 1973.

I ordered [*my troops to march to Damascus*]—This is the typical formula indicating the start of a campaign; see further discussion in Text no. 2.03.

Mari᾿ [I locked up] in Damascus—The name of the king is discussed in Text no. 2.01.

100 talents of gold, 1,000 talents of silver—The amounts of precious metals paid are different from those given in Text nos. 2.01 and 2.03, and in general, there is a tendency for the amount of tribute and spoils to grow from one edition to the next. Here the number of talents of gold is unlikely large, and the number of talents of silver is smaller than that given in the texts from Calah and Tell al-Rimaḥ.

2.03—THE SUBMISSION OF WESTERN KINGS— TELL AL-RIMAḤ STELA

This royal stela of marble was discovered in 1967 at Tell al-Rimaḥ (ancient Zamaḫu), about 60 km west of Mosul; it had been set up near the podium within the Assyrian shrine at the site; see Fig. 6. It measures 130 cm in height and 60 cm wide at its base, and was found in an excellent state of preservation, except for the purposeful mutilation of the last 9 lines of text (see below). The figure of the king attired in typical royal dress is engraved on the face of the stela; the king holds a scepter in his left hand, while his right hand is positioned before his face in the customary gesture signifying divine adoration. The gods are depicted by eight symbols that surround the king's head, front and back. An inscription of 21 lines runs across the skirt of the king, its last part having been effaced in antiquity. There are sufficient remnants to suggest a reading of these lines and the reason of their effacement. They reported the royal grant of numerous cities and their villages to Nergal-eresh, governor of vast territories west of Assyria. It would seem that when Nergal-eresh fell out of favor, perhaps after the death of Adad-nerari III, his opponents sought to erase the memory of this influential official. Of special interest is that of all the reports of the western campaigns of Adad-nerari III, only the Tell al-Rimaḥ stela records the name of Joash, king of Israel, as vassal of Assyria.

Text edition: Grayson 1996:209–212, no. 7.
Translations: *TPOA* 94–95; *TUAT* 1/4, 368; *COS* 2, 275–276, *HTAT* 275–276.
Photograph: Page 1968: plate xxxviii.

1–2 To the god Adad, the greatest lord, the hero of the gods, the brave one, son of the god Anu, unique, awesome, exalted, canal-inspector of heaven and earth, who rains down abundance, who dwells in Zamaḫu, great lord, his lord.

3 Adad-nerari, strong king, king of the universe, king of Assyria, son of Shamshi-Adad, king of the universe, king of Assyria, son of Shalmaneser, king of the four quarters.

4–8 I mustered (my) chariots, troops and camps and ordered (them) to march to the land of Ḫatti. In one year, I submitted at my feet the land of Amurru and the land of Ḫatti in its entirety. I imposed tax and tribute upon them forever. He received 2,000 talents of silver, 1,000 talents of bronze, 2,000 talents of iron, 3,000 multicolored linen garments as tribute from Mariʾ of Damascus. He received the tribute of Joash of Samaria, of (the people of) Tyre and Sidon.

9–12 I marched to the great sea in the West. I erected my lordly image in Arvad, which is in midst of the sea. I ascended Mount Lebanon and cut down 100 mighty cedar timbers needed for my palace and temples. He received the tribute of all the kings of the land of Nairi.

4–8 **In one year, I subdued to my feet the land of Amurru and the land of Ḫatti in its entirety**—The time-indication "in one year" is a literary formulation lacking chronological significance. It is used to introduce summations like the one here. The ensuing paragraph brings together data from a number of campaigns waged by Adad-nerari III in the West. According to the Eponym Chronicle (see Text no. 10.01), he fought in northern Syria between the years 805–803 BCE and possibly also in 802. But it was not until 796 BCE that he reached the vicinity of Damascus. This is indicated by the notation in the Eponym Chronicle that the Assyrian army camped at Manṣuate, identified with Magdal ᶜAnjar in the Beqaᶜ of Lebanon, astride the road between Beirut and Damascus (though other sites have been suggested for Manṣuate—in northern Syria at Tell Barsip by Dalley 1996–1997:68–70; at Maṣyaf, 45 km west-southwest of Ḥamā, by Lipiński 2000:306–310). This, then, would have been the year that Joash paid tribute to his Assyrian overlord (cf. Tadmor 1973).

He received 2,000 talents of silver—The inelegant interchange between first-person to third-person verbs is indicative of the source from which the list of tribute was copied. The amount of silver and other items is not identical with those given in the king's other inscriptions (Text nos. 2.01 and 2.02), and is an example of the numerical exchanges that are commonplace in royal inscriptions; see De Odorico 1995:67–74.

He received the tribute of Joash of Samaria—Or "Joash the Samarian" (Akkadian *Iuʾasu Samirināya*); see the discussion of the cuneiform transcription in Malamat 1971. The term "Samarian" for the Israelite king appears here in Assyrian texts for the first time, and it continues in use through the 8th century; see, e.g., "Menahem the Samarian" (Text no. 4.02). Assyrian intervention in the affairs of Israel at this point in time is not mentioned in the Bible; yet it is reasonable to detect Assyria and Adad-nerari behind the term "deliverer" in 2 Kgs 13:5: "So the Lord gave Israel a deliverer and they were freed from the authority of Aram. The Israelites lived peacefully as in former times." This deliverance is set in the days of Jehoahaz, the immediate predecessor of Joash, probably towards the end of his reign. By intervening in the affairs of the Syrian kingdoms, Adad-nerari III put pressure on Damascus, thus relieving Israel from the heavy hand of the Arameans; Joash submitted as stated by the al-Rimaḥ stela (see Weippert 1992).

9–12 **He received the tribute of all the kings of the land of Nairi**—The reference to Nairi, in the vicinity of Diyabakir in southeastern Turkey, seems out of place in the context of kingdoms that were all located in the West. Following the suggestion of Tadmor (1973), perhaps it was added in order to fill in a blank space in the line enumerating the king's victories.

References

Dalley, Stephanie M.
1996–1997 Neo-Assyrian Tablets from Til Barsib, *Abr-Nahrain* 34:66–99.

DeOdorico, Marco
1995 *The Use of Numbers and Quantifications in the Assyrian Royal Inscriptions*, SAAS 3, Helsinki.

Ephʿal, Israel and Joseph Naveh
1989 Hazael's Booty Inscriptions, *IEJ* 39:192–200.

Grayson, A. Kirk
1996 *Assyrian Rulers of the Early First Millennium BC. II (858–745 BC)*, RIMA 3, Toronto.

Hasegawa, Shuichi

2008 Adad-Nērārī III's Fifth Year in the Saba'a Stela. Historiographical Background, *RA* 102:89–98.

Lipiński, Edward

2000 *The Aramaeans. Their Ancient History, Culture, Religion*, Leuven.

Millard, Alan R.

1973 Adad-nirari, Aram, and Arpad, *PEQ* 105:161–164.

Millard, Alan R. and Hayim Tadmor

1973 Adad-Nirari III in Syria, *Iraq* 35:57–64.

Page (Dalley), Stephanie

1968 A Stela of Adad-Nirari III and Nergal-Ereš from Tell Al Rimaḥ, *Iraq* 30:139–153.

Malamat, Abraham

1971 On the Akkadian Transcription of the Name of King Joash, *BASOR* 204:37–39.

Schramm, Wolfgang

1972 War Semiramis assyrische Regentin? *Historia* 21:513–521.

Tadmor, Hayim

1973 The Historical Inscriptions of Adad-Nirari III, *Iraq* 35:141–150 (= pp. 321–335 in H. Tadmor, *"With my many chariots I have gone up the heights of mountains": Historical and Literary Studies on Ancient Mesopotamia and Israel*, M. Cogan [ed.], Jerusalem 2011).

Weinfeld, Moshe

1991 Semiramis: Her Name and Her Origin. Pp. 99–103 in Mordechai Cogan and Israel Eph^{c}al (eds.), *Ah Assyria... Studies Tadmor, ScrHier* 33.

Weippert, Manfred

1992 Die Feldzüge Adadniraris III. nach Syrien. Voraussetzungen, Verlauf, Folgen, *ZDPV* 108:42–67.

Yamada, Keiko

2005 "From the Upper Sea to the Lower Sea"—The Development of the Names of Seas in the Assyrian Royal Inscriptions, *Orient* 40:31–55.

Fig. 9. Face of the Pazarcik Stela (*Kahramanmaraş Museum, Turkey*).

CHAPTER 3

Shalmaneser IV

Few inscriptions of Shalmaneser IV (783–773 BCE) have been recovered. The Eponym Chronicle (Text no. 10.01) records six campaigns against Urartu during his reign; yet this obvious concern with the northern border of Assyria did not mean abandonment of the West, for the Chronicle tells of a march to "the Cedar Mountain" (in 775) and "to Damascus" (in 773). This was a period when the influence of powerful governors and officials was much in evidence.

For much of the first half of the eighth century, Jeroboam, son of Joash, reigned as king of Israel (788–747 BCE, including four years as coregent). He is reported to have extended his influence into central Syria: "He restored the boundaries of Israel from Lebo-Hamath to the Sea of the Arabah" (2 Kgs 14:25). The date and the length of time of Israel's resurgence are unknown, but this presence in the area of Hamath could only have come about with the acquiescence of Assyria which continued to attend to its interests throughout the period.

No. 3.01—TO DAMASCUS—THE PAZARCIK STELA

This stela was discovered near the town Maraş during construction work on the Pazarcik dam in southeastern Turkey. Two inscriptions are engraved on the stone; the earlier one on the face of the monument, from the reign of Adad-nerari III, confirmed the boundary between Kummuḫ and Gurgum (see Fig. 9); the later one on the reverse, from the reign of Shalmaneser IV, confirmed this same border and also reported on a campaign to Damascus by Shamshi-ilu, the commander-in-chief, in 773 BCE.

Text edition: Grayson 1996:239–240, no. 1.
Translations: *COS* 2, 283–284; *TUAT* NF II, 67; *HTAT* 276–277.
Photographs: Donbaz 1990, figs. 9–16.

1–3 Shalmaneser, strong king, king of Assyria, son of Adad-nerari, strong king, king of the universe, king of Assyria, king of the four quarters.

4–10 When Shamshi-ilu, the commander-in-chief, marched to Damascus—the tribute of Ḫadianu of Damascus, silver, gold, copper, his royal bed, his royal couch, his daughter with her extensive dowry, the property of his palace without number, I received from him.

11–20 On my return (from Damascus), I gave this boundary stone to Ushpilulume, king of the Kummuḫites. Whoever takes (it) from Ushpilulume, his sons, his sons' sons, may the gods Ashur, Marduk, Adad, Sin, Shamash not stand at his lawsuit (and) and not listen to his prayers. May his country [be broken?] quickly like a brick. May he not give advice to the king. Taboo of Ashur, my god (and) Sin, who dwells in Harran.

4–10 **When Shamshi-ilu, the commander-in-chief, marched to Damascus**—Shamshi-ilu was one of the most prominent officials in Assyria during the first half of the 8th century BCE; he served as eponym three times (in the years 780, 770, 752). He erected stelae that commemorated his personal achievements and whose texts resembled the style of royal inscriptions (see Ikeda 1999:281–290). An oblique reference to this powerful governor just might be behind the unnamed "one who holds the scepter from Beth-eden (=Bit-Adini)" in Amos 1:5 given that the provincial seat of Shamshi-ilu was at Til-Barsip (Kar-Shalmaneser) in the territory of the former Aramean kingdom of Bit-Adini; see Malamat 2001.

The commander-in-chief—The Akkadian term *turtānu* means "the second-in-command." Several *turtānu*s are mentioned in the Bible, one who led the Assyrian army against Ashdod (Isa 20:1) and the other who was part of the Assyrian delegation that negotiated with Hezekiah in 701 BCE (2 Kgs 18:17).

Marched to Damascus—The event referred to is the central event of the year 773 BCE according to the Eponym Chronicle; see Text no. 10.01.

The tribute of Ḫadianu of Damascus—The place of Ḫadianu in the line of succession of the kings of Damascus is unclear. At the end of the 9th century, Ben-hadad, son of Hazael, ruled over the kingdom of Damascus, and it is not known whether there was another king between him and Ḫadianu (that is, if Mari[ʾ], referred to by Adad-nerari III, is Ben-hadad; see Text no. 2.01). The Hebrew transcription of the name is חֶזְיוֹן, a name borne by one of the early kings of Damascus; see 1 Kgs 15:18.

11–20 **On my return (from Damascus), I gave this boundary stone to Ushpilulume, king of the Kummuḫites**—This king is also mentioned on the face of the stela in the text of Adad-nerari III.

May the gods Ashur, Marduk, Adad, Sin, Shamash not stand at his lawsuit (and) and not listen to his prayers. May his country [be broken?] quickly like a brick. May he not give advice to the king—These curses are drawn from the corpus of traditional imprecations that reach back to the days of Hammurabi, king of Babylon in the early 2nd millennium BCE, in which the gods are called upon to punish the violator of oaths and sacred obligations. The gods will not protect offenders and will turn a deaf ear to their prayers. The last two curses are not at all clear because of the bad state of preservation of the stone; for other readings, see Zaccagnini 1993.

References

Donbaz, Veysel

1990 The Neo-Assyrian Stelae in the Antakya and Kahramanmaraş Museums, *ARRIM* 8:5–24.

Grayson, A. Kirk

1996 *Assyrian Rulers of the Early First Millennium BC. II (858–745 BC)*, RIMA 3, Toronto.

Ikeda, Yutaka

1999 Looking from Til Barsip on the Euphrates: Assyria and the West in Ninth and Eighth Centuries B.C. Pp. 271–302 in K. Watanabe (ed.), *Priests and Officials in the Ancient Near East*, Heidelberg.

Malamat, Abraham

2001 Amos 1:5 in the Light of the Til Barsip Inscriptions. Pp. 366–369 in idem, *History of Biblical Israel. Major Problems and Minor Issues*, Leiden.

Timm, Stefan

1993 König Hesion II. von Damascus, *WO* 24:53–84.

Zaccagnini, Carlo

1993 Notes on the Pazarcik Stela, *SAAB* 7:53–72.

Fig. 10. The Iran Stela of Tiglath-pileser III (*Israel Museum*).

CHAPTER 4

TIGLATH-PILESER III

The reign of Tiglath-pileser III (745–727 BCE) ushered in what was surely the most aggressive period of Assyrian expansion. Tiglath-pileser III came to the throne after decades during which the position of the king as head of state had diminished, due in part to the usurpation of power by high officials. He began the imperial renewal by circumscribing the territories of the provincial governors and their responsibilities, and followed this with a series of military campaigns that brought Assyria back to its former predominant position "from the Upper Sea (=Mediterranean) to the Lower Sea (=Persian Gulf)."

The history of Tiglath-pileser III has suffered in modern historical writings because of the sorry state of preservation in which his inscriptions were found. A large part of them had been discovered in the early days of Mesopotamian archaeology during the excavations conducted by Austin Henry Layard at Tell Nimrud (ancient Calah) in 1845. In the southwest palace of Shalmaneser III, Layard discovered a burnt building on the verge of collapse, on whose walls were large reliefs with their inscriptions facing inward. Parts of other reliefs were found stacked on the floor. Layard surmised that the reliefs had been brought from another part of the mound and had been meant for secondary use in the building in which they were discovered. When he reached the central palace and discovered a pile of about 100 additional reliefs, he correctly concluded that Esarhaddon had appropriated the reliefs for his new palace. Layard copied some of the reliefs, made paper squeezes of their inscriptions, and then sawed off the inscriptions from the reliefs so that he could ship "the pictures" to the British Museum in London. Thus was the "official history" of Tiglath-pileser III almost entirely lost.

The early editors of the texts did not note that the original texts belonged to different recensions. Some of the texts were inscribed between two bands of reliefs and differed in the number of lines—somewhere between 7 and 12 lines each—depending on the room in which they were set up; others were inscribed directly on the engraved images—here the number of lines was 16, 20 or more. In addition, the editors did not know that the reliefs came from different rooms in the palace. Hayim Tadmor, who studied Layard's notebooks, unravelled these complexities and published all the inscriptions of Tiglath-pileser III in a new edition that reconstructs their original settings (Tadmor 1994).

No. 4.01—THE AZRIYAU AFFAIR—ANNAL FRAGMENT FROM 738 BCE

The events of the year 738 BCE survive in a fragmentary annal text; they concern a rebellion against Assyria led by a certain Azriyau that took place in the vicinity of Hamath. In the first publication of this text (in 1869), George Smith, one of the fathers of Assyriology, joined a broken clay tablet (K 6205) to the annal text on the basis of the name of a person "*xxx*-yau of Iaudi" who was taken to be Azriyau mentioned in the annals. Now *Iaudu* is the usual Assyrian transcription of the name of the kingdom of Judah and according to Smith, Azriyau was none other than Azariah-Uzziah, king of Judah (cf. 2 Kgs 15:1–7; 2 Chr 26). In the course of the following century, scholars debated the correctness of this identification, pointing out that *Iaudi* was also the name of the kingdom of Samʾal in northern Syria (Tadmor 1961). The matter was partially settled by the discovery made in 1974: the fragment K 6205 was joined to another tablet fragment and it became clear that the new combined text does not belong to the corpus of Tiglath-pileser III (see Na'aman 1974, and Text no. 5.10). Thus, Azriyau of the annals of Tiglath-pileser III remains without a sure identification, neither as to his origin or his kingdom. What is clear is that Hamath was the center of the disturbances in 738 and the engagement there ended with deportation of its residents and the annexation of the territory to Assyria. The text is badly broken and the partial restorations are suggested on the basis of parallel formulations in the annal fragments of the same year (Annals 22 and 26).

Text editions: Tadmor 1994:58–63, Annals, No. 19*; Tadmor and Yamada 2011:42–43.

Translations: *ARAB* 1, §770; *DOTT* 54; *TGI* 54–55; *ANET* 282–283; *TPOA* 97–98; *TUAT* 1/4, 370–371; *COS* 2, 285.

1–12 [...] ... [...] Azriyau [... I] seized and [...] tribute like that [of the Assyrians ...] the city *x* [...] his help. The city El[ ] ... [the city Usn]u, the city Siannu, the city Ma[ ], the city Kashpuna, [which are on the sea]coast, together with the cities [... up to Mount Saue,] which touches [Mount Lebanon,] Mount Ba[ʾali-]ṣapuna, up to Mount Ama[na]na, the boxwood mountain, Mount Sa[ue in its entirety, the district of Kar-Adad, the city of Ḫatarikka, the district] of Nuqudina, [Mount Ḫa]su[atti], together with the cities [in its environs, the city Ara ... on both their sides, the cities of] their environs, Mount Sarbua in its entirety, [the city Ashḫani, the city Yaṭabi, Mount Yaraqu in its entirety...] the city Elitar[bi, the city Zitanu, up to the city Atin[ni ... the city Bumame, 19 districts of Hamath,] together with the cities in its environs, [which are on the sea]coast of the West, [which in rebellion were seized by Azriyau,] I annexed [to the territory of Assyria]. I placed two of my eu[nuchs] over them as governors. [...] 83,000 [...] from those cities, I organized in the province of Tush[ḫan]. 1,223 I settled in the province of Ulluba.

1–12 **[...] Azriyau**—This name is Israelite; this can be determined by the theophoric element -*yahu*, the name of the God of Israel, regularly transcribed in Assyrian cuneiform as -*yau*. As already noted in the introduction to this text, in the first publication of the annals of Tiglath-pileser III, a tablet fragment was joined to the annals; it is now known that the tablet belongs either to Sargon II or Sennacherib (see Text no. 5.10) and what remains of the name of the king in rebellion against Assyria on the tablet: "-yahu, king of Judah," refers most likely to Hezekiah, king of Judah. Therefore, Azriyau of the days of Tiglath-pileser III lacks a sure identification, as there is no information concerning him other than his name. It has been suggested that he was king of Ḫatarikka, biblical Hadrach (Na'aman 1978), but the transcription of the name points to its being an Israelite name. Had Azriyau been an Aramean from north Syria, the transcription would have been **Idriyau*. Still the presence of an Israelite of seeming stature in Hamath remains puzzling; see Cogan and Tadmor 1988:165–166.

1–3 The very fragmentary opening lines apparently tell of the capture of Azriyau and putting down the rebellion he led. The area was reorganized as an Assyrian province.

5–12 **[the city Usn]u, the city Siannu**—For the identifications of these cities, see Text no. 1.01.

The city Kashpuna, [which are on the sea]coast—Perhaps to be identified with Kusbā near Wadi Qadisha, 15 km south of Tripoli.

Mount Ba[ʾali-]ṣapuna—Jebel el-Aqraᶜ in northern Syria; known as Mount Ḫazi in Hittite and Akkadian texts and Mons Casius in classical sources; in the Bible as Zaphon: "the summit of Zaphon" (Isa 14:13; cf. Ps 48:3).

Mount Ama[na]na—Mount Amana, a height in the southern Anti-Lebanon; see Text no. 1.01.

Mount Sa[ue in its entirety—Identified with Jebel Zawiye, east of Tripoli.

The district of Kar-Adad—Perhaps Aleppo, the cult center of the god Adad.

The city of Ḫatarikka—Perhaps Tell Afis, about 40 km southwest of Aleppo. At Tell Afis, the stela of Zakur, king of Hamath and Luᶜash, was discovered; it commemorates the victory over Ben-hadad III and his allies (for the inscription, see *KAI* 204; *COS* 2, 155; for the identification of Ben-hadad III, see Text no. 2.01, lines 15–21).

I placed two of my eu[nuchs] over them as governors—The annexed territories were divided into two provinces.

[...] 83,000 [...] from those cities, I organized in the province of Tush[ḫan]—The vast majority of rebels were transferred to the territory of Tushḫan on the headwaters of the Tigris.

1,223 I settled in the province of Ulluba—In Urartu/Ararat, north of Assyria. According to the Eponym Chronicle, Ulluba was captured in 739 BCE (Text no. 10.01); the resettlement of this group of exiles took place in the following year, after the defeat of Azriyau.

No. 4.02—LIST OF TRIBUTE BEARERS IN 738 BCE—ANNAL FRAGMENT

The list of western monarchs who rendered tribute to Tiglath-pileser III in his 8th year (738 BCE) follows Text no. 4.01, and about 16 lines separated the two texts. These lines, now lost, would have described the battles with Arameans east of the Tigris. The line that comes immediately after it and opens the next unit determines the date of the list; it reads: "In the 9th year of my reign. . . ." Among the tributaries in 738 was Menahem of Samaria. This is not the first appearance of an Israelite king as Assyrian vassal; see Text no. 2.03. For a somewhat earlier list of Tiglath-pileser's vassals, see Text no. 4.03.

Text editions: Tadmor 1994:68–71, Annals 13*, lines 10–12; Annals 14*, lines 1–5; Tadmor and Yamada 2011:46–48.

Translations: *ARAB* 1, §772; *DOTT* 54–55; *TGI* 55; *ANET* 283; *TPOA* 98–99; *TUAT* 1/4, 371; *COS* 2, 285–286; *HTAT* 289.

13*, 10–12; 14*, 1–5

I received the tribute of Kushtashpi of Kummuḫ, Rezin of Damascus, Menahem of Samaria, Hiram of Tyre, Sibitti-biʾil of Byblos, Urikki of Que, Pisiris of Carchemish, Eni-il of Hamath, Panammu of Samʾal, Tarḫulara of Gurgum, Sulumal of Melid, Dadi-ilu of Kaska, Uassurme of Tabal, Ushḫitti of Tuna, Urballa of Tuḫana, Tuḫamme of Ishtunda, Urimmi of Ḫubishna, Zabibe, queen of the Arabs: gold, silver, tin, iron, elephant hides, ivory, multicolored garments, linen garments, blue-purple and red-purple wool, ebony, boxwood, all kinds of precious things from the royal treasure, live sheep whose wool is dyed red-purple, birds of the heavens whose wings are dyed blue-purple, horses, mules, cattle and sheep, she-camels, together with their young. In the 9th year of my reign, the god Ashur supported me and I marched to . . .

The list of tributaries is constructed on the basis of geographic units that may reflect actual regional alliances of kingdoms holding common interests. Kummuḫ is always mentioned first, attributable to its century-long loyalty to Assyria. Afterwards, the order is: central and southern Syria, north Syria, the far North and Northwest. This listing is preserved in all copies of the list.

Rezin of Damascus—Rezin is known to have spearheaded the combined attack of Damascus and Samaria on Jerusalem (2 Kgs 16:5) that took place a few years after the present reference of his submission to Tiglath-pileser III. His name is transcribed here *Raḫianu* and in Text no. 4.03 *Raqianu*. These two forms point to the Old Aramaic form רַצְיָן*; in Hebrew it is represented as רְצִין. The original pronunciation was preserved as late as the 1st century BCE as seen in the form רציאן in the Qumran Isaiah scroll 1QIsa[a] at Isa 9:10. The meaning of the name is "desired, satisfied, pleasant." There was probably an as-yet-unknown monarch in Damascus between Ḫadianu, king of Damascus, in the seventh decade of the 8th century (see Text no. 3.01) and Rezin. On Rezin's later rebellion against Tiglath-pileser III, see Text no. 4.05, lines 3–4.

Menahem of Samaria—Or "the Samarian" (*Meniḫimme Samerināya*). The title "Samarian" had been used earlier with regard to Joash; see Text no. 2.03. The story of Menahem's submission to Tiglath-pileser III in which he paid "1,000 talents of silver," related in 2 Kgs 15:19–20, is not necessarily the tribute payment in the present annal text; see the discussion in Cogan and Tadmor 1988, ad loc.

Hiram of Tyre—For full discussion, see Text no. 4.05, line 8.

Sibitti-biʾil of Byblos—In the mid-9th century, Byblos had opposed Assyrian penetration into the Phoenician coast; see Text no. 1.01, lines 87–96. The Phoenician form of the name was שפטבעל.

Urikki of Que—The name Urikki appears in the bilingual inscription of Azitawada (in Phoenician and hieroglyphic Luwian) from Karatepe (*KAI* 26; *COS* 2, 148–150) as Awariku-Warikus, but there has been some question as to whether Urikki at Karatepe is the king of Que during the reign of Tiglath-pileser III. A new inscription in Phoencian and Luwian by King Warikas, telling of his benevolent submission to Assyria, confirms the identification; see Dion 2006:140–142. Que is the area of the city of Adana in Cilicia. It is referred to as one of the sources for horses traded by King Solomon's dealers; cf. 1 Kgs 10:28.

Pisiris of Carchemish—The kingdom of Carchemish was centered on the upper Euphrates, at Jerablus, 100 km northeast of Aleppo, on the border between Syria and Turkey. Cf. Jer 46:2.

Eni-il of Hamath—The kingdom of Hamath assumed Assyrian vassalage after the defeat of Azriyau; see Text no. 4.01.

Panammu of Samʾal—He is Panammu II mentioned in the Aramaic inscription of his son Bar-rakib who relates that his father, as vassal of Tiglath-pileser III, fell in the battle of Damascus serving his overlord (733/32 BCE); see *KAI* 215; *COS* 2, 158–160.

Samʾal—The name of the kingdom as well as the capital that was located at Zenjirli, northwest of Aleppo, at the foot of Mount Amanus.

Tarḫulara of Gurgum, Sulumal of Melid, Dadi-ilu of Kaska—Neo-Hittite kingdoms in southeast Turkey.

Uassurme of Tabal—Situated in southwest Turkey north of the Taurus mountain range. Tabal (biblical Tubal) is listed among the sons of Japheth in Gen 10:2; cf., also, Ezek 27:13; 38:2–3; 39:1.

Ushḫitti of Tuna, Urballa of Tuḫana, Tuḫamme of Ishtunda, Urimmi of Ḫubishna—All four are small neo-Hittite kingdoms in central Anatolia.

Zabibe, queen of the Arabs—With Assyria dominating the Syro-Phoenician heartland, the desert nomads, who played a key role in the trade that traversed the King's Highway from Damascus to north Syria and its western arm through the kingdom of Israel to Tyre, recognized Tiglath-pileser III as hegemon. The center of the Arabs referred to here was in North Arabia and not the far South, as the latter was still outside Assyria's political horizon. On the Arab tribes, see further Text no. 4.06, lines 19–34; Eph^{c}al 1982: 82–83.

No. 4.03—LIST OF TRIBUTE BEARERS IN 740 BCE—THE IRAN STELA

Only one stela from the reign of Tiglath-pileser III is known; it was apparently discovered near Kermanshah in western Iran. Three fragments of the stela have surfaced; two are now in the Israel Museum, Jerusalem, the third is in a private collection (Fig. 10). The stela was erected in the course of the campaign to the Zagros Mountains in 737 BCE, the last year reported in the historical section of the stela.

The list of monarchs who were tributaries to Tiglath-pileser III comes at the end of the historical survey of the king's nine years in the field, and before the blessings and curses that traditionally conclude a royal inscription. Several items indicate that the list is not dated to the year 737, the year of the Zagros campaign, but was composed prior to it. In the list from 738 (see Text no. 4.02), the king of Tyre is Hiram; Hiram continued to rule over Tyre until 734 as shown by the list of tributaries from that year (see Text no. 4.04). Hence Tubaʾil, king of Tyre, mentioned in the stela, ruled prior to Hiram. In addition to this, the king of Hamath is not included among the vassals enumerated in the stela, and it seems that at the time the list was drawn up, the rebellion in Hamath had not yet been put down; this was accomplished only in 738 in the campaign against Azriyau (see Text no. 4.01). This being so, the list of tributaries in the stela predates that of the annals (Text no. 4.02), and apparently was drawn up sometime between 740 and 739 BCE. The scribes, who accompanied the army on the campaign, had taken along material in anticipation of their having to compose a text for a royal inscription that would be set up in one of the conquered territories. It was customary to commemorate the king's victories with a stela, and to that end, they came equipped with a ready-made tribute list.

Text editions: Tadmor 1994:106–109, Stela III A; Tadmor and Yamada 2011:86–87.
Translations: *TPOA* 98; *TUAT* 1/4, 378; *COS* 2, 28; *HTAT* 289.
Photograph: Tadmor 1994:91.

1–23 The kings of the land of Ḫatti, the Arameans of the western seacoast, the Kedarites (and) the Arabs, Kushtashpi of Kummuḫ, Rezin of Damascus, Menahem of Samaria, Tubaʾil of Tyre, Sibitbaʾil of Byblos, Urik of Que, Sulumal of Melid, Uassurme of Tabal, Ushḫitti of Atuna, Urballa of Tuḫana, Tuḫamme of Ishtunda, Urimmi of Ḫubishna, Dadiʾil of Kaska, Pisiris of Carchemish, Panammu of [Sa]mʾal, Tarḫularu of [Gur]gum, Zabibe, queen of the Arabs—I imposed upon them tax and tribute, silver, gold, tin, iron, elephant hides, ivory, blue-purple and red-purple garments, multicolored garments, linen garments, camels and she-camels.

24–30 As for Iranzu from Mannea, Dalta from Ellipi, (and) the city rulers of Namri and Singibu[tu] (and) all the eastern mountains, I imposed upon them horses, mules, Bactrian camels, cattle and sheep, to be received annually in Assyria.

1–23 **The Kedarites (and) the Arabs**—The term "Arab" is the generic term for all the nomads in the Syrian Desert. This is the first reference in the Assyrian sources to the Arab tribes since the Kurkh Monument of Shalmaneser III (Text no. 1.01).

Kedarites—Akkadian *Qidri*; Hebrew קֵדָר. This tribe or confederation of nomadic tribes spread to many parts of the Syro-Arabian desert. Its center was the oasis at Dumah (Jauf), in eastern Wadi Sirhan. During the Persian

Period, the Kedarites reached as far as the border of Egypt, as is evidenced by the Aramaic inscription on a silver bowl from Tell el-Maskhuṭa in Wadi Tumeilat that mentions "Qainu, son of Geshem, king of Kedar" (*COS* 2, 176); he might be Geshem the Arab, one of Nehemiah's rivals (cf. Neh 2:19). In the Bible, Kedar is one of the sons of Ishmael (Gen 25:13; also Isa 60:7, Jer 49:28). See Ephᶜal 1982:223–227.

Rezin of Damascus—For the various transcriptions of his name, see Text no. 4.02, and also Weippert 1973:46, n. 83.

Menahem of Samaria—*Meniḫimme Samerināya.* Following the date suggested above for this list, Menahem was an Assyrian vassal in 740 BCE, if not earlier.

Tubaʾil of Tyre—The length of his reign is unknown. Other than that he was followed by Hiram who was king in 738 (see Text no. 4.02), there are no other references in the sources to Tubaʾil. The name, in its Hebrew form, is אֶתְבַּעַל; cf. 1 Kgs 16:31. The Assyrian transcription of the name and the one used by Josephus (*Antiquities* 8.317)—*Ithobalos*—reflect the Phoenician form.

Sibitbaʾil of Byblos—In Text no 4.02, the name is transcribed as Sibittibiʾil.

Zabibe, queen of the Arabs—Considering the generic nature of the term "Arabs" (see note above), Zabibe may have been queen of the tribe of Kedar.

24–30 **As for Iranzu from Mannea, Dalta from Ellipi, (and) the city rulers of Namri and Singibu[tu] (and) all the eastern mountains**—This summary of the tributaries from the eastern mountains repeats what had already been reported in the stela concerning the outcome of the campaign in the king's second year.

No. 4.04—LIST OF TRIBUTE BEARERS IN 734 BCE—SUMMARY INSCRIPTION No. 7

This tribute list is part of a summary inscription of Tiglath-pileser III that is inscribed on a large clay tablet of which only about half is extant. The king's conquests "from my accession year until the 17th year of my reign" (745–729 BCE) are related in geographical order from east to west, after which there is a list of all the lands subservient to him. Though the inscription was composed in 729, the list reflects the extent of Assyrian domination in 734. This date is suggested by the inclusion of Mitinti, king of Ashkelon and Ḫanunu, king of Gaza, among the tribute bearers. Both of these kings were in rebellion against Tiglath-pileser during his campaigns to the West in 734–732 BCE, at the end of which Ḫanunu was returned to his former position and Mitinti replaced. Likewise, missing from the list are the kingdoms of Damascus, Israel and Tyre, which were in rebellion against Assyria during those years. From a literary point of view, the list can be divided into two units; the first one includes the monarchs as they appeared in the lists from 740 and 738 (see Text nos. 4.02 and 4.03), the second is new, and it includes the kings of Phoenicia, southern Syria and Judah. Two more recent events are added at the end of the list, as an appendix; they relate the submission of the rulers of Tabal and Tyre who were not included in the list.

Text editions: Tadmor 1994:170–171, Summary 7; Tadmor and Yamada 2011: 122–123.

Translations: *ARAB* 1, §§801–803; *DOTT* 55–56; *TGI* 59; *ANET* 282; *TPOA* 104–105; *TUAT* 1/4, 374–375; *COS* 2, 289; *HTAT* 289.

Rev. 7′ [The tribute] of Kushtashpi of Kummuḫ, Urik of Que, Sibitti-biʾil of [Byblos …],

[Eni]-il of Hamath, Panammu of Samʾal, Tarḫulara of Gurgum, Sulu[mal of Melid …],

[U]assurme of Tabal, Ushḫitti of Tuna, Urballa of Tuḫana, Tuḫam[me of Ishtunda …],

[Ma]tanbiʾil of Arvad, Sanipu of Beth-Ammon, Salamanu of Moab, […],

[Mi]tinti of Ashkelon, Jehoahaz of Judah, Qaushmalaka of Edom, Muṣ-*x*-[…],

[Ḫa]nunu of Gaza: gold, silver, tin, iron, lead, multicolored garments, linen garments, red-purple garments of their lands,

[all kinds of] costly items, the produce of sea (and) land, the commodities of their lands, royal treasures, horses, mules broken to the yo[ke . . . I received].

[U]assurme of Tabal behaved as if he was equal to Assyria and did not appear before me. My eunuch, the chief [eunuch, I sent to Tabal …]

CAMPAIGNS OF TIGLATH-PILESER III, 734–732 BCE

15′ [Ḫ]ulli, son of nobody, I placed on his throne. 10 talents of gold, 1,000 talents of silver, 2,000 horses, [... mules, his tribute I received].

My eunuch, the chief eunuch, I sent to Tyre. From Metenna of Tyre, 150 talents of gold, [(and) 2,000 talents of silver his tribute I received].

10′ **[Ma]tanbi'il of Arvad**—The second unit of new tributaries begins here. **Sanipu of Beth-Ammon, Salamanu of Moab, [...], [Mi]tinti of Ashkelon, Jehoahaz of Judah, Qaushmalaka of Edom, Muṣ-*x*-[. . .], [Ḫa]nunu of Gaza**—The kings of the Transjordan, Philistia and Judah appear for the first time in the inscriptions of Tiglath-pileser III.

Sanipu of Beth-Ammon—The name is known from an Ammonite inscription; cf. Aḥituv 2008:360–370.

Jehoahaz of Judah—Akkadian *Iauḫazi Iaudāya*, i.e., Hebrew יְהוֹאָחָז. This is the full form of the name Ahaz, king of Judah (2 Kgs 16:1). According to the report in 2 Kgs 16:7, the submission of Ahaz to Tiglath-pileser III was meant to save him from the siege that had been set on Jerusalem by Rezin of Damascus and Pekah of Samaria; for the Assyrian viewpoint concerning this event, see comment to Text no. 4.05. According to the Eponym Chronicle (Text no. 10.01), the Assyrian campaign to the southern Levant lasted three years, 734–732 BCE, which suggests that the attack on Judah preceded the arrival of the Assyrian army in the area.

Qaushmalaka of Edom—The reconstructed Moabite equivalent would be קוסמלך*, "the god Kos is king."

12′ **[Ḫa]nunu of Gaza**—Akkadian *Ḫanunu Ḫazzatāya*. The varying transcriptions of the city-name Gaza permits determining the original first consonant: In Akkadian *ḫet*, in Hebrew *ʿayin* (עַזָּה), in Greek transcription *gamma* (Γάζα), and in Arabic غ (غزة); the initial consonant was *ġ*. As to the vowel of the second syllable, it is given here as *Ḫazzatu* (also Text nos. 4.12, 14′; 4.13, 8′); but in other texts, it is *Ḫazzutu* (Text 4.13, line 9′). This interchange of *â›ô/û* is also documented in Hebrew, e.g., the name of the Red Sea coast town of Elath/Eloth (2 Kgs 16:6).

14′ **[U]assurme of Tabal**—He had been one of Tiglath-pileser's loyal vassals in the early years of the decade (see Text nos. 4.02 and 4.03), but he rebelled and was removed.

My eunuch, the chief [eunuch, I sent to Tabal . . .]—The Assyrian title *rab ša rēši* (in the Hebrew Bible: Rabsaris) means "chief eunuch"; he held high positions in the Assyrian military, at times serving as commander-in-chief (Tadmor 1983). A Rabsaris was a member of the delegation that negotiated with Hezekiah; see 2 Kgs 18:17.

10 talents of gold, 1,000 talents of silver—These very large sums (300 kg of gold and 30,000 kg of silver) may be compared to the amount received from Metenna of Tyre, and they are indicative of the payments made by usurpers in order to secure their thrones. Menahem, king of Israel, made a similarly large payment—1,000 talents of silver—"so he (Tiglath-pileser) would support him in holding on to the kingdom" (cf. 2 Kgs 15:19–20).

16′ **Metenna of Tyre**—Metenna took the throne sometime after 734 BCE, when Hiram was removed (see Text no. 4.05, line 5).

150 talents of gold, [(and) 2,000 talents of silver his tribute I received]—4,500 kg of gold and 60,000 kg of silver.

No. 4.05—SUMMARY INSCRIPTION No. 9

The fragments of a large clay tablet were recovered in the temple of the god Nabu at Calah; they were inscribed with a typical summary inscription of Tiglath-pileser III, in which the events were organized in geographical order. A small tablet fragment (Summary 10; Tadmor 1994:192) in the British Museum may belong to Summary 9; but the physical join cannot be checked as the tablet is in Baghdad. The conquests in the West during the years 738, 734-732 BCE are presented in brief statements, and are parallel to similar summaries in Text nos. 4.06 and 4.07. Indeed, the three texts complement one another, which aids in reconstructing the broken lines in each, as well as in identifying the individual events (though some remain unclear). The paragraph division is original; the scribe drew a dividing line on the tablet between events. All the summary inscriptions were composed in 729 or slightly thereafter, as is shown by the opening statement: "From my accession year until the 17th year of my reign." The following excerpt treats north Syria, Israel and Philistia.

Text editions: Tadmor 1994:186–189, Summary 9; Tadmor and Yamada 2011:131–132.

Translations: *ARAB* 1, §§815–817; *TGI* 57–58; *TPOA* 102–103; *TUAT* 1/4, 376–378; *COS* 2, 291–292; *HTAT* 294–295.

Rev.

[The city of Ḫata]rikka, as far as Mount] Sa[ue], the city Kashpuna on the shore of the Upper Sea [and the cities Ṣimirra and Arqa]

[to] the territory of Assyria I added. Two of my eunuchs as governors [I placed over them.

The wide [land of Bit-]Ḫazaʾili in its entirety, from [Mount Leb]anon up to the city Gilea[d, Abel-*x*-*x* …]

[on the b]order of land of Bit-Ḫumria, I added to the territory of Assyria. My eunuch [as governor I placed over them.]

[Hi]ram of Tyre, who conspired together with Rezin [ ]

[The city] Maḫalab, his fortified city, together with (other) strong cities, I captured. [Their] spoil […]

He came before me and kissed my feet. 20 talents [of gold …]

Multicolored [garments], linen garments, eunuchs, male and female singers, *x* [horses of] Egy[pt … I received.]

[The land of Bit-Ḫumria] to its limit [I conquered … with their] possessions, [I brought to Assyria.]

[Hoshea] as king over them [I placed.]

[To the city] Sarabanu before me [he/they brought]

[From …] *x* + 100 talents of silver I took away and [brought to Assyria.]

[Ḫanunu of Gaza was frightened by my powerful weapons] and fled [to Egypt … Gaza]

[An image of the great gods, my lords, and my royal image of gold] I made [and set it up] in the palace of Gaza.

[I counted them among the gods of his land. … He,] like a bird, [flew back] from Egypt

[ ] his [... I made into] an Assyrian customs-house.

Fifteen very fragmentary lines follow, which tell of battles with Arabs (as in Text nos. 4.06 and 4.07) and of the gifts paid by other western monarchs.

Rev. 1 Events associated with the year 738.

[The city of Ḫata]rikka, as far as Mount] Sa[ue]—See Text no. 4.01.

The city Kashpuna on the shore of the Upper Sea—See Text no. 4.01. The "Upper Sea" is the Assyrian designation for the Mediterranean Sea. In this case, the scribe erred; he wrote "Lower Sea," that is, the Persian Gulf.

3–4 The capture of Damascus was accomplished after a lengthy two-year siege in 733 and 732 BCE (see Eponym Chronicle, Text no. 10.01); the restorations are based on Text no. 4.06. Rezin, king of Damascus, was party to the rebellion against Assyria together with Tyre, Israel, Ashkelon and Gaza. The attack on Jerusalem by Rezin and Pekah, reported in 2 Kgs 15:37; 16:5–9; Isa 7:1–9, was apparently aimed at applying pressure on Ahaz to join the anti-Assyrian camp. For another view on this assault on Judah's capital, see Oded 1972.

The wide [land of Bit-]Ḫazaʾili in its entirety—Besides the two appellations encountered in the inscriptions of Shalmaneser III (*ša māt imērišu; Dimašqi*), the kingdom of Damascus was also known as "the land of the House of Hazael." From the description given here, it emerges that on the eve of Tiglath-pileser's campaign, the borders of Damascus in northern Transjordan reached as far as the city of Gilead. Now the report in 2 Kgs 14:28 credits Jeroboam II of Israel with having recovered this area and extended Israel's hegemony beyond Damascus into northern Syria. Apparently sometime after his death, the northern Transjordanian territories ("the Bashan," cf. Deut 3:1–7) came under Aramean control again (see Tadmor 1962).

From [Mount Leb]anon up to the city Gilea[d, Abel-*x-x* . . .] [on the b]order of land of Bit-Ḫumria—Restored on the basis of Text no. 4.06, line 6. If correct, Gilead is to be identified with one of the towns south of the River Yarmuk, either Jabesh-gilead or Ramoth-gilead, both in the district of Gilead. A city named "Gilead" is not known, though the prophet Hosea, who lived

Fig. 11. Assyrian soldiers taking away captives and spoils from "the city of Astartu"; palace relief of Tiglath-pileser III (*Courtesy of the Trustees of the British Museum*).

at this time, did rebuke Gilead as being "a city of evildoers, tracked up with blood" (Hos 6:8).

The partial information available from the annals on battles in northern Transjordan is supplemented by a palace relief showing the capture of a city and the taking of captives and spoils; it is identified by the caption: "The city of Astartu"; i.e., Ashtaroth, Tell ^{c}Ashtarah in the Bashan (see Fig. 11). In biblical tradition, Ashtaroth was the residence of Og, king of the Bashan (Deut 1:4; 3:1).

I added to the territory of Assyria. My eunuch [as governor I placed over them.]—The incorporation of Damascus into the Assyrian provincial system marked the end of the monarchy of Damascus.

5–8 Tyre submitted during the first stage of the campaign in 734 BCE, as the Assyrian army made its way down the seacoast towards Philistia, the main goal of that year (see Text no. 10.01).

5 **[Hi]ram of Tyre**—The name Hiram is spelled here in an unusual form, *Ḫirimmu* instead of the form *Ḫirummu* used in other texts. Biblical texts also preserve two forms of the name: Hiram (2 Sam 5:11; 1 Kgs 5:15) and Hirom (1 Kgs 7:40). The form with *o*/*u* apparently reflects the Phoenician form of the name (חרום).

Who conspired together with Rezin—This short item attests to the broad support for the rebellion against Tiglath-pileser III. While the Bible speaks only of Rezin and Pekah, the Assyrian inscriptions attest to the inclusion of Hiram and Ḫanunu of Gaza (see line 13) among the breakaway vassals.

[The city] Maḫalab, his fortified city—Located at el-Maḫalab, about 6 km northeast of Tyre. The town is mentioned by Sennacherib (Text no. 6.01) and also as Ahlab in Judg 1:3; in Josh 19:29 (where the text reads erroneously מחבל for מחלב).

[Horses of] Egy[pt . . . I received.]—Egyptian horses were apparently of a special breed and were considered worthy gifts by Assyrian kings; cf. Text no. 5.09.

9–11 These very broken lines refer to the battles in the kingdom of Israel during 734–732 and can be restored with the help of Text no. 4.06, lines 15–18.

[Hoshea] as king over them [I placed.]—The change of rulers in Samaria is described in 2 Kgs 15:30: "Hoshea, son of Elah, conspired against Pekah, son of Remaliah. He attacked and killed him; and succeeded him as king." The Assyrian text relates the confirmation of Hoshea by Tiglath-pileser III as king and vassal.

[To the city] Sarabanu before me [ ]—This city, in the district of Bit-Shilani in southern Babylonia, was the site of battles by Tiglath-pileser III in 731. In that year, Hoshea sent his gifts to his overlord (as a sign of his continued loyalty?); see Borger and Tadmor 1982.

12 The surrender of a city, perhaps in Philistia, whose identity is irretrievable; for the suggestion that it was Ashkelon, see Tadmor 1994.

13–16 The surrender of Gaza.

16 **[... I made into] an Assyrian customs-house**—The founding of a customs-house in Philistia, one of the innovations of Tiglath-pileser III, clearly points to the strong economic drive at the base of Assyrian expansion, whose goal was the domination of international trade. Gaza sat astride the road that led from Egypt northward and its port served the export of goods from south Arabia that reached the coast after having passed through the Negeb desert.

Gaza's special status is seen in the erection of a gold (!) statue of the king in the city's palace, which, following Tadmor's suggestion, portrayed the king wearing on his chest the symbols of the gods. The requirement that the residents of Gaza honor the sovereign's gods together with their own gods does not mean that the worship of Assyrian gods was imposed upon them; rather it was a sign of the obeisance due the hegemon, especially following the increased Assyrian presence in the city. On the question of the imperial cult, see Cogan 1993 and further below in Text no. 4.07.

No. 4.06—SUMMARY INSCRIPTION No. 4

This summary inscription was inscribed on a large pavement stone, only part of which was discovered by Layard in the excavations at Calah. The paper squeezes of the fragments that were made on site were subsequently lost, and the text is known only from the reconstruction made by George Smith, and now corrected by Tadmor on the basis of the copies in Smith's notebooks. The extant text parallels the summaries in other texts (see Text nos. 4.05 and 4.07); the date of composition is, like the other summary inscriptions, 729 BCE.

Text editions: Tadmor 1994:136–143, Summary 4; Tadmor and Yamada 2011: 105–107.

Translations: *ARAB* 1, §§815–819; *DOTT* 55; *TGI* 58–59; *ANET* 283–284; *TPOA* 101–102; *TUAT* 1/4, 373–374; *COS* 2, 287–288; *HTAT* 292, 294.

[...] which [...] the city of Ḫatarikka up to Mount Sau[e]
...[ ] Byb[los ... Ṣi]mirra, Arqa, Zimar[ra]
...] Usnu, [Siannu, Ma]ʾaraba, Riʾiṣu[ri]
...] the cities [...] *x x* [of the Upper [Sea], I ruled. Six of [my] eunuchs
[as governors over] them I appointed. [. . . Kash]puna, which is on the shore of the Upper Sea
[*up to* the city *Qa*]nite, Gil[ead and]Abel- *x-x*, which are on the border of Bit-Ḫumri[a]
[the] wide [land of Bit-Ḫazaʾi]li in its entirety, I added to the territory of Assyria.
[*x* eunuch]s of mine as governors [over them I app]ointed. Ḫanunu of Gaza

[who before] my weapons fle[d and to] Egypt escaped—Gaza
[*I entered/captured*]. His property (and) [his] gods [I took as spoil. The image of the gods,] my lords and my royal image
[of gold I made], in the palace [of Gaza I set it up] and I counted them among the gods of his land.
...] I established. [ov]erwhelmed him and like a bird
[out of Egypt] flew [ ] I returned him to his position.
[... I made into an Assyrian customs-]house. [Gold,] silver, multicolored garments, linen garments,
large [horses], ... [I re]ceived. The land of Bit-Ḫumria
...his] auxiliary [troops...] all of its people
...to] Assyria I carried off. Pekah, their king, [I/they ki]lled *x-x* and Hoshea
[as king] I appointed over them. 10 talents of gold, *x* talents of silver, [with] their [property] I received from them and
[to Assyria I carried] them off. As for Samsi, the queen of the Arabs, at Mount Saqurri
9,400 (of her people) I defeated. 1,000 people, 30,000 camels, 20,000 cattle
...] 5,000 (containers) of various spices, *xxx* pedestals of her gods,
[weapons (and) staffs of her goddess,] and her property, I seized. And she, in order to save her life,
...to the de]sert, a place of thirst, like a wild ass
[headed. The rest of her possessions,] her [ten]ts, her people's protection, within her camp
[I set on fire. And *Samsi*] was frightened [by] my mighty [weapon]s; camels, she-camels
[with their foals, to Assyria, before] me she brought. I appointed an inspector over her and
[10,000 soldiers...] The people of Massaᵓ, Tema, Sabaᵓ,
[Ḫayappâ, Badanu], Ḫatte, Idibaᵓilu,
...] on the border of the western lands
[of whom no one knew and whose place] is far, the fame of my lordship
[... they heard and they *beseeched*] my lordship. Gold, silver,
[camels, she-camels, various spices,] their tribute, as one,
[they brought before me and kissed] my feet.
[Idibiᵓilu as gatekeeper to]wards Egypt, I appointed.
[the weapon of the god of A]shur I placed therein.
...] I made and
...] the yoke of the god Ashur, my lord

[I placed on them … in all the lands through which] I had marched.

1′ **[…] which […] the city of Ḫatarikka up to Mount Sau[e]**—Cf. Text no. 4.05, line 1.

2′–4′ **…] Byb[los … Ṣi]mirra, Arqa, Zimar[ra] …] Usnu, [Siannu, Ma]ʾaraba, Riʾiṣu[ri]**—Cf. text no. 4.07, lines 8′–9′. In the Iran stela, the name of the city Riʾiṣu[ri] is given as Reshi-ṣuri, that is, "Top of the Rock."

5′ **[. . . Kash]puna, which is on the shore of the Upper Sea**—Along the Phoenician coast. The common reading "Rashpuna" (see, e.g., *ANET* 283b) is a scholarly error; see Tadmor 1985.

6′ **[*up to* the city *Qa*]nite, Gil[ead and]Abil- *x-x*, which are on the border of Bit-Ḫumri[a]**—Qanite is identified with modern Qanawat in the Hauran (Jebel ed-Druz), biblical Kenath (Num 32:42; 1 Chr 2:23). It was a large city in the Bashan, the region in northern Transjordan that was the point of contention between Israel and Damascus over several centuries and that changed hands a number of times.

Gilead—Cf. Text no. 4.05, line 3.

Abel- *x-x*—There are two broken cuneiform signs that are undecipherable. A number of suggestions have been made to complete the name of this town that consists of the West-Semitic geographic term Abel, which means "stream of water." For example, Abel-beth-maachah (2 Kgs 15:29), a site in the Upper Galilee quite distant from the others mentioned. A possible reading is Abel-shittim, a town in the plain of Moab (cf. Num 33:49); but this locates the border of Damascus quite far south and would imply the elimination of the Israelite rule in the Gilead, in contradiction to the claim of 2 Kgs 15:29. See, too, Na'aman 1995.

12′–13′ **[ov]erwhelmed him and like a bird [out of Egypt] flew [ ] I returned him to his position**—Ḫanunu's speedy return from Egypt indicates that he could not find refuge there, a sign that at this juncture Egypt's rulers sought to avoid entanglement with Assyria. From the Assyrian perspective, the importance of stability in this vital trade area explains the re-installment of Ḫanunu to his former position (cf. Weippert 1982:397).

15′-17′ **The land of Bit-Ḫumria [. . . his] auxiliary [troops . . .] all of its people [. . . to] Assyria I carried off**—This is the earliest reference to the forced induction of Israelite soldiers into the Assyrian army; cf. the later incorporation of charioteers from Samaria into Sargon's royal guard, Text no. 5.02.

17′–18′ **Pekah, their king, [I/they ki]lled and Hoshea [as king] I appointed over them. 10 talents of gold, *x* talents of silver, [with] their [property] I received from them**—This description parallels the report of Hoshea's usurpation of the throne in Samaria in 2 Kgs 15:30; the Assyrian account speaks of confirmation of Hoshea by Tiglath-pileser III.

19′–20′ **As for Samsi, the queen of the Arabs, at Mount Saqurri 9,400 (of her people) I defeated**—According to Text no. 4.08, line 18, Samsi had sworn allegiance to Tiglath-pileser III and here she is reported to have joined the rebellion against Assyria. The Assyrian army pursued her to Mount Saqurri—perhaps Jebel ed-Druz (so Ephᶜal 1982:85)—a first step in an attempt to impose Assyrian authority over these desert dwellers. The army, however, did not continue the pursuit into the heart of the desert. With the defeat of Damascus, Samsi came to terms with Assyria (line 25′) and delivered her rich tribute as a gesture of submission.

27′–34′ The text is completed in part by Summary Inscription no. 7 (Tadmor 1994:168–169).

27′–29′ **The people of Massaᵓ, Tema, Sabaᵓ, [Ḫayappâ, Badanu], Ḫatte, Idibaᵓilu, [. . .] on the border of the western lands**—Massaᵓ, Tema, and Idibaᵓilu (Hebrew אַדְבְּאֵל) appear in the list of the sons of Ishmael in Gen 25:13–15.

Tema—The name of an Arab tribe (cf. Isa 21:14), as well as a major oasis in northern Arabia on the way to the countries of the Fertile Crescent. See further Text no. 11.05, col. ii, line 5.

Sabaᵓ—Perhaps to be identified with the important south Arabian kingdom of Sheba within the territory of modern-day Yemen, which in the 1st millennium BCE was noted for its trade in luxury goods—spices, gold and precious stones. These items appear repeatedly in the lists of gifts that Assyrian kings received from the Arab tribes. Note, too, that the Queen of Sheba who visited King Solomon bore similar riches (1 Kgs 10:1–3; cf., too, Isa 60:6). Though Sheba was located in the far south, it would have had an interest in the affairs in the Fertile Crescent, especially that section of the King's Highway that passed through Transjordan to Damascus and on to north Syria; and perhaps there were Sabeans who settled in that area (Ephᶜal 1982:83–91).

[Ḫayappâ]—The biblical Ephah (עֵיפָה) was one of the descendants of Keturah (Gen 25:4), all of whom were settlers of the northern Sinai Peninsula.

[Badanu], Ḫatte—These tribes are not mentioned in any other source, but it is reasonable to think that they were settled in the same areas as the other nomads.

34′ **[Idibiʾilu as gatekeeper to]wards Egypt, I appointed**—The tribe of Idibaʾil was integrated into the Assyrian administration of northern Sinai as "gatekeeper," that is, overseer of the traffic that moved in the area between Philistia and Egypt.

No. 4.07—SUMMARY INSCRIPTION No. 8

This fragment of a large clay tablet was found at Calah in 1950; the remains of 27 lines, part of a detailed summary inscription, are recoverable. It may have been part of the same tablet as Summary Inscription No. 7 (Tadmor 1994:154–175) on which the list of tributaries in 734 BCE appears (see Text no. 4.04). Parallel texts are Text nos. 4.05 and 4.06, which supply many of the reconstructions.

Text editions: Tadmor 1994:176–179, Summary 8; Tadmor and Yamada 2011:126–128.

Translations: *TGI* 56; *TPOA* 103–104; *TUAT* 1/4, 375–376; *COS* 2, 290–291; *HTAT* 292.

…] *x* […

…] his […] on dry land […]

…] I made (them) pour out [their lives (?)]. That city to[gether with…]

…] in the midst of the sea I overwhelmed them into [oblivion…]

…] and his heart pounded. He put on sackcloth […]

…] of ivory, ebony inlaid with (precious) stones, gold with […]

…] ivory, fine oil, all sorts of spices, horses from E[gypt . . .]

…] *x x* from Kashpuna, which is on the shore of the [Upper] Sea…]

…] under the control of my eunuch, the governor of the city Ṣi[mirra I placed. …]

…like gr]ass, with the bodies of their warriors, I filled [the plain.…]

…together with] their possessions, their cattle, their sheep, their asses […]

…] within his palace […]

…*atone*]*ment* of their sins I accepted, and their country [*I spared* …]

…Ḫan]unu of Gaza was frightened by my powerful weapons and [he fled to Egypt]

…*Gaza* …*I conquered* x *talents of*] gold, 800 talents of silver, people together with their possessions, his wife, [his] sons, [his daughters…]

…His property (and) his gods *I took as spoil.*] The image of the great gods, my lords (and) my royal image of gold [I made],

…in the palace of Gaza I set it up and I counted them among the gods of his land.] Their […] I established. And he, like a bird out of Egypt [flew]

…I returned him to his position. […] into an [Assyrian (customs-)house] I made. My royal stela in the city of the Wadi of Egypt, a river[-bed *without water*…I set up.]

…From…*x* + 100 talents of] silver I took away and [brought] to Assyria.

…to the kings] who preceded me had not submitted and had not sent them greetings, about the conquest of Ḫa[tti (?) he…heard …]

…] and was frightened. His envoys to do obeisance to me [he sent…]

…] Siruatti, the Me'unite, whose [dwelling is] below Egypt […]

…] exalted, about my extensive conquests he he[ard…]

…] at Mount Saqurri 9,400 (of her people) I defea[ted.…]

…] her [gods,] weapons, staffs of her goddess(es), […]

…to the desert, a place of thirst, like a wild a]ss she headed. The rest [of her possessions…]

…] she-camels [with their foals.…]

4′ **…] in the midst of the sea I overwhelmed them into [oblivion…]**—The identification of the subject of this passage is difficult. If the kingdom referred to is Tyre, which was situated on an island opposite the coast (as suggested by Eph^{c}al 1982), then the order of events in this summary inscription differs from the others. It is perhaps preferable to identify the enemy here as Arvad, which also was an island kingdom.

7′ **Horses from E[gypt…]**—Cf. Text no. 4.05, line 8.

8′–9′ **From Kashpuna, which is on the shore of the [Upper] Sea . . .] under the control of my eunuch, the governor of the city Ṣi[mirra I placed. . . .]**—Kashpuna was annexed to the province of Ṣimirra.

10′–13′ **Like gr]ass, with the bodies of their warriors, I filled [the plain . . . together with] their possessions, their cattle, their sheep, their asses [. . .] within his palace [. . . *atone*]*ment* of their sins I accepted, and their country [I *spared* . . .]**—The identity of this engagement is doubtful. For a suggestion that the reference is to the assassination of Pekah by Hoshea in the palace of Samaria, see Na'aman 1986:72–73.

16′–17′ **The image of the great gods, my lords (and) my royal image of gold [I made, in the palace of Gaza I set it up and I counted them among the gods of his land.]**—According to Tadmor's suggestion (1994), only one statue was set up, that of the king bearing on his chest the symbols of the gods. In any case, placing the king's statue in a conquered city is quite unusual and this is the only example of this practice from the days of Tiglath-pileser III; similar acts are accredited to Shalmaneser III. The significance of this act is not altogether clear; perhaps the palace at Gaza also served as a shrine, but there is no evidence for the ascription of divine status to Assyrian kings. For sure the very presence of the king's image in one of the major cities of Philistia clearly marked its new position as an important Assyrian center.

18′ **My royal stela in the city of the Wadi of Egypt, a river [. . . I set up.]**—In biblical cartography, the Wadi of Egypt (נַחַל מִצְרַיִם) marked the southern border of Canaan, cf. Num 34:5; Ezek 47:19; it is commonly identified with Wadi el-ᶜArish. For a different identification, see Na'aman 1979, and the counter-arguments of Rainey 1982. See also the discussion in Text no. 8.03, lines 39–42.

22′ **Siruatti, the Me'unite, whose [dwelling is] below Egypt**—The Me'unites were an Arab tribe that ranged in the northern Sinai Peninsula. The geographic indication "below Egypt" recognizes Egyptian influence in the area south of Raphia. A late biblical tradition tells of King Uzziah, who reigned slightly earlier than Tiglath-pileser III, as having fought "against the Philistines, against the Arabs who lived in Gur-baal, and the Meunites" (2 Chr 26:39–41); see the discussions of Tadmor 1971; Ephᶜal 1982:91–92; 219–220.

No. 4.08—SUMMARY INSCRIPTION No. 13

This inscription was originally inscribed upon a large bas-relief, which was discovered mostly destroyed. The unusual order of events in the text suggests that it is a variant summary inscription. The components discernible are: the submission to Tiglath-pileser III in Calah of an unnamed king, the Arabian campaigns, the surrender of Hoshea.

Text editions: Tadmor 1994:198–203, Summary 13; Tadmor and Yamada 2011:111–112.
Translations: *ARAB* 1, §§778–779; *ANET* 283; *TUAT* 1/4, 372; *COS* 2, 292.

…] *x* […
…*he sent*] to Calah befo[re me *to do obeisance*…]
…As for Samsi, queen of] the Arabs, at Mount Sa[qurri…]
…] her [en]tire camp […   ]
…by] my [weapons] was frightened […]
…brought to As]syria in[to my presence…]
…an inspector over her I ap]pointed and ‹10,000› soldie[rs…]
…at] my [feet] I had them submit. The people of [Massaʾ,]
[Tema, Sab]aʾ, Ḫaya[ppâ,]
[Badanu, Ḫat]te, I[dibaʾilu,]
…on the bor]der of the western lands […]
…the fa]me of my lordship (and) [my heroic] de[eds]
…*they heard*…] Gold, silver, camels,
[she-camels,] various spices, their tribute, as [one, before me
[they brought and kis]sed [my] feet. Their gifts […]
…] Idibiʾilu as [gatekeeper] towards [Egy]pt, I appointed.
[The land of Bit-Ḫumria,] all of [whose] cities, in my former campaign, I had lev[elled,]
[ ] its livestock I took as spoil and Samaria alone I spar[ed. Pek]ah, their king

---

1′–2′ **…*he sent*] to Calah befo[re me *to do obeisance*…]**—Tadmor suggests that the tribute mentioned here was from a king of Egypt and was received in 730 BCE, a year during which the king stayed "in the land," that is, did not take part in a campaign (see Text no. 10.01).

3′–15′ **...As for Samsi, queen of] the Arabs, at Mount Sa[qurri...]**—A short version of the battles conducted against the nomads, given in fuller form in Text no. 4.06, lines 19′–36′.

16′–17′ **[The land of Bit-Ḫumria,] all of [whose] cities, in my former campaign, I had lev[elled,]**—The reference to earlier campaigns against Israel may refer to the taking of the Galilee and the Gilead. This could have occurred during 733 BCE, the first year of the siege of Damascus (see Text no. 10.01). In any case, it seems clear that there was more than one thrust against Israel.

A palace relief, known only in a copy from Layard's notebooks, depicts the assault on "the city of Gezer" (Akkadian *Gazru*) in the Aijalon Valley; see Fig. 12. This Israelite city was most likely taken in the 734 phase of the western campaign, as the Assyrian army advanced on Philistia; see Cogan 2015.

Fig. 12. Attack on the city of Gezer; drawing of a relief from Calah (now lost).

Samaria alone I spar[ed. Pek]ah, their king—Restored on the basis of Text no. 4.06, line 17′.

No. 4.09—DEFEAT OF DAMASCUS IN 732 BCE—ANNAL FRAGMENT

This annal fragment treats the war against Rezin of Damascus and it is the most detailed one concerning this front that has survived. The date of the battles is set by the Eponym Chronicle (Text no. 10.01) in which the entry "to Damascus" is given for the years 733 and 732 BCE. The fragment is no longer extant and the text is available only in the notebooks of the first editors. The Assyrian report complements the laconic biblical reference concerning the fall of Damascus: "The king of Assyria marched against Damascus and captured it. He exiled it (i.e., its inhabitants) to Kir and put Rezin to death" (2 Kgs 16:9).

Text editions: Tadmor 1994:78–81, Annals, no. 23; Tadmor and Yamada 2011:57–59.
Translations: *ARAB* 1, §776–777; *ANET* 283; *TPOA* 100; *TUAT* 1/4, 372; *COS* 2, 286; *HTAT* 292–293.

[of] Rezin [of Damascus…
[he]avy […] his advisor […
[the blood of his] war[riors, the river […] raging
[I pa]inted re[d…] his [cour]tiers
charioteers and […]—their weapons I broke.
[ ]*x* their horses *x* […] his warriors, his archers,
shield- and lance-bearers I myself captured and their battle-array
[I scatt]ered. He, in order to save his life, fled alone,
[and like] a mongoose entered the gate of his city. His chief ministers, alive
I impaled, and had (the people of) his land behold them. For 45 days, my camp
I set up around his city and locked him up like a bird in a cage. His gardens
[ ] his orchards without number I cut down; I did not leave a single one.
[the town of]ḫadara, the ancestral home of Rezin of Damascus,
[the pl]ace of his birth, I invested and captured. 800 persons with their possessions,
their cattle (and) their sheep, I took as spoil. 750 captives from Kuruṣṣa
(and) Sama, 550 captives from Metuna I took. 591 cities
from the 16 districts of Damascus I destroyed like mounds after the Flood.
Samsi, queen of the Arabs, who broke the oath of the god Shamash

8′–9′ **He, in order to save his life, fled alone, [and like] a mongoose entered the gate of his city**—It is not unusual to find the Assyrian scribes employing colorful images like the present one that aim at belittling the enemy king: in the face of Assyria's overwhelming might, Rezin fled like a small, defenseless animal to seek refuge. For a discussion of this literary feature of the Assyrian royal inscriptions, see Marcus 1977.

10′–11′ **My camp I set up around his city and locked him up like a bird in a cage**—Damascus was sealed off from the outside world. This same image appears with reference to Sennacherib's investment of Jerusalem; see Text no. 6.01. Tadmor views this simile "as a face-saving device," hiding the fact that the city under siege withstood the attack and did not fall to the Assyrians. Indeed, Damascus held out for two years.

11′–12′ **His gardens [ ] his orchards without number I cut down; I did not leave a single one**—The willful destruction of a major economic source was an oft-used tactic against defiant cities. Tiglath-pileser III punished his enemies in southern Babylonia in similar fashion, as seen in the relief that depicts soldiers cutting down date palms in Babylonia; see Barnett and Falkner 1962: pl. xxxiii. Cf., too, Shalmaneser III's actions in the district of Hauran reported in Text no. 1.03, lines 14–21.

13′–14′ **[the town of]ḫadara, the ancestral home of Rezin of Damascus, [the pl]ace of his birth**—The town has not been identified; perhaps el-Ḥadar, 53 km southwest of Damascus (Forrer 1920:62). The reference to the ancestral town may infer that Rezin did not belong to the main line of succession in Damascus.

15′–16′ **750 captives from Kuruṣṣa (and) Sama, 550 captives from Metuna I took**—A review of the suggested locations of these cities by Lipiński 2000:364–365 shows them all to be very speculative.

16′–17′ **591 cities from the 16 districts of Damascus I destroyed like mounds after the Flood**—Surely such a large number of cities includes many towns and villages in the environs of Damascus. Their total destruction "like mounds after the Flood," is verbal hyperbole, making up somewhat for not having broken through the defenses of the capital. Yet, in the end, Damascus did surrender to Tiglath-pileser III.

18′ **Samsi, queen of the Arabs, who broke the oath of the god Shamash**—This is all that remains of the episode concerning the Arabs; see Text no. 4.06, lines 19′–38′. The mention of the god Shamash, rather than the chief god Ashur, before whom oaths of loyalty were usually taken, is likely due to the scribe's wish to create a pun of the name Samsi.

No. 4.10—CONQUEST OF THE GALILEE—ANNAL FRAGMENTS

Two annal fragments, both very broken, preserve the report of events in the kingdom of Israel in 733–732 BCE. The few remaining lines tell of deportations from the Lower Galilee and complement the statement in 2 Kgs 15:29 that notes towns captured in the Upper Galilee: "In the days of Pekah, king of Israel, Tiglath-pileser, king of Assyria, came and took Ijon, Abel-beth-maachah, Janoah, Kedesh, Hazor—the Galilee and the Gilead—all the land of Naphtali. He exiled them." These actions took place during the two years that Damascus was under siege. The translation that follows is based on the two fragments that, according to the reconstruction of Tadmor (1994:220–221), come from two different recensions of the annals; Annals 18 is the main text and Annals 24 (given in bold print) provides a number of restorations.

Text editions: Tadmor 1994:80–83, Annals No. 18 || No. 24; Tadmor and Yamada 2011:61–63.

Translations: *ARAB* 1, §779; *ANET* 283; *TPOA* 100–101; *TUAT* 1/4, 372–373; *COS* 2, 286; *HTAT* 293–294.

[ ] *x* [ ] *ti* [ ]

[like] fog *x* [ ] it.

[...**of sixteen**] districts of the land of Bit-[*Ḫumria*], *I ut*[*terly destroyed* ...]

[*x* captives from the city]bara, 625 captives from the city of [..., **226 *captives from*** ...]

[*x* captives from the city of] Hannathon, 650 captives from the city of Ku[..., **400 *captives from*** ...]

[*x* captives from the city of Ia]ṭbite, 656 captives from the city Sa-[*x* **13,520** (people)... **with their possessions** ...]

[...] the city Aruma, the city Marum **[(*that were in*) difficult mountains ...]**

[...**Mitinti of**] Ashkelon, his loyalty oath [*he broke* **and rebelled against me** ...]

[. . . the defeat of Re]zin he saw and in an attack [*of panic* (?) . . . **he became frightened** . . .]

[**Rukibti, son of** . . .] sat on his throne as [king . . .]

[. . .] he wandered about and beseeched me. 500 [. . .]

[. . .] I entered his city. 15 citi[es . . .]

[I]dibiʾilu the Arab [. . .]

3′ **[. . . of sixteen] districts of the land of Bit-[*Ḫumria*]**—The districting of the kingdom of Israel is only attested in this passage. There is a report of the twelve-part division of the United Kingdom ascribed to Solomon (see 1 Kgs 4:7–19), but it is not related to the present matter. Because the number of districts—sixteen—is also ascribed to Damascus (see Text no. 4.09, line 17), some suggest that the reconstructed reading should be: Bit-[*Ḫazaʾili*]; see, e.g., Oded 1970:196–197. This would imply that in the period prior to Tiglath-pileser's campaign, the Galilee had come under the control of Damascus, an assumption that is at odds with the information in 2 Kgs 15:29. An alternate suggestion takes the two annal texts as close, but not completely parallel, with only Annals 18 recording the depopulation of the Galilee; see Galil 2000:514–515.

4′ **[*x* captives from the city]bara**—Several suggestions have been made as to the restoration of this toponym: [Ga]bara, Roman Gabara, today Kh. Kabara in the Lower Galilee (Forrer 1920:61); [Ak]bara, Akbara, south of Safed (Mazar 1933:3); and even [Beth]-barah, on the River Jordan, mentioned in Judg 7:24.

5′ **[*x* captives from the city of] Hannathon**—This town was located at Tell el-Bediwîyeh in the Beth-Netophah Valley and was assigned to the tribe of Zebulun (Josh 19:14).

6′ **[*x* captives from the city of Ia]ṭbite**—Perhaps the city Jotbah referred to in 2 Kgs 21:19. Much later, in the time of the Great Revolt against Rome, Iotapata was the headquarters of Josephus (*Jewish War* 3. 7. 7 et al.); today Kh. Jifât.

656 captives from the city Sa-[ ]—A possible restoration is Sa[runa], Kh. Saruna in the Lower Galilee (Forrer 1920:61); another possible reading is Sam[ḫuna], Kh. Seimûniyeh (Tel Shimron), biblical Shimron; cf. Josh 11:1 (so Na'aman cited by Tadmor 1994:82).

13,520 . . . with their possessions . . .]—Apparently the number refers to the total of persons exiled from the Galilee. This figure, together with those given of the individual towns, are the only written evidence for the size of the population from the days of the kingdom of Israel; for a discussion of population size from the archaeological perspective, see Shiloh; Broshi and Finkelstein.

7′ **[. . .] the city Aruma**—Perhaps Rumah, Kh. er-Rûmeh in the Beth-Netophah Valley; cf. 2 Kgs 23:36.

The city Marum—Identified as Merom (Josh 11:5), evidently Tell el-Khirbeh, at the foot of Marûn er-Râs in the Lebanese Galilee opposite Kibbutz Yiron.

8′–10′ **[. . . Mitinti of] Ashkelon, his loyalty oath [*he broke* and rebelled against me . . . the defeat of Re]zin he saw and in an attack [*of panic* (?) . . . he became frightened . . . Rukibti, son of . . .] sat on his throne as [king . . .]**—The anti-Assyrian coalition was broad-based, and included Damascus, Israel, Ashkelon, Gaza (see Text no. 4.06, line 13), as well as Tyre (see Text no. 4.05, line 5); this is in contrast to the impression given by the biblical text (2 Kgs 16:6–9) that only Samaria and Damascus had thrown off the yoke of Tiglath-pileser III. Mitinti was an Assyrian vassal until 734 BCE (see Text no. 4.04), but apparently had been enticed to join the rebels. Following the downfall of Rezin, the backbone of the coalition, Mitinti may have committed suicide or perhaps he was killed. His successor Rukibti remained loyal to Assyria up until the rebellion against Sennacherib. Rukibti's son was appointed king at the end of the battles in 701 BCE (see Text no. 6.01).

11′–12′ **[. . .] he wandered about and beseeched me. 500 [. . .] I entered his city. 15 citi[es . . .]**—The subject may be Rukibti and the payment he transferred to Tiglath-pileser III; see the discussion of Wazana 2003:113–114.

13′ **[I]dibiʾilu the Arab [. . .]**—For this episode, see Text no. 4.06, line 34.

References

Aḥituv, Shmuel
2008 *Echoes from the Past*, Jerusalem.

Barnett, Richard D. and Margarete Falkner
1962 *The Sculptures of Tiglath-pileser III (745–727 B.C.)*, London.

Borger, Rykle and Hayim Tadmor
1982 Zwei Beiträge zur alttestamentlichen Wissenschaft auf Grund der Inschriften Tiglathpileser III, *ZAW* 94:244–251.

Broshi, Magen and Israel Finkelstein
1992 The Population of Palestine in Iron Age II, *BASOR* 287:47–60.

Cogan, Mordechai
1973 Tyre and Tiglath-pileser III, *JCS* 25:96–99.
1993 Judah Under Assyrian Hegemony: A Reexamination of Imperialism and Religion, *JBL* 112: 403–414.
2015 When Was Gezer Captured by Tiglath-pileser III?, *IEJ* 65:96–99.

Cogan, Mordechai and Hayim Tadmor
1988 *II Kings*, Anchor Bible 11, Garden City.

Dion, Paul-Eugene
2006 Ahaz and Other Willing Servants of Assyria. Pp. 133–145 in J. R. Wood, J. E. Harvey, M. Leuchter (eds.), *From Babel to Babylon. Essays on Biblical History and Literature in Honour of Brian Peckham*, New York-London.

Eph^{c}al, Israel
1982 *The Ancient Arabs*, Jerusalem.

Forrer, Emil
1920 *Provinzeinteilung des assyrischen Reiches*, Leipzig.

Galil, Gershon
2000 A New Look at the Inscriptions of Tiglath-pileser III, *Bib* 81:511–520.

Kessler, Karlheinz
1975 Die Anzahl der assyrischen Provinzen des Jahres 738 v. Chr. in Nordsyrien, *WO* 8:49–63.

Levine, Louis D.
1972 Menahem and Tiglath-pileser: A New Synchronism, *BASOR* 206:40–42.

Lipiński, Edward
2000 *The Aramaeans. Their Ancient History, Culture, Religion*, Leuven.

Marcus, David
1977 Animal Similes in Assyrian Royal Inscriptions, *Or* 46:86–106.

Mazar, Benjamin
1933 The Campaign of Tiglath-pileser III to the Land of Israel in 732 BCE, *BJPES* 1:1–6 (Hebrew).

Na'aman, Nadav
1974 Sennacherib's "Letter to God" on His Campaign to Judah, *BASOR* 214:25–39.
1978 Looking for *KTK*, *WO* 9:220–239.

1979 The Brook of Egypt and Assyrian Policy on the Border of Egypt, *Tel Aviv* 6:61–68.

1986 Historical and Chronological Notes on the Kingdoms of Israel and Judah in the Eighth Century B.C., *VT* 36:71–92.

1995 Rezin of Damascus and the Land of Gilead, *ZDPV* 111:105–117.

Oded, Bustenay

1971 Darb el-Hawarneh, An Ancient Route, *ErIsr* 10:191–197 (Hebrew).

1972 The Historical Background of the Syro-Ephraimite War Reconsidered, *CBQ* 34:153–165.

1974 Phoenician Cities and the Assyrian Empire in the Time of Tiglath-pileser III, *ZDPV* 90:38–49.

Rainey, Anson F.

1982 Toponymic Problems (cont.), *Tel Aviv* 9:131–132.

Shiloh, Yigal

1981 The Population of Iron Age Palestine in the Light of Urban Plans, Areas, and Population Density, *ErIsr* 15:274–282 (Hebrew).

Tadmor, Hayim

1961 Azriyau of Yaudi, *ScrHier* 8:232–271.

1962 The Southern Border of Aram, *IEJ* 12:114–122.

1971 The Me'unites in the Book of Chronicles in the Light of an Assyrian Document. Pp. 222–230 in *Bible and Jewish History* (*Studies Liver*), Benjamin Uffenheimer (ed.), Tel-Aviv (Hebrew). (= English translation, pp. 793–804 in H. Tadmor, *"With my many chariots I have gone up the heights of mountains": Historical and Literary Studies on Ancient Mesopotamia and Israel*, M. Cogan [ed.], Jerusalem 2011.)

1983 Rab-saris or Rab-shakeh in 2 Kings 18. Pp. 279–285 in Carol L. Meyers and M. O'Connor (eds.), *The Word of the Lord Shall Go Forth*, Winona Lake, IN.

1985 "Rashpuna"—A Case of an Epigraphic Error, *ErIsr* 18:180–182 (Hebrew).

1994 *The Inscriptions of Tiglath-pileser III King of Assyria*, Jerusalem.

Tadmor, Hayim and Shigeo Yamada

2011 *The Royal Inscriptions of Tiglath-pileser III (744–727 BC) and Shalmaneser V (726–722 BC), Kings of Assyria*, RINAP 1, Winona Lake, IL.

Wazana, Nili

2003 "I Removed the Boundaries of Nations" (Isa. 10:13): Border Shifts as a Neo-Assyrian Tool of Political Control in Ḫattu, *ErIsr* 27:110–121 (Hebrew).

Weippert, Manfred

1973 Menahem von Israel und seine Zeitgenossen in einer Stelainschrift des assyrichen Königs Tiglathpileser III. aus dem Iran, *ZDPV* 89:26–53.

1982 Zur Syrienpolitik Tiglathpilesers III. Pp. 395–408 in H.-J. Nissen and J. Renger (eds.), *Mesopotamien und seine Nachbarn*, vol. 2, Berlin.

Fig. 13. Statue of winged bull from the palace of Sargon II at Khorsabad (*Courtesy of the Trustees of the British Museum*).

CHAPTER 5

Sargon II

Sargon II (722–705 BCE) ascended the throne in Assyria after the death of Shalmaneser V. Most historians hold that Sargon was not the legitimate successor, although recent restudy of the sources has suggested that he was of royal blood, being a son of Tiglath-pileser III. Only after a struggle to solidify support for his rule was Sargon able to undertake military campaigns whose aims were to reestablish Assyrian hegemony over the kingdoms that had rebelled on the death of Shalmaneser V.

Many of the questions concerning Sargon II's activities in Israel and Philistia have no definitive solution because of the poor state of preservation of the inscriptions, as well as their many internal contradictions. One of the knotty issues is the fixing of absolute dates for events during his reign, made especially difficult due to the difference of one year between the dates given in the Khorsabad annals and those in the Nineveh prisms. Hayim Tadmor explained this as the result of the reworking of the material by the scribes at Khorsabad who transferred events from later years to earlier ones in order to cover up the fact that the king did not undertake military activity each year. It seems, therefore, that the dating used in the Nineveh prisms is preferable.

Two of Sargon's major encounters are treated in the following sections, the conquest and the exile of Samaria, and the operations at Ashdod. Sargon II's claim to have captured Samaria is contradicted by the short biblical report that ascribes the fall of Samaria to Shalmaneser V; indeed Sargon is not mentioned at all.

> Shalmaneser, king of Assyria, marched against him, and Hoshea became his vassal and rendered him tribute. But when the king of Assyria discovered that he was part of a conspiracy, for he had sent envoys to Sais, ‹to› the king of Egypt and withheld the yearly tribute to the king of Assyria, the king of Assyria arrested him and put him in prison. The king of Assyria invaded the whole country; he marched against Samaria and laid siege to

> it for three years. In the ninth year of Hoshea, the king of Assyria captured Samaria. He exiled Israel to Assyria and resettled them in Halah and on the Habor, the river of Gozan, and in the cities of Media (2 Kgs 17:3–6).

There seems to be little doubt that this Israelite account is wanting and it needs to be supplemented by the Assyrian evidence. The relevant Assyrian texts relating to this issue are treated below. For recent discussions and suggested reconstructions of the course of events, see Cogan and Tadmor 1988:195–201; Na'aman 1990; Hayes and Kuan 1991; Becking 1992; Galil 1995a; Younger 1999.

No. 5.01—THE FALL OF SAMARIA AND ASHDOD—KHORSABAD SUMMARY INSCRIPTION

This Summary Inscription was composed in c. 707 BCE, two years before the death of Sargon II. It was incised on the walls of five different rooms in the king's palace in the newly constructed capital of Dur-Sharrukin (Khorsabad). The presentation of events lack chronological order as is typical of this genre; their dates can be established on the basis of an analysis of the various recensions of the annals.

Text edition: Fuchs 1994:196–198, 219–222.
Translations: *ARAB* 2, §§55, 62; *DOTT* 60; *TGI* 62–64; *ANET* 284–286; *TPOA* 107–109, 113–114; *TUAT* 1/4, 383–385; *COS* 2, 296–297; *HTAT* 302, 306–307.

23–27 From accession year to the fifteenth year of my reign, I defeated Ḫumbanigash, king of Elam, in the district of Der. I besieged and captured Samaria. I took as spoil 27,290 people who live there; I organized (a contingent of) 50 of their chariots and I instructed the rest of them in correct conduct. I appointed my eunuch over them and imposed upon them the tribute of the former king. Ḫanunu, king of Gaza, and Reᵓe, the commander-in-chief of Egypt, marched against me to wage war and battle at Raphia. I defeated them. Reᵓe was frightened by the sound of my weapons and he fled, and his place is undisclosed. I captured with my own hand Ḫanunu of Gaza. I received the tribute of Pharaoh, the king of Egypt, Samsi, queen of the Arabs, Itᵓamara, the Sabaean: gold, dust of the mountains, horses and camels.

33–36 Yaubiᵓdi of Hamath, a low-class person, with no right to the throne, an evil

Hittite, schemed to become king of Hamath. He caused Arpad, Ṣimirra, Damascus and Samaria to rebel against me, and he came to an agreement with them and prepared for battle. I mobilized the numerous troops of Assyria; at Qarqar, his beloved city, I besieged him and his troops, and I captured him. I set fire to Qarqar. I flayed him. I killed the rebels of those cities and established order. I organized (a contingent of) 200 chariots and 600 riding horses from among the people of Hamath, and added them to my royal corps.

90–109 Azuri, king of Ashdod, plotted not to deliver tribute and sent seditious words concerning Assyria to the kings in his neighborhood. Because of the crimes he committed against the people of his land, I abolished his rule. I appointed Aḫimiti, his favorite brother, as king. But the people of Ḫatti, speakers of lies, disliked his kingship and they elevated Yamani, who had no right to the throne, and like them, did not respect my authority. In my fury, I did not gather my numerous troops and did not mobilize my soldiers; with (only) my warriors, who even in [frie]ndly ar[eas] do not leave my side, I marched to Ashdod. And, he, Yamani, heard from afar the approach of my campaign, and he fled to the border of Egypt in the district of Meluḫḫa, and his place is undisclosed. I besieged Ashdod, Gath, and Ashdod-yam, and captured (them). I counted as spoil his gods, his wives, his sons and his daughters, property (and) possessions, the treasures of his palace, together with the people of his land. I reorgan[ized] these cities. People from the lands that I had conquered with my own hand, that were in the eastern [*district*], I set[tled in them], and I appointed [my eunuch as gov]ernor over th]em. I counted them with the people of Assyria and they bear my yoke.

109–112

The king of Meluḫḫa, who in [*x x* the land of] Uriṣṣu, an out-of-the-way place, [ ] *x* [from] distant [times] until now, his forefathers had not sent a messenger to the kings, my forefathers, in order to inquire of their well-being, [heard] from afar of the might of the gods Ashur, Nabu and Marduk; the awesome splendor of my kingship overwhelmed him and he was seized by panic. He put him (Yamani) in manacles and iron fetters and they brought (him) before me to Assyria (after) a l[ong] journey.

23–27 **From accession year to the fifteenth year of my reign**—This is the typical opening formula of a Summary Inscription; cf. introduction to Text no. 4.05.

The term "accession year" (Akkadian *rēš šarrūti*) refers to the period time from the king's taking the throne until the beginning of his first year that was counted from the Assyrian New Year celebrated in the month of Nisan. The accession year is not counted in the total number of years of the king's reign. The equivalent term in biblical Hebrew is שְׁנַת מָלְכוֹ; cf. 2 Kgs 25:27. In Aramaic documents from Wadi Daliyeh, the term appears as ראש מלכות.

I defeated Ḫumbanigash, king of Elam, in the district of Der—The report in the Babylonian Chronicle contradicts this statement: The Elamites "caused the Assyrians to retreat; he inflicted a great defeat upon them" (Text no. 11.01, lines 33–35). Sargon's claim of victory is overstated; as a result of a setback at Der, Sargon did not interfere in the affairs in the south for the next ten years. It is possible that the Elamites were bribed by the Chaldean Merodach-baladan to attack the Assyrians at Der; for this reconstruction of the events, see the discussion of Grayson 1965:341–342.

Der—Located at Tell ^{c}Aqar, near Badrah, c. 130 km east of Baghdad, on the Iraq-Iran border.

I besieged and captured Samaria—The Assyrian form of the name—Samerina—reflects the Aramaic pronunciation *Šamarayîn* (cf. שָׁמְרַיִן in Ezra 4:10); see, too, the discussion in Text no. 11.01, obv. col. 1, line 28.

I took as spoil 27,290 people who live there—A variant reads 27,280. This figure is too large for the population of the city Samaria alone and probably included persons from the entire district of Samaria (Younger 1998). At the same time, one should not credit the biblical verse: "The King of Assyria captured Samaria; he exiled Israel to Assyria" (2 Kgs 17:5b–6a), as if a total depopulation of Israel had been undertaken.

I organized (a contingent of) 50 of their chariots—A variant reading: 200 chariots.

I instructed the rest of them in correct conduct—The residents of Samaria who remained in the land were instructed in the proper behavior expected of Assyrian citizens. This included "to revere god and king," i.e., rendering homage to the imperial god Ashur and the reigning king as his earthly representative. Experts were sent to Samaria to oversee the instruction of the surviving Israelites and the exiles that were brought to the newly founded province of Samerina (see further in Text no. 5.02). For a discussion of the

Fig. 14. Assyrians and Cushites battle at Raphia (P. E. Botta–E. Flandin, *Monument de Ninive* II, Paris 1849, pl. 88).

methods and goals of Assyrian exile, the deportation and exchange of population, see Oded 1979.

Ḫanunu, king of Gaza, and Reʾe, the commander-in-chief of Egypt, marched against me to wage war and battle at Raphia—Tiglath-pileser III had reappointed Ḫanunu as king in Gaza after an earlier rebellion (see Text no. 4.05, lines 13–16). At the same time, Egyptian support of anti-Assyrian elements in Philistia remained a repeated phenomenon in the relations between the Assyrian empire and its southern vassals. It is not known which of the kings of the Delta sent a task force to support the rebels in Gaza. However, if the reliefs in Sargon's palace (Room v, nos. 3 and 4; see Fig. 14) depict the battle at Raphia, then the scene of Cushite fighters fleeing from Assyrian soldiers suggests that the king of Egypt who sent troops to aid Ḫanunu was Shabaka, who had come to the throne in Cush upon the death of Pi(ᶜankh)y and later overran the Delta before Sargon reached Gaza (see Kahn 2001). Two other reliefs, from the same series that depicts the battles in Philistia and the Judean Shephelah in 720, bear short inscriptions above cities under attack: *Gabbutunu* (Room v, no. 5), Gibbethon, Tell Melāt, west of Gezer (cf. Josh 19:44, in which Gibbethon is assigned to the tribe of Dan); and *ʾAmqar*[*r*]*una* (Room v, no. 10), Ekron. For the dating of the palace reliefs at Khorsabad to the various campaigns of Sargon, see the studies of Reade 1976; Franklin 1994; Russell 1999:114–123.

I received the tribute of Pharaoh, the king of Egypt—The king may be either Tefnakht of Sais or Osorkon IV of Tanis (see Text no. 5.09).

Samsi, queen of the Arabs—Samsi had recognized Assyrian hegemony during the rule of Tiglath-pileser III, more than a decade earlier (see Text no. 4.06, lines 19–20).

Itʾamara, the Sabaean—Perhaps the leader of a Sabaean colony in north Arabia. The strengthening of Assyrian presence in the border areas of the West led the three rulers mentioned here to recognize Sargon's rule.

33–36 **Yaubiʾdi of Hamath, a low-class person, with no right to the throne, an evil Hittite, schemed to become king of Hamath**—Yaubiʾdi appears as Ilubiʾdi in Text no. 5.03. The form Yaubiʾdi has been interpreted as containing the theophoric element *yahu-*, the name of the God of Israel, and taken as evidence for Israelite influence in northern Syria (see, e.g., Dalley 1990). But this is contradicted by the other form of the name, Ilubiʾdi, leaving the meaning of Yaubiʾdi unexplained (see van der Toorn 1992). For a survey of Yahwistic names in Neo-Assyrian texts, see Younger 2002.

He caused Arpad, Ṣimirra, Damascus and Samaria to rebel against me—The uprisings against Sargon II in the West included Assyrian provinces throughout Syria and as far south as Israel. The description of the conquest of Samaria that leads off the list of victories above was a later stage in the campaign in 720 BCE that began with the battle against Yaubiʾdi; see further Text no. 5.04. (The text on a fragmentary stela from Ashrane, on the River Orontes, downstream from Qarqar, seems to suggest that Ḫatarikka also participated in the anti-Sargon uprising; see Tadmor 1958:137, n. 137.)

At Qarqar, his beloved city, I besieged him and his troops—Qarqar was the site of the battle between Shalmaneser III and the western coalition in 853; see Text no. 1.01, lines 87–96.

90–112 **Azuri, king of Ashdod, plotted not to deliver tribute**—For another description of the Ashdod campaign, see Text no. 5.08.

They elevated Yamani, who had no right to the throne—In Sargon's annals, Yamani is referred to as Yadna. Yamani is a West-Semitic name (and does not mean "a Greek," as given in *ANET* 286, n. 12); cf. the similar Hebrew names Imnah (Gen 46:17) and Jamin (1 Chr 4:24). Yamani had usurped the throne, and as such, his rule is described as being improper; cf. the expression "son of nobody" in Text no. 1.02, lines 97–99.

He fled to the border of Egypt in the district of Meluḫḫa—Yamani sought refuge in Upper Egypt, the stronghold of the Cushite rulers of Egypt. Meluḫḫa, an antiquated geographical designation, stands for Cush; see further Text no. 9.01. Cush was an independent kingdom in the vicinity of Jebel Barkal close to the Fourth Cataract of the Nile. In the second half of the 8th century, the Cushite kings made repeated efforts to seize all of Egypt; Shabaka (721–707 BCE) succeeded in doing so by moving on Memphis in 720, thus dominating Upper and Lower Egypt.

I besieged Ashdod, Gath, and Ashdod-yam, and captured (them).

Ashdod—Tel Ashdod, c. 7 km south of the city of Ashdod and 4 km inland from the present-day coastline.

Gath—One of the five major Philistine cities, Gath was located at Tel Ẓafit (Tell eṣ-Ṣafi), on the southern bank of Naḥal Elah, 2 km south of Kefar Menaḥem. For the history of the disputed identification of Gath and the now recognized location, see Rainey 1975.

Ashdod-yam—"Ashdod of the sea," the port of Ashdod. Its remains lay buried c. 5 km northwest of Ashdod.

I reorgan[ized] these cities . . . and I appointed [my eunuch as gov]ernor over th]em—Ashdod became an Assyrian province, an unusual measure in Assyrian provincial organization, considering that the city had no contiguous border with any other imperial territory. Moreover, it seems that a unique arrangement was set in place in Ashdod: alongside the Assyrian governor, a local king continued to rule. This emerges from the reference to Mitinti, king of Ashdod, in the inscriptions of Sennacherib (see Text no. 6.01), a loyal vassal of Assyria.

109–112 **The king of Meluḫḫa, who in [*x x* the land of] Uriṣṣu, an out-of-the-way place**—The reference is to Upper Egypt; the name in Egyptian means "the southern district."

He put him (Yamani) in manacles and iron fetters and they brought (him) before me to Assyria (after) a l[ong] journey—The extradition of Yamani by the Cushite king is reported in another of Sargon's inscriptions, the rock relief in Iranian Kurdistan recently discovered:

> I took spoil from the city of Ash[do]d. Yamani, its king, was frightened by [my] we[apons]...he fled to the district of Meluḫḫa and dwelt (there) like a thief...Shapataka, king of Meluḫḫa, heard of the power of the god Ashur, Nabu and Marduk, which [ ] I [ ] in all the lands (?), (and) he put him in manacles and fetters...and brought him to me. (Frame 1999: lines 19–21)

The inscription dates from 706 BCE, incised at the end of campaign against Karalla. It is the only text that reports on Yamani's extradition by Shabatka (= Shapataka). This datum provides *terminus ante quem* for Shabatka's taking the throne in Egypt, i.e., towards the end of 707 BCE. His gesture towards Egypt's northern rival replaced the hostile anti-Assyrian policy of his predecessor Shabaka; see the full discussion in Kahn 2001.

No. 5.02—THE FALL OF SAMARIA—CALAH SUMMARY INSCRIPTION

The description of Sargon II's activities in Samaria as recorded on a prism discovered at Calah are, for the most part, identical with those given in the annals; a number of recensional differences may be noted: the number of exiles from Samaria and the size of the force enlisted in the Assyrian army. As is customary in summary inscriptions, the order of presentation follows a geographical order, without any consideration given to chronology.

Text edition: Gadd 1954:179–180, cols. iv, lines 25–49.
Translations: *DOTT* 60; *TGI* 60–61; *TPOA* 109–110; *TUAT* 1/4, 382; *COS* 2, 295–296; *HTAT* 301–302.

Col. iv, 25–49

[The Sa]marians, who had come to an agreement with a [*hostile*?] king not to do service or to render tribute to me, did battle. In the strength of the great gods, my lords, I fought with them; 27,280 people, together with [their] char[iots] and the gods in whom they trust, I counted [as] spoil. 200 chariots I organized as a royal contingent from among them and the rest of them I settled in Assyria. I resettled Samaria more (densely) than before (and) brought there people from the lands of my conquest. I appointed my eunuch over them as governor and counted them as Assyrians. I spread the splendor of the god Ashur, my lord, over the Egyptians and the Arabs, and at the mention of my name, their heart beat fast and they let down their hands. I opened the sealed [po]rt of Egypt and let the [people] of Assyria and Egypt mingle together, and [had them] trade with each other.

Col. iv, 25–49

[The Sa]marians, who had come to an agreement with a [*hostile*?] king not to do service or to render tribute to me, did battle—The reference to the rebellious inhabitants of the city—Samarians—and not to its king seems to imply that there was no reigning monarch in Samaria. This unusual state of affairs may have arisen after the imprisonment of King Hoshea (cf. 2 Kgs 17:4) and the surrender of the city to Shalmaneser V at the end of 722 BCE (see Text no. 11.01, lines 24–28). The unexpected death of Shalmaneser may have rekindled Israelite resistance to Assyria, this time led by army officers, as no further king is known to have ruled in Samaria after Hoshea. The reference to the king with whom Samaria conspired is likely Yaubiʾdi of Hamath who is the sole person mentioned by name in Sargon's texts when speaking of affairs in the West.

27,280 people—The figure in the Khorsabad inscriptions is 27,290.

The gods in whom they trust, I counted [as] spoil—It was common practice for the Assyrian army to carry off divine images from a captured city (see Cogan 1974:22–41). The "gods" taken from the territory of Samaria may refer to the golden calf that was in the sanctuary of Bethel; cf. Hos 10:5–6: "The inhabitants of Samaria fear for the calf of Beth-aven (i.e., Bethel); its people shall mourn for it...for the glory that has departed from it. It too shall be brought to Assyria as tribute to a Great King." For the suggestion that the broken relief in the palace at Dur-Sharrukin (Khorsabad), Room 5, 6–8, depicts Assyrian soldiers taking away the Israelite images, see Uehlinger 1998:768–770.

200 chariots I organized as a royal contingent from among them—The figure in the Khorsabad inscriptions is 50. Assyrian administrative texts relate to the service of the Samarian charioteers, who served along with other recruits in a Samarian unit. For these "Horse List" texts, see Cogan 2013:42–45.

The rest of them I settled in Assyria—The complementary biblical text relates: "He exiled Israel to Assyria and resettled them in Halah and on the Habor, the river of Gozan, and in the cities of Media" (2 Kgs 17:6). The Assyrian text prompts the suggestion that the unnamed "king of Assyria" in

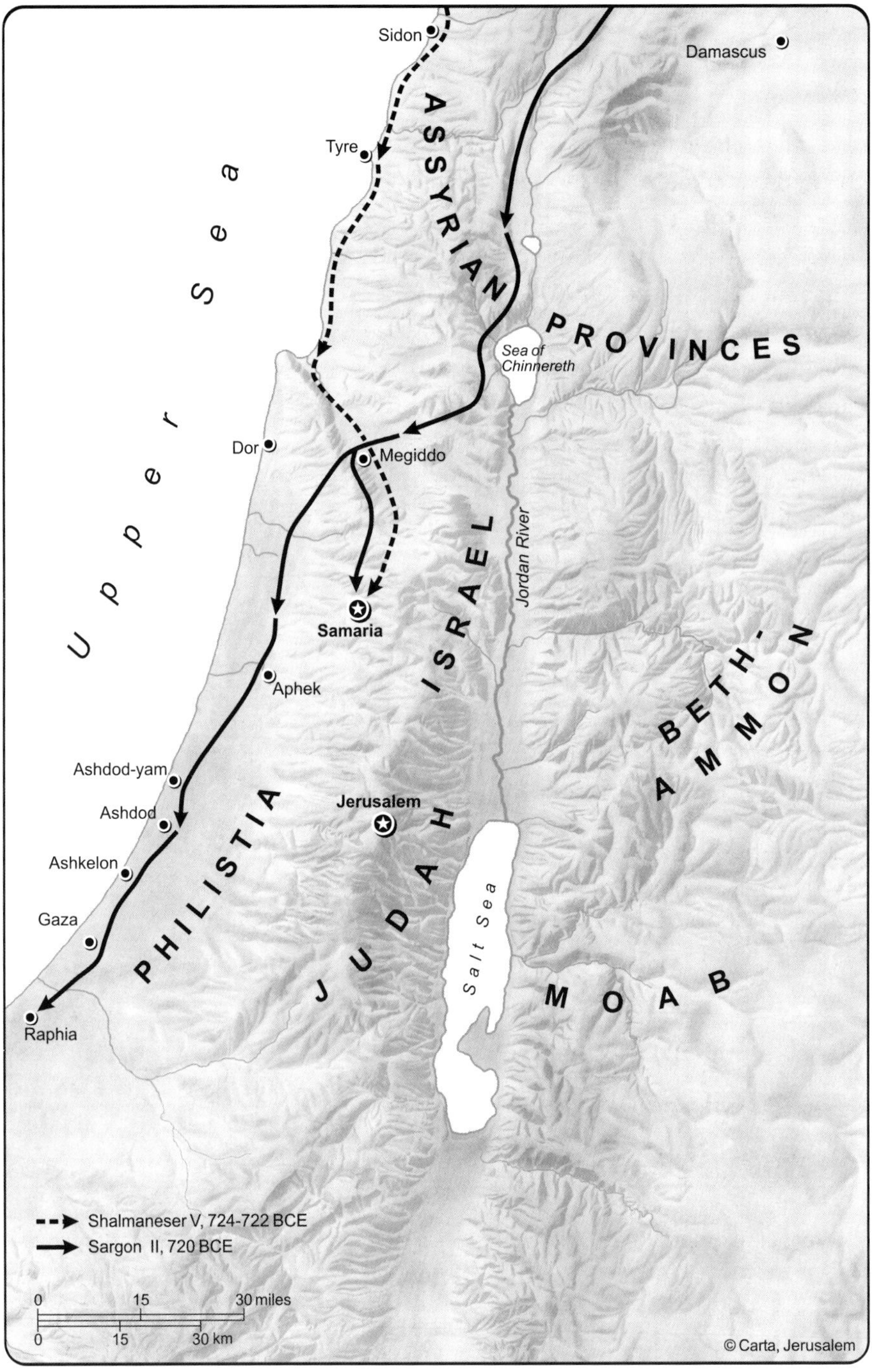

ASSYRIAN CAMPAIGNS TO ISRAEL, 724–720 BCE

2 Kings 17 was Sargon II and not Shalmaneser V, who died before formally annexing the city. For the later whereabouts of the exiled Samarians, see the discussions by Eph^{c}al 1991; Oded 2000; Cogan 2013:34–35.

I resettled Samaria more (densely) than before (and) brought there people from the lands of my conquest—The re-population of Samaria took place in stages over several years. For example, Sargon reports transferring desert-dwelling Arabs to the new province; see Text no. 5.03, lines 120–125; and see Na'aman and Zadok 2000. Biblical texts also relate to this process. In 2 Kgs 17:24: "The king of Assyria then brought (people) from Babylon, Cutha, Avva, Hamath, Sepharvaim, and settled them in the cities of Samaria in place of the Israelites"; Ezra 4:2 and 9–10 refer to the Assyrian kings Esarhaddon and Osnappar (i.e., Ashurbanipal) who "deported and settled (peoples) in the city of Samaria." On these reports, see Cogan 1988. In the center of the city of Samaria, the new provincial capital, a royal stela was erected, proclaiming Sargon's victories; a single fragment of this stela has survived, see Appendix.

I opened the sealed [po]rt of Egypt—The exact location of this port is nowhere given. Several identifications, based upon archaeological findings, have been put forward: (1) Tell Abu Salima, on the coast between Raphia and el-^{c}Arish, a fortress with an Assyrian-type shrine of the 8th–7th century BCE (Reich 1981); (2) Ruqeish, a fortified settlement on the coast of Deir el-Balaḥ, south of Gaza (Oren 1993).

I let the [people] of Assyria and Egypt mingle together, and [had them] trade with each other—A little more than a decade earlier, Tiglath-pileser III had founded a customs depot in this same area (Text no. 4.05, line 16). Sargon re-enforced this policy of imperial economic aggrandizement in Philistia.

No. 5.03—THE FALL OF SAMARIA AND ASHDOD—KHORSABAD ANNALS

The annals of Sargon II were inscribed on the walls of a number of rooms in the king's palace at Khorsabad, and even though there are duplicate copies, several large sections remain irretrievable due to the poor preservation of the reliefs. The annals, like the summary inscriptions, were composed to mark the inauguration of the palace in 707 BCE. In the following selections, the suggested restorations are based on parallels from the Khorsabad Summary Inscription (Text no. 5.01) and the Calah Prism (Text no. 5.02).

Text edition: Fuchs 1994:86–87, 89–90, 110, 132–135.
Translations: *ARAB* 2, §4; *DOTT* 59, 61; *TGI* 63; *ANET* 285–286; *TPOA* 108, 112; *TUAT* 1/4, 378–381; *COS* 2, 293–294; *HTAT* 303–304, 305.

10–18 In [my] acc[ession year ... the Samar]ians [about 2 lines are missing] that bring me victory, wi[th them I fought ... 27,290 people who live there] I took as spoil. [I organized] 50 chariots as a royal contingent from [among them ... Samaria more (densely)] than before I resettled, (and) people from the lands of my con[quest I brought there ... tax] and tribute I imposed upon them like Assyrians. The [sealed] po[rt of Egypt I opened and let the people of Assyria and Egypt] mingle together, and had them trade with each other.

23–57 In the second year of my reign, Ilubiʾ[di of Hamath ...] numerous [...] he assembled at Qarqar, and the oath [of the great gods ... Arpad, Ṣimirra,] Damascus (and) Samaria he caused to rebel [against me ... about 25 lines are missing ... he s]et and Reʾe, his [commander-in-chief,] gave him aid and marched against me to wage war and battle. In the name of the god Ashur, my lord, I inflicted a defeat upon them, and [Reʾe,] like a shepherd whose sheep were stolen, escaped alone. I captured [Ḫa]nunu with my own hand and brought him bound to Ashur, my city. I destroyed, demolished, and burnt Raphia. I took as spoil 9,033 people together with their many possessions.

101, 120–125

In the seventh year of my reign. . . . The Tamudi, [Iba]didi, Marsimani, Ḫayappâ, the far-off Arabs, desert dwellers who do not know overseer (and) commander, who had not brought any king their tribute, I defeated them with the aid of Ashur, my lord; I exiled their remnant (and) settled (them) in Samaria. I received tribute from the Pharaoh of Egypt, Samsi, queen of the Arabs, Itʾamara, the Sabaean, and from kings of the seashore and desert: gold, ore of the mountains, precious stones, ivory, ebony seeds, aromatics of all kinds, horses (and) camels.

234, 241–255

In the eleventh year of my re[ign] ... Azuri, king of Ashdod, plotted not to deliver tribute [...] and sent sediti[ous words] concerning Assyria to the kings in his neighborhood. Because of the crimes he committed against the people of his land, I aboli[shed] his rule. I appointed Aḫimiti, his favorite brother, as king. But the people of Ḫatti, speakers of lies, disliked his kingship and they elevated Yadna, who had no right to the throne, and like them, did not respect authority. In my rage, I marched to Ashdod, his royal city, with my personal chariot and my horsemen, who even in friendly areas do not leave my side. I besieged Ashdod, Gath, and Ashd[od-yam,] and captured (them). I counted as spoil the gods who dwell there, him, together with the people of his land, gold, silver, the property of his palace. I reorganized these cities. People from the lands that I had conquered with my own hand, I settled (in them). I appointed my eunuch as governor over them. I counted them with the people of Assyria and they bear my yoke.

10–18 **In [my] acc[ession year**—According to the Babylonian Chronicle, Sargon II took the throne on the 12th of Tebeth (see Text no. 11.01, line 31); accordingly, his accession year lasted all of 2 months and 18 days, i.e., the period of time until the Assyrian New Year on the first of Nisan. A campaign to Samaria could not have been undertaken in such a short period; besides the rebellions in other kingdoms in the West would have had to been quelled before taking on Samaria. The report on the campaign against Samaria was moved up from the king's second year (720 BCE) to his accession year in order to cover up the fact that during these few months, Sargon had not undertaken military activity and was engaged with the consolidation of his rule.

23–57 **In the second year of my reign, Ilubiʾ[di of Hamath . . . numerous [. . .] he assembled at Qarqar**—The first stage in the reconquest of the West was subduing Ilubiʾdi (or Yaubiʾdi); for the events, see Text no. 5.01, lines 33–36. From Hamath, Sargon proceeded south to Damascus, then on to Samaria and finally to Gaza.

The large gap of about twenty-five lines cannot be restored at present, even with the help of parallel texts. Some have speculated that what followed the description of the submission of Samaria were reports of battles in other parts of Israel, perhaps including an encounter with Hezekiah, king of Judah; for discussion, see Text no. 5.07, lines 7–9.

[Reʾe,] like a shepherd whose sheep were stolen, escaped alone—The Assyrian scribe has punned on the name of Egyptian commander. The loss of troops by Reʾe is described as being like that of a shepherd, *rēʾû* in Akkadian, who has lost his flock.

I captured [Ḫa]nunu with my own hand—Ḫanunu had been recognized as king of Gaza by Tiglath-pileser III (see Text no. 4.05).

101, 120–125

In the seventh year of my reign . . . The Tamudi, [Iba]didi, Marsimani, Ḫayappâ, the far-off Arabs . . . I exiled their remnant (and) settled (them) in Samaria—The activities of the year 716 BCE point to Sargon's ongoing attention to affairs in the West. Four years after Samaria was conquered, desert-dwelling Arabs were settled in the province of Samerina. This is a rather puzzling move. For one, it is hard to envision a military undertaking into the heart of the desert to the encampments of these Arab tribes; moreover, there is little sense in relocating nomads to an agricultural territory. Perhaps, as Eph^cal suggests (1982:105–108), this "exile" of Arabs is a somewhat exaggerated description; in actuality, it refers to an economic arrangement reached by Sargon with these tribes who were involved in the south Arabian trade. The nomads were settled in Samerina in order to engage in the transfer of goods through the former kingdom of Israel to Tyre and other coastal cities.

234, 241–255

In the eleventh year of my re[ign] . . . Azuri, king of Ashdod, plotted not to deliver tribute—The picture given in the annals of the affairs in Ashdod—the repeated uprisings that called for Assyrian intervention—follows, for the most part, the one in the Summary Inscription (Text no. 5.01). Although all the events described are gathered under the rubric "in the eleventh year of my reign," it seems more than likely that they occurred over several years, with the final battle and incorporation of Ashdod taking place in 711 BCE. For the problem of this date, see Text no. 5.08, Introduction.

Yadna, who had no right to the throne—The name Yadna has yet to be explained, but it is clear that he is the Yamani of the Summary Inscription (Text no. 5.01, line 90ff.). In the present description, Sargon claims to have captured him outright, but other texts make it clear that Yamani fled to Egypt before the arrival of the Assyrian troops and only years later was he handed over to Sargon; see discussion in Text no. 5.01.

No. 5.04—THE ASHUR CHARTER

The activities of Sargon II during the first years of his reign are summarized on a large clay tablet, now very fragmentary, discovered at Nineveh. The text has become known as "The Ashur Charter," referring to the privileges of the city of Ashur treated therein. The text opens with Sargon's rendering thanks to the god Ashur for his selection as king, and in return, Sargon restores ancient privileges to the city of Ashur, the god's sacred precinct, which he claims were violated by his predecessor Shalmaneser V. Hereafter, the residents of the city will be exempt from army service and corvée, civic dues required of other Assyrian citizens. In a separate passage, the events of the king's second regnal year (720 BCE) are summarized. In that year, Sargon marched to the West in order to suppress the uprisings that had broken out a year and a half earlier when he took the throne. This record, coming as it does from a non-historiographical text, supports the suggestion that the annal report of a battle in Samaria in Sargon's accession year (see Text no. 5.03, lines 10–18) lacks "historical reliability" (Tadmor 1958:32).

Text edition: Saggs 1975.
Translations: *ARAB* 2, §§133–135; *TPOA* 106–107; *TUAT* 1/4, 387; *COS* 2, 295; *HTAT* 302–303.

16–28 In the second year of my reign, when I had seated myself on my royal throne and had been [crowned] with the lordly crown, I dispersed the forces of Ḫumbanigash, king of Elam. I defeated Ilu[biʾdi] of Hamath, with no right to the throne and unworthy of the palace, and in shepherding (his) people [did not…] their fate (?). He sought evil and not good for the god Ashur, his land (and) his people. He scor[ned …]. He gathered together Arpad (and) Samaria, and brought them over to his side […] He killed and did not leave a person […] I raised [my hands to the god Ashur] and to conquer the land of Hamath […] the wi[de land of Amur]ru, I came (*before him*?). The god Ashur hea[rd *my prayer*(?)] and received my supplication. My [vast] f[orces …] I set [on the road to Am]urru. The land of Ha[math…] *From days* of old had learned the fame […] I subdued [the people (?) of Am]urru at my feet […] and I brought them to my city Ashur.

Ḫumbanigash, king of Elam—See Text no. 5.01, line 23.

Ilu[biʾdi] of Hamath, with no right to the throne and unworthy of the palace—This implies that Ilubiʾdi was not the legitimate ruler of Hamath.

He gathered together Arpad (and) Samaria, and brought them over to his side—Despite the defeat of Samaria after a long siege and the capture of King Hoshea (cf. 2 Kgs 17:4–5), the death of Shalmaneser V cut short the incorporation of Samaria into the imperial provincial network; the residents of the city continued to resist, requiring a further Assyrian campaign against Samaria in Sargon's second year. See Text no. 5.03, lines 23–57.

The wi[de land of Amur]ru—This is the standard expression in Assyrian royal inscriptions used when referring to the West in general, and to southern Syria and Israel in particular.

No. 5.05—CYLINDER INSCRIPTION No. 1

A large number of inscribed cylinders were discovered over the years at Khorsabad; they are now scattered in museums in Paris, London and Chicago. The inscription on the cylinders appears in both short and long versions. Several lines relate briefly to Sargon II's activities in Israel.

Text edition: Fuchs 1994:31–32, 34.
Translations: *ARAB* 2, §§116–118; *TPOA* 112–113; *TUAT* 1/4, 386; *COS* 2, 298; *HTAT* 306.

1–2 Sargon, representative of the god Enlil, priest, desired one of the god Ashur, chosen of the gods Anu and Dagan, great king, powerful king, king of the universe, king of Assyria, king of the four quarters (of the world)...

19–20 who makes the wide land of Bit-Ḫumria tremble, who defeats Egypt at Raphia, and brings Ḫanunu, king of Gaza, bound to (my) city of Ashur, who captures the Tamudi, Ibadidi, Marsimani, Ḫayappâ (and) whose remainder I transferred and set down in the land of Bit-Ḫumria.

Full descriptions of the events alluded to in the cylinder inscription can be found in Text no. 5.01, lines 23–27, and Text no. 5.03, lines 10–18, 23–57, 120–125.

No. 5.06—THE CYPRUS STELA

This stela was erected on the island of Cyprus whose seven kings recognized Sargon II as hegemon in c. 708 BCE, after an Assyrian force had intervened to settle a dispute between the local rulers and the Phoenician colonies on the island. The exact find spot of the stela is not known and according to one source, it was discovered at Larnaka (see Tadmor 1996); today the stela is on display at the National Museum in Berlin.

The selection presented describes the suppression of the rebellion against Sargon at the outset of his rule.

Text edition: Winckler 1889:178, col. ii, lines 51–65.
Translations: *ARAB* 2, §§183; *ANET* 284; *TUAT* 1/4, 385–386; *HTAT* 304.

Col. ii, 51–65

I swept over the land of Hamath [to its entire] extent like the flood. Yaubiʾdi, ki[ng of Hamath,] together with his family and [his] warriors, the spoil of their land, bound, I bro[ught them] to Assyria. From among them, I organized (a contingent of) 300 chariots, 600 horse[men], shield- and lan[ce-] bearers, and added them to my royal corps. 6,300 Assyrians, gui[lty persons,] I set[tled] in Hamath. I appointed my eunuch as [governor] over them and imposed tax and tr[ibute] on them.

Col. ii, 51–65

Yaubiʾdi, ki[ng of Hamath,] together with his family and [his] warriors, the spoil of their land, bound, I bro[ught them] to Assyria—The battle in north Syria is dated to 720 BCE; see Text no. 5.03, line 23; Text no. 5.04. A relief in the palace of Khorsabad depicts the punishment inflicted upon Yaubiʾdi and bears the inscription: "Yaubiʾdi of Hamath, I flayed him" (Room viii, no. 25).

6,300 Assyrians, gui[lty persons,] I set[tled] in Hamath—A further description of this episode appears on the Ḥama stela (Lambert 1981; Hawkins 2004):

> 6,300 Assyrians, guilty ones, I cleared (them of) their sin and I had mercy on them; I settled them in the land of Hamath. Tax and tribute, bearing the basket (and) going on campaign, I imposed upon them like the kings my fathers had imposed upon Irḫuleni of Hamath.

The reference to "guilty" Assyrians is apparently to those who opposed Sargon's assumption of the throne. Sargon pardoned them, but distanced them from Assyria's heartland, resettling them in Hamath. Their civic duties were those of all Assyrian citizens. The reference to Irḫuleni of Hamath is to the king of Hamath during the reign of Shalmaneser III, a century earlier; his submission to Assyria is not known from any other source (see Text no. 1.01).

No. 5.07—STONE SLAB FROM CALAH

The following excerpt is from a short summary inscription, preserved on two stone slabs commemorating the completion of renovations on the palace of Ashurnasirpal II at Calah. The names of the countries that were conquered or had submitted to Sargon suggest that the text was composed in c. 716 BCE. It is the sole text from Sargon's reign that speaks of the submission of the kingdom of Judah.

Text edition: Winckler 1889:168–172.
Translations: *ARAB* 2, §§137–138; *ANET* 287; *TPOA* 110–111; *TUAT* 1/4, 387; *COS* 2, 298–299.

7–9 Pious ruler, who met Ḫumbanigash, king of Elam, in the district of Der and inflicted a defeat upon him; subduer of the land of Judah, whose place is far off; deporter of (the people of) Hamath, whose hands captured Yaubiʾdi, their king; who repulses the land of Kakme, the wicked enemy; who sets in order the chaotic land of Mannea; who pleases his country; who extends the border of Assyria.

10–12 Prudent king, the net (which entraps) the unsubmissive; who captured with his own hand Pisiris, king of Ḫatti, and appointed his own person over Carchemish, his center; deporter of (the people of) the city Shinutu, who brought Kiakki, king of Tabal, to Ashur, his sacred precinct, and imposed his yoke on the land of Mushki; conqueror of the land of Mannea, the land of Karallu, (and) the land of Paddiru; avenger of his land; who defeats the distant land of Media as far as the rising sun.

7–9 **Who met Ḫumbanigash, king of Elam, in the district of Der and inflicted a defeat upon him**—See the discussion in Text no. 5.01, lines 23–27.

Subduer of the land of Judah, whose place is far off—It is generally held that this phrase refers to the voluntary submission of Hezekiah to Sargon

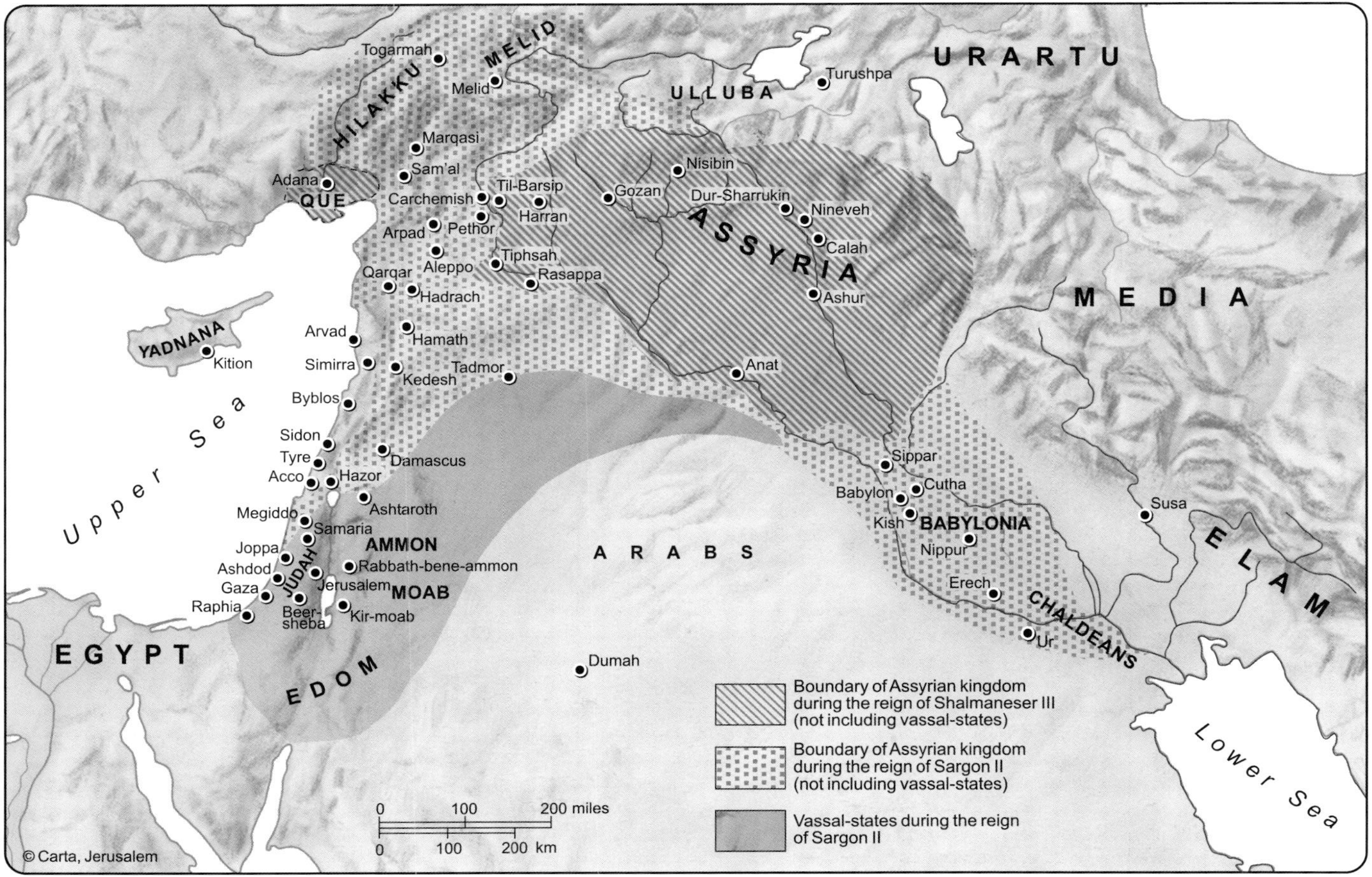

The Expansion of the Assyrian Empire, Mid-9th to End of 8th Centuries

during the campaign in 720 and not to a military engagement between Assyria and Judah, inasmuch as there is no reference to one in any extant text. Yet the counter-proposal that such an encounter did take place should not be ruled out. In the annal inscription referring to the military activities of the king's second regnal year, 720 BCE, there is a large lacuna of some twenty-five lines after the the description of Samaria's fall and before the battle at Raphia, enough space to have described the use of force against Hezekiah (see Text no. 5.03, lines 23–57). The present phrase would, then, refer to that postulated battle and defeat. See, in full, Fuchs 1994:314; Frahm 1997:232.

Yaubiʾdi—Led the rebellion in the West at the time of Sargon's accession, see Text no. 5.01, lines 33–36.

10–12 **Who captured with his own hand Pisiris, king of Ḫatti, and appointed his own person over Carchemish, his center**— The annals place the conquest of Carchemish in Sargon's fifth year, 717 BCE.

Who brought Kiakki, king of Tabal, to Ashur, his sacred precinct, and imposed his yoke on the land of Mushki—According to the annals, Pisiris of Carchemish had tried to instigate the kings of Tabal and Mushki to revolt against Assyria. They were conquered in the campaign against Tabal in 718 BCE, Sargon's fourth year. The neighboring kingdoms Tabal and Mushki were located in southwestern Anatolia; they are referred in the "Table of Nations" in Gen 10:2 as sons of Japheth. The prophet Ezekiel appropriated the names of these kingdoms for his apocalyptical warrior-king, "Gog, the chief prince of Meshech and Tubal" (Ezek 38:2).

Conqueror of the land of Mannea, the land of Karallu (and) the land of Paddiru—These mountain kingdoms to the east and north of Assyria were conquered in 716 BCE.

Mannea—The kingdom of Mannea was located south of Lake Urmia and at times extended its sway as far as the sources of the River Diyala. It had a checkered history of relations with Assyria, alternating between allegiance and rebellion. In the Bible, Mannea appears among the enemies of Babylon: "Assemble kingdoms against her—Ararat, Minni [=Mannea] and Ashkenaz.... Appoint nations for war against her—the kings of Media ..." (Jer 51:27–28).

No. 5.08—THE ASHDOD CAMPAIGN—NINEVEH ANNAL PRISM

Part of a detailed report of the Assyrian campaign to Ashdod survives on a very fragmentary annal prism discovered at Nineveh that was likely edited in 711 BCE. With relation to affairs in Ashdod, it tells of Sargon II marching at the head of his royal contingent in order to put down the rebellion that had broken out in the city.

The Ashdod episode is variously dated in the sources. The Khorsabad annals group all events in the king's eleventh regnal year. The Nineveh prism records them as having occurred in the king's ninth year. The discrepancy between these dates stems from the different starting point used by the authors of the texts. They both wrestled with the uncomplimentary opening years of Sargon II's reign and the fact that the king did not take to the field until 720 BCE, his second regnal year. As noted earlier (Text no. 5.3, lines 10–18), the late Khorsabad annals, composed in c. 707 BCE, covered up this fact by moving items up to Sargon's accession and first years, while the earlier Nineveh prism inscription is closer to the actual dates. In either case, it should also be noted that the Eponym Chronicle (Text no. 10.01) records "the king (remained) in the land (of Assyria)" in 712 BCE. This year was apparently skipped over altogether in the annal counting. By both methods, Ashdod was captured in 711 BCE.

A further datum from this period is preserved in the heading to Isaiah's prophecy concerning Ashdod: "In the year that the commander-in-chief (תַּרְתָּן) came to Ashdod—having been sent by Sargon, king of Assyria—he fought against Ashdod and took it" (Isa 20:1). Assuming the accuracy of this datum, the claim of a royal victory at Ashdod is another example of appropriation by the king of an achievement accomplished by his army. At the end of the engagement and with the annexation of Ashdod, a royal stela was erected in the city, pieces of which were unearthed in excavation (see Tadmor 1971; Horowitz and Oshima 2006:40–41; and Appendix).

Text edition: Fuchs 1998:44–46, 73–74.
Translations: *ARAB* 2, §§193–195; *ANET* 287; *TPOA* 114–115; *TUAT* 1/4, 381–382; *HTAT* 307–308.

Col. viia, 13–16; viib 1–48

In the ninth year of my reign, I ma[rched] to [Ashdod that is on the coast] of the Great Sea [. . .] Ashdod [. . .] A break of few lines Because of [the crimes he committed...I removed him] from Ash[dod]. Aḫimiti [...], his beloved brother, over [the people of Ashdod,] I elevated and pl[aced him on the throne . . .] Tax and tribute [. . .] like that of the kings [my fathers I imposed] on him. But [they,] the evil [people of Ḫatti] . . . not to bear tri[bute . . . they pl]otted evil, [against] their ruler, [they rev]olted, and like one who sheds blood, [out of Ashdod] they expelled him. *x x x* [. . .] Yamani, a person of low-cl[ass, with no right to the throne, they set] over themselves as king and placed [him on] his lordly [throne]. . . . their city [after 4 lines] around it a moat [. . .] 20 cubits its depth [. . .] they reached ground water. To the k[ings] of Philistia, Judah, Ed[om,] Moab, (and) the residents of the sea(coast), who bear the tax and gifts of the god Ashur, my lord, (they sent) seditious words and slander, to make them hostile towards me. They sent bribes to Pharaoh, king of Egypt, a king who cannot save them, to seek his aid. I, Sargon, righteous prince, who fears the oath of Shamash (and) Marduk, who heeds the word of Ashur, I had my troops cross the Tigris (and) Euphrates in full flood, in the high waters of spring, as if on dry land. He, Yamani, their king, who trusted in his own strength and did not sub[mit] to my lordship, heard from [afar about the m]arch of my campaign, and the splendor of Ashur, my lord, overwhelmed him. [. . . like roots] by the bank of a river [he swayed (with fright) . . .] in deep water [like fish] take refuge [. . .] far [. . .] he fled [. . .] Ashdod [. . .] [. . .]

---

20 cubits its depth [. . .] they reached ground water—The description refers to the strengthening of the city's defenses in anticipation of the expected Assyrian attack. In particular, a moat was excavated around the city in order to prevent digging through the city's walls by the attackers; on this technique, see Eph^{c}al 2008.

To the k[ings] of Philistia, Judah, Ed[om,] Moab, (and) the residents of the sea(coast), who bear the tax and gifts of the god Ashur, my lord, (they sent) seditious words and slander, to make them hostile towards me—It is not known whether Yamani's call to Ashdod's neighbors to join in the anti-Assyrian rebellion bore fruit. The annals report only on a battle against Ashdod, although it is possible that at an early stage, Ashdod found support in other kingdoms, perhaps even Judah; this might explain the interest of the prophet Isaiah in the events in Ashdod; see Isa 20.

They sent bribes to Pharaoh, king of Egypt, a king who cannot save them, to seek his aid—The solicitation of Egyptian aid is not surprising, as the kings of the Nile Delta (and later the Cushite rulers) saw the Assyrian domination of the coastal cities of Philistia as contravening their own interests in the area. The Pharaoh referred to by this title may have been Bocchoris, king of Sais. But unlike the later revolt against Sennacherib, during which Egyptian troops fought in Philistia (see Text no. 6.01), there is no evidence of their engagement at Ashdod in the reign of Sargon. In the end, Yamani found himself seeking refuge in Cush (see Text no. 5.01).

No. 5.09—TO THE BORDER OF EGYPT—ASHUR ANNAL PRISM

A large prism fragment containing the bottom parts of three columns of an annal text was discovered in the courtyard of the Ashur Temple in the city of Ashur. The inscription belongs to a recension of the annals of Sargon II that differed from the Khorsabad annals in the numbering of his military campaigns. Parts of the fifth through eighth years are extant. The final section of the fifth year (716 BCE) reports Assyrian military activity on the Egyptian border in the northern Sinai Peninsula that is so far unparalleled in other texts.

Text edition: Fuchs 1998:28–29, 57; earlier Weidner 1940–44; Tadmor 1958:77–84.
Translations: *TGI* 62; *ANET* 286; *TPOA* 111–112; *TUAT* 1/4, 382–383; *HTAT* 305.

Col. ii, 1–11

Together with [...] and sheep [...] from the midst [...] in the land of [...] that is on the border of the city of the Wadi of E[gypt, a district on the] western [seacoast] I sett[led. I put them under the control of my appointee,] the sheikh of the city Laban. Shilkanni, king of Egypt, whose p[lace is far,] the awesome splendor of the god Ashur, my lord, [overwhelmed him]; twelve large Egyptian horses, whose like do not exist in my land, he brought as his gift.

From the midst [...] in the land of [...] that is on the border of the city of the Wadi of E[gypt, a district on the] western [seacoast] I sett[led—The area of the northern Sinai Peninsula near the Wadi of Egypt, modern el-ᶜArish, was resettled with captives taken during a previous campaign. By this move, Sargon strengthened the Assyrian hold on this vital commercial link, following the lead of Tiglath-pileser III who had founded a customs depot in the same area (see Text no. 4.05, line 16). Sargon himself had fought at Raphia in 720, at which time he declared a "free-trade" zone between the cities of Philistia and Egypt (see Text no. 5.02). Based upon an analysis of the personal names found on a number of sherds from Tell Jemmeh (c. 13 km south of Gaza on Naḥal Besor), it has been suggested that the settlers were brought from Mannea in western Iran where Sargon had fought earlier in the same year; see Naveh 1985; Na'aman and Zadok 1988; and for a different interpretation of the names as Philistine, see Kempinski 1987.

The sheikh of the city Laban—In handing over the supervision of the settlers to a local chieftain, Sargon was again following the example of Tiglath-pileser III, who had integrated the nomads in the Assyrian administration of Philistia and northern Sinai (see Text no. 4.06, line 34'). The city Laban is unidentified. In the itinerary of the Egyptian king Shishak, the name Raban appears after Raphia, and might be Laban; for its identification with Tell Abu Salima, see Aḥituv 1984:129.

Shilkanni, king of Egypt—Osorkon IV, who ruled in the eastern Delta (c. 730–715 BCE), was the last king of the 22nd dynasty; see Kitchen 1973:372–376.

Twelve large Egyptian horses—Egyptian horses were highly prized in Assyria, and with this gift, Osorkon courted Assyria for support against the threat to his rule from the Cushites who had invaded the Delta.

No. 5.10—THE AZEKAH INSCRIPTION

The account of an Assyrian campaign against King Hezekiah of Judah and the attack on the Judean town of Azekah are preserved on the remains of a clay tablet discovered at Nineveh. The two fragments of the tablet were originally treated separately and assigned to two different Assyrian kings, one (K 6205) to Tiglath-pileser III, the other (BM 82-3-23, 131) to Sargon II; the two fragments were subsequently rejoined (see Na'aman 1974). The poetic style and figurative language of the text resemble Sargon II's "Letter to the God," which was composed after his campaign to Urartu, leading to the likelihood that the present text was also a "Letter to the God," this one written after Sargon's campaign in Philistia or Israel. A number of dates for the events have been suggested: (1) 720 BCE, Sargon's campaign against the western rebels (see Fuchs 1994:314, followed by Frahm 1997:229–232); (2) 712 BCE, Sargon's campaign to Philistia (Tadmor 1958:80–84). For a later date, at the completion of Sennacherib's campaign to Judah in 701 BCE, see Na'aman 1974.

Text edition: Na'aman 1974; Frahm 1994:230.
Translations: *TPOA* 123–124; *COS* 2, 304–305; *HTAT* 336–337.

1–2 (scattered signs)

[Ashur, my lord, support]ed me and to the land of Ju[dah I marched. In] the course of my campaign, the tribute of the ki[ngs of . . ., I received.]

[by the mig]ht (?) of Ashur, my lord, the district [of Hezek]iah of Judah, like [ ]

[ ] the city of Azekah, his stronghold, which is between my [*royal contin*]*gent* and the land of Judah [ ]

[ ] located on a mountain peak, like countless pointed ir[on] daggers, reaching to high heaven

[ ] were strong and rivaled the highest mountains; at its sight, as if from the sky [

[by packed-down ra]mps, and applying mighty(?) battering rams, infantry attacks by min[es]

[the approach of my cav]alry they saw, and heard the sound of Ashur's mighty troops and they were afraid [ ]

[I besieged(?)] I conquered, I carried off its spoil. I tore down, I destroyed [ ]

[the city *x* ,] a royal [city] of the Philistines, which He[zek]iah had taken and fortified for himself [ ]

[ ] (scattered signs) [ ] like a tree [ ]

[ ] surrounded by great t[o]wers, most difficult [ ]

[ ] a palace, like a mountain, was barred in from of them, high [ ]

[ ] it was dark, and the sun never shone on it, its waters were located in dar[kn]ess, its outflow [ ]

[ ] its mo[uth(?)] was cut with axes and a moat was dug around it [ ]

[soldiers] skilled in battle, he stationed in it, he girded his weapons, in order to [ ]

[ ] I had the people of Amurru, all of them, carry earth [ ]

[against them. For a third time, [ ] great, like a pot [I smashed]

20 [cattle and sh]eep, from its midst I t[ook out, and as] spo[il I counted.]
(illegible signs)

---

5 **The city of Azekah, his stronghold, which is between my [*royal contin*]*gent* and the land of Judah [ ]**—Azekah, Tell Zakarîyeh, is situated northwest of the entrance of the Elah Valley into the Judean Shephelah (cf. Josh 15:35).

11 **[the city *x* ,] a royal [city] of the Philistines**—Several suggestions as to the identity of this town have been put forward: Gath (Na'aman 1974); Ekron (Galil 1995b; Na'aman 1994b). But it is difficult to reconcile the topography described in the text with the location of these two cities.

Which He[zek]iah had taken and fortified for himself [ ]—The summary note on Hezekiah's rule in 2 Kgs 18:8 also reports that "he defeated the Philistines as far as Gaza and its border areas, from watchtower to fortified city."

15 **[ ] it was dark, and the sun never shone on it, its waters were located in dar[kn]ess, its outflow [ ] its mo[uth(?)] was cut with axes and a moat was dug around it [ ]**—The city's water system seems to be the subject of wonderment. At nearby Beth-shemesh, an underground reservoir in use at the end of the 8th century BCE was excavated; see Bunimovitz and Lederman 2003:7–20.

18 **[ ] I had the people of Amurru, all of them, carry earth [ ]**—This line describes the mobilization of the local population to work on the construction of the siege ramp thrown up against the city under attack.

No. 5.11—ATHALIAH, THE WIFE OF SARGON

The subterranean burial chamber under the floor of a room in the domestic quarter of the North-West Palace of Ashurnasirpal II (Tomb II) held a sarcophagus with the remains of two women. An inscribed slab and a stone funerary text identified the chamber as originally belonging to one of the interred, Yabâ, the wife of Tiglath-pileser III. Among the many objects in the chamber were gold bowls incised with the names of Yabâ, as well as Baniti, wife of Shalmaneser V, and Athaliah, wife of Sargon II.

The names of two of the queens, Yabâ and Athaliah, are West-Semitic names and point to their holders as being of foreign, that is, non-Assyrian

Fig. 15. Gold bowls of queens, from Nimrud. Top left: Athaliah; top right: Yabâ; bottom: Baniti (Curtis, et al. 2008: Plate IV).

origin. These royal women could have arrived at the court in Nimrud as captives after an Assyrian campaign or as hostages guaranteeing the loyalty of the rulers in their native lands.

Three objects belonged to Athaliah: a gold bowl, a jar of rock crystal, a mirror of electron. They all bear the same inscription.

Text edition: Al-Rawi 2008:138.
Photographs: Curtis et al. 2008: Plates III a–d; IV a.

Belonging to Athaliah, queen of Sargon, king of Assyria

Athaliah, queen of Sargon—The name Athaliah clearly looks like a Hebrew name as determined by the Israelite theophoric element *-yahu* יהו, this despite the irregular shortened cuneiform spelling *A-tal-ia-a* / *A-ta-li-a*. (For the suggestion that the name is of Arabic derivation and that Athaliah was an Arab princess, see Zadok 2008:327–329.) The date and the circumstances of her arrival in Nimrud are unknown. If she were Israelite, that is, from Samaria, she would have come during the last decade of the kingdom of Israel, prior to its fall in 722. If she were Judean, she could have arrived any time after the submission of King Ahaz to Tiglath-pileser III in 734 BCE; see Text no. 4.04.

The presence of an Israelite-Judahite woman at the side of Sargon has led to speculation on her role in influencing her husband's policy towards Judah, as well as that of Sennacherib, especially with regard to the concluding accord reached with Hezekiah (her half-brother?) at the conclusion of the campaign of 701 BCE; see Dalley 2004; 2008.

References

Aḥituv, Shmuel

1984 *Canaanite Toponyms in Ancient Egyptian Documents*, Jerusalem.

Al-Rawi, Farouk N. H.

2008 Inscriptions from the Tombs of the Queens of Assyria. Pp. 119–138 in J. E. Curtis, et al. (eds.), *New Light on Nimrud. Proceedings of the Nimrud Conference 11th–13th March 2002*, London.

Becking, Bob

1992 *The Fall of Samaria. An Historical and Archaeological Study*, Leiden.

Bunimovitz, Shlomo and Zvi Lederman

2003 The Final Destruction of Beth Shemesh and the Pax Assyriaca in the Judean Shephelah, *Tel Aviv* 30:3–26.

Cogan, Mordechai

1974 *Imperialism and Religion*, SBLMS 19, Chico, CA.

1988 "For We, Like You, Worship Your God"—Three Biblical Portrayals of Samaritan Origins, *VT* 38:286–292.

2013 *Bound for Exile: Israelites and Judeans Under Imperial Yoke—Documents from Assyria and Babylonia*, Jerusalem.

Cogan, Mordechai and Hayim Tadmor

1988 *II Kings*, Anchor Bible 11, Garden City.

Curtis, J. E., et al.

2008 *New Light on Nimrud. Proceedings of the Nimrud Conference 11th–13th March 2002*, London.

Dalley, Stephanie

1985 Foreign Chariotry and Calvary in the Armies of Tiglath-pileser III and Sargon II, *Iraq* 47:31–48.

1990 Yahweh in Hamath in the 8th century BC: Cuneiform Material and Historical Deductions, *VT* 40:21–32.

2004 Recent Evidence from Assyrian Sources for Judaean History from Uzziah to Manasseh, *JSOT* 28:387–401.

2008 The Identity of the Princesses in Tomb II and a New Analysis of Events in 701 BC. Pp. 171–175 in J. E. Curtis, et al. 2008.

Damerji, Muayyad Said

2008 An Introduction to the Nimrud Tombs. Pp. 81–82 in J. E. Curtis, et al. 2008.

Elat, Moshe

1978 The Economic Relations of the Neo-Assyrian Empire with Egypt, *JAOS* 98:20–34.

Eph^{c}al, Israel

1982 *The Ancient Arabs*, Jerusalem.

1991 The "Samarians" in the Assyrian Sources. Pp. 36–45 in *Ah Assyria. . . Studies Tadmor*, Mordechai Cogan and Israel Eph^{c}al (eds.), *ScrHier* 33.

2008 *The City Besieged*, Jerusalem.

Frahm, Eckart

1997 *Einleitung in die Sanherib-Inschriften*, AfO Beiheft 26, Wien.

Frame, Grant

1999 The Inscription of Sargon II at Tang-i Var, *Or* 68:31–57.

Franklin, Norma

1994 The Room V Reliefs at Dur-Sharrukin and Sargon II's Western Campaigns, *Tel Aviv* 21:255–275.

Fuchs, Andreas

1994 *Die Inschriften Sargons II. aus Khorsabad*, Göttingen.

1998 *Die Annalen des Jahres 711 v. Chr.*, SAAS 8, Helsinki.

Gadd, C. J.

1954 Inscribed Prisms of Sargon II from Nimrud, *Iraq* 16:173–201.

Galil, Gershon

1992 Judah and Assyria in the Sargonid Period, *Zion* 57:111–133 (Hebrew).

1995a The Last Years of the Kingdom of Israel and the Fall of Samaria, *CBQ* 57:52–65.

1995b A New Look at the "Azekah Inscription," *RB* 102:321–329.

Grayson, A. Kirk

1965 Problematical Battles in Mesopotamian History. Pp. 337–342 in *Studies in Honor of Benno Landsberger on His Seventy-fifth Birthday, April 21, 1965*, Chicago.

Hawkins, J. D.

2004 The New Sargon Stele from Hama. Pp. 151–164 in G. Frame (ed.), *From the Upper Sea to the Lower Sea, Studies on the History of Assyria and Babylonia in Honor of A. K. Grayson*, Leiden.

Hayes, John H. and John K. Kuan

1991 The Final Years of Samaria (730–720 BC), *Bib* 72:153–181.

Horowitz, Wayne and Takayoshi Oshima

2006 *Cuneiform in Canaan. Cuneiform Sources from the Land of Israel in Ancient Times*, Jerusalem.

Kahn, Dan'el

2001 The Inscription of Sargon II at Tang-i Var and the Chronology of Dynasty 25, *Or* 70:1–18.

Kempinski, Aron

1987 Some Philistine Names from the Kingdom of Gaza, *IEJ* 37:20–34.

Kitchen, Kenneth A.

1973 *The Third Intermediate Period in Egypt (1100–650 B.C.)*, Warminster.

Lambert, W. G.

1981 Portion of Inscribed Stela of Sargon II, King of Assyria. P. 125 in O. Muscarella (ed.), *Ladders from Heaven*, Toronto.

Na'aman, Nadav

1974 Sennacherib's "Letter to God" on His Campaign to Judah, *BASOR* 214:25–39.

1990 The Historical Background to the Conquest of Samaria (720 BC), *Bib* 71:206–225.

1994a The Historical Portion of Sargon II's Nimrud Inscription, *SAAB* 8:17–20.

1994b Ahaz's and Hezekiah's Policy Toward Assyria in the Days of Sargon II and Sennacherib's Early Years, *Zion* 59:5–30 (Hebrew).

Na'aman, Nadav and Ron Zadok

1988 Sargon II's Deportations to Israel and Philistia (716–708 B.C.), *JCS* 40:36–46.

2000 Assyrian Deportations to the Province of Samerina in the Light of Two Cuneiform Tablets from Tel Hadid, *Tel Aviv* 27:159–188.

Naveh, Joseph

1985 Writing and Scripts in Seventh-Century BCE Philistia: The New Evidence from Tell Jemmeh, *IEJ* 35:11–15.

Oded, Bustenay

1979 *Mass Deportations and Deportees in the Neo-Assyrian Empire*, Wiesbaden.

2000 The Settlements of the Israelite and the Judean Exiles in Mesopotamia in the 8th–6th Centuries BCE. Pp. 91–103 in *Studies in Historical Geography and Biblical Historiography Presented to Zecharia Kallai*, Gershon Galil and Moshe Weinfeld (eds.), VTSup 81.

Oren, Eliezer

1993 Ruqeish. Pp. 1293–1294 in vol. 4 of *NEAEHL*.

Reade, Julian E.

1976 Sargon's Campaigns of 720, 716, and 715 B.C.: Evidence from the Sculptures, *JNES* 35:95–104.

Reich, Ronnie

1981 On the Identification of the "Sealed Kāru of Egypt," *ErIsr* 15:283–287 (Hebrew).

Russell, J. M.

1999 *The Writing on the Wall. Studies in the Architectural Context of Late Assyrian Palace Inscriptions*, Winona Lake, IL.

Saggs, H. W. F.

1975 Historical Texts and Fragments of Sargon II of Assyria I. The "Assur Charter," *Iraq* 37:11–20.

Spalinger, Anthony

1973 The Year 712 B.C. and Its Implications for Egyptian History, *JARCE* 10:95–101.

Tadmor, Hayim

1958 The Campaigns of Sargon II of Assur: A Chronological-Historical Study, *JCS* 12:22–40, 77–100 (= pp. 239–319 in H. Tadmor, *"With my many chariots I have gone up the heights of mountains": Historical and Literary Studies on Ancient Mesopotamia and Israel*, M. Cogan [ed.], Jerusalem 2011).

1971 Fragments of an Assyrian Stele of Sargon II, *Atiqot*, English Series 9–10:192–197.

1996 Notes on the Stele of Sargon II from Cyprus, *ErIsr* 25:286–289 (Hebrew).

Uehlinger, Christoph

1998 ". . . und wo sind die Götter von Samarien?" Die Wegführung syrisch-palästinischer Kultstatuen auf einem Relief Sargons II. in Ḫorṣābād / Dūr-Šarrukīn. Pp. 739–776 in "Und Mose schreib dies Lied auf," *Studien zum Alten Testament und zum Alten Orient. Festschrift für Oswald Loretz*, Münster.

van der Toorn, Karl

1992 Anat-Yahu, Some Other Deities, and the Jews of Elephantine, *Numen* 39:80–101.

Weidner, Ernst

1940–44 Šilkan(ḫe)ni, König von Muṣri, ein Zeitgenosse Sargons II., *AfO* 14:40–53.

Winckler, Hugo

1889 *Die Keilschrifttexte Sargons*, Leipzig.

Younger, K. Lawson

1998 The Deportations of the Israelites, *JBL* 117:201–227.

1999 The Fall of Samaria in Light of Recent Research, *CBQ* 61:461–482.

2002 Yahweh at Ashkelon and Calah? Yahwistic Names in Neo-Assyrian, *VT* 52:207–218.

Zadok, Ran

2008 Neo-Assyrian Notes. Pp. 312–330 in Mordechai Cogan and Dan'el Kahn (eds.), *Treasures on Camels' Humps. Historical and Literary Studies from the Ancient Near East Presented to Israel Ephᶜal*, Jerusalem.

Fig. 16. Prism of Sennacherib (*Israel Museum*).

CHAPTER 6

SENNACHERIB

Upon acceding to the throne of Assyria following the death of Sargon II in battle, Sennacherib (705–681 BCE) faced two major insurrections: in the West, a coalition of a number of Phoenician and Syrian kingdoms led by King Hezekiah of Judah, and in the South, the combined forces of the Chaldeans and Elamites under the leadership of Merodach-baladan. A single campaign to the West in 701 BCE ended in a decisive victory by the Assyrian army. But this success was not matched on the Babylonian front where war continued on and off from 703 until 689 BCE. In that year, Sennacherib pressed on to victory against Babylon, which was followed by the wanton destruction of the city. In 681, Sennacherib was murdered by his son, Arda-Mullissu, who had been passed over by his father who chose Esarhaddon as his successor (cf. 2 Kgs 19:37; Babylonian Chronicle no. 1 [Text no. 11.01, lines 34–35]).

NO. 6.01—THE CAMPAIGN TO THE WEST IN 701 BCE

The events of the year 701 BCE are among the most discussed in biblical research. Since the discovery of Sennacherib's inscriptions at the beginning of Assyriological research in the mid-19th century, countless reconstructions of the Assyrian campaign to Judah have been proffered, without any scholarly agreement having been reached, except perhaps in the most general terms. One suspects that it is the uncommon multiplicity of written sources referring to the events that gives rise to so many differing reconstructions. These sources include: the narratives in 2 Kgs 18–19; Isa 36–37; 2 Chr 32, as well as various prophecies of Isaiah; the Assyrian annal report; a wall relief from the palace of Sennacherib depicting the investiture and surrender of the Judean town of Lachish.

The Assyrian document presented here, known as the Rassam Cylinder, is the earliest source; its colophon reads: "Month of Iyyar, (eponymate of)

Mitunu, governor of Isana," i.e., spring 700 BCE. This date, when compared with those of earlier texts that report just two campaigns, helps establish the date of the "third campaign," the campaign to Judah, to 701 BCE.

From the Assyrian point of view, the military operations in Judah were undertaken to quell the revolt of vassal states in the West that had broken out upon the death of Sargon II four years earlier. The literary nature of narrative, in which events are arranged topically rather than chronologically, i.e., they are grouped under the rubrics of "the submissive" or "the defeated," does not permit reconstructing the itinerary of the campaign. It should also be kept in mind that this report is a part of the royal annals, which sought to magnify and memorialize the achievements of Sennacherib on the battlefield and in civil affairs. Thus, setbacks, if such there were, inevitably appear as Assyrian advances; see in detail Tadmor 2011; Cogan 2014; also Laato 1995.

The biblical account, on the other hand, is more complex than the Assyrian one; it is composed of multiple sources that have been juxtaposed in the present text, causing much tension between them. In the Book of Kings, three distinct units of different genres and different ages are identifiable: 2 Kgs 18:13–16, a chronicle-like report; 2 Kgs 18:17–19:37, two intertwined prophetic accounts.

The greatest point of discrepancy—indeed the bone of contention of most studies—lies in the contradictory endings to the campaign reported by each of the contending sides. The biblical account tells of the miraculous defeat of the Assyrian army (2 Kgs 19:35), while the Assyrian annals portray Sennacherib as having roundly defeated Hezekiah, who submitted to his overlord and sent a substantial tribute payment to Nineveh at the conclusion of the campaign. For the present, let it suffice to reiterate that there is no record of Sennacherib having undertaken a second western campaign during his reign, and considering the development of events in the West during the first quarter of the 7th century, all the events described in our sources refer to a single campaign in 701 BCE; see Cogan 2001. For thorough critical discussions of the events of year 701, see the studies of Gonçalves 1986 and Gallagher 1999.

Text editions: Frahm 1997:53–55, lines 32–58; Grayson and Novotny 2012: 63–66.
Translations: *ARAB* 2, §§239–240, 284; *DOTT* 66–67; *TGI* 67–68; *ANET* 287–288; *TUAT* 1/4, 388–390; *COS* 2, 302–303; *HTAT* 329–333.

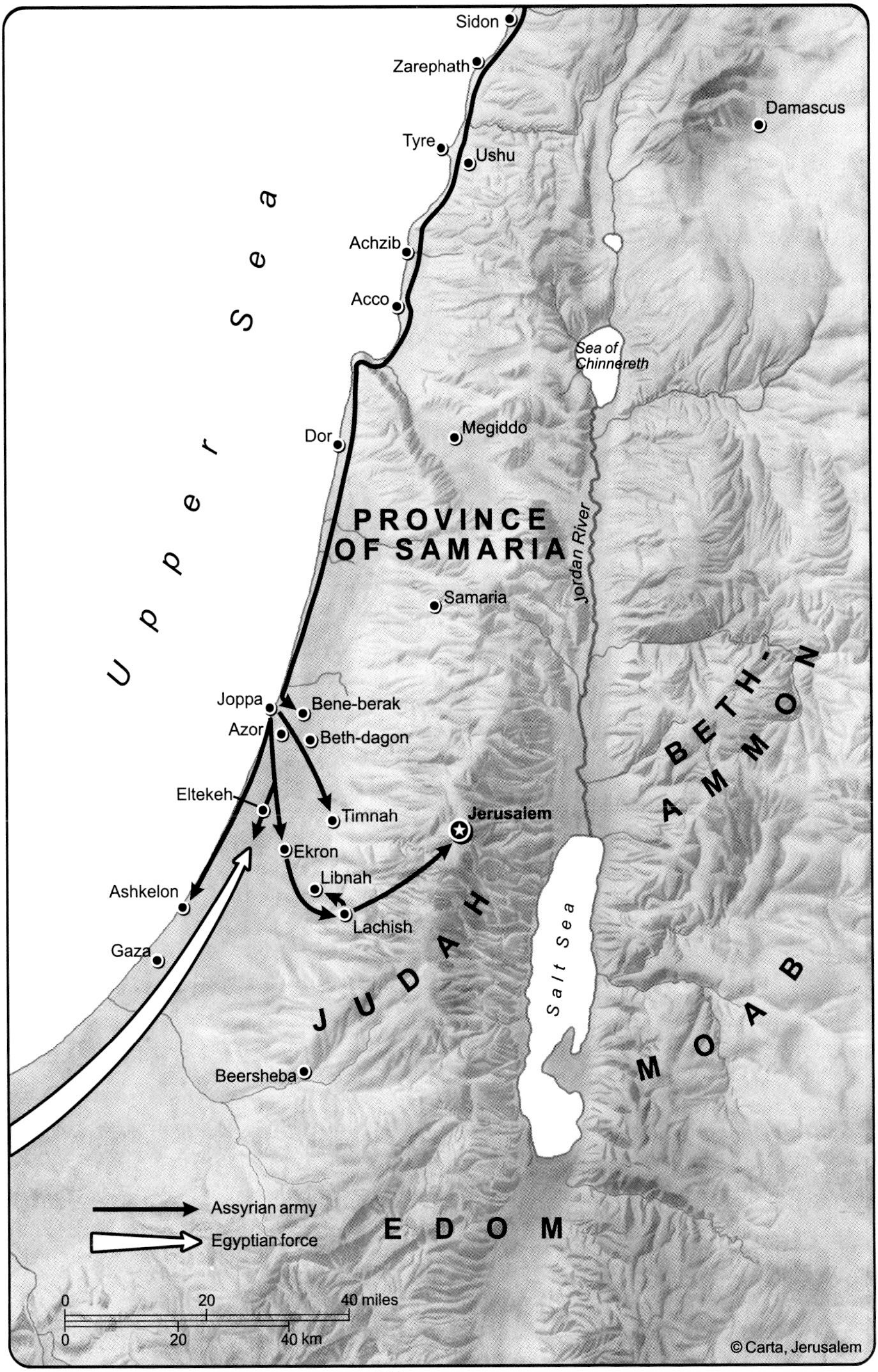

Sennacherib's Campaign to the West, 701 bce

32–35 In my third campaign, I marched to Ḫatti. The awesome splendor of my lordship overwhelmed Luli, king of Sidon, and he fled overseas far-off. The terrifying nature of the weapon of (the god) Ashur my lord overwhelmed his strong cities, Greater Sidon, Little Sidon, Bit-zitti, Ṣariptu, Maḫaliba, Ushu, Achzib, Acco, walled cities (provided) with food and water for his garrisons, and they bowed in submission at my feet. I installed Tubaʾlu on his royal throne over them and imposed upon him tribute and dues for my lordship (payable) annually without interruption.

36–38 The kings of Amurru, all of them—Minuḫimmu of Samsimuruna, Tubaʾlu of Sidon, Abdiliʾti of Arvad, Urumilki of Byblos, Mitinti of Ashdod, Puduʾilu of Beth-Ammon, Chemosh-nadbi of Moab, Ayarammu of Edom—brought me sumptuous presents as their abundant audience-gift, fourfold, and kissed my feet.

39–41 As for Ṣidqa, king of Ashkelon, who had not submitted to my yoke—his family gods, he himself, his wife, his sons, his daughters, his brothers, and (all the rest of) his descendants, I deported and brought him to Assyria. I set Sharru-lu-dari, son of Rukibti, their former king, over the people of Ashkelon and imposed upon him payment of tribute (and) presents to my lordship; he (now) bears my yoke. In the course of my campaign, I surrounded and conquered Beth-Dagon, Joppa, Bene-berak, Azor, cities belonging to Ṣidqa, who did not submit quickly, and I carried off their spoil.

42–48 The officials, the nobles, and the people of Ekron who had thrown Padi, their king, (who was) under oath and obligation to Assyria, into iron fetters and handed him over in a hostile manner to Hezekiah, the Judean, took fright because of the offense they had committed. The kings of Egypt, (and) the bowmen, chariot corps and cavalry of the king of Cush assembled a countless force and came to their (i.e., the Ekronites) aid. In the plain of Eltekeh, they drew up their ranks against me and sharpened their weapons. Trusting in the god Ashur, my lord, I fought with them and inflicted a defeat upon them. The Egyptian charioteers and princes, together with the charioteers of the Cushites, I personally took alive in the midst of the battle. I besieged and conquered Eltekeh and Timnah and carried off their spoil. I advanced to Ekron and slew its officials and nobles who had stirred up rebellion and hung their bodies on watchtowers all about the city. The citizens who committed sinful acts, I counted as spoil, and I ordered the release of the rest of them, who had not sinned. I freed Padi, their king, from Jerusalem and set him on the throne as king over them and imposed tribute for my lordship over him.

49–54 As for Hezekiah, the Judean, I besieged 46 of his fortified walled cities and surrounding smaller towns, which were without number. Using packed-down ramps and applying battering rams, infantry attacks by mines, breeches, and siege machines (or perhaps: storm ladders), I conquered (them). I took out 200,150 people, young and old, male and female, horses, mules, donkeys, camels, cattle, and sheep, without number, and counted them as spoil. He himself, I locked up within Jerusalem, his royal city, like a bird in a cage. I surrounded him with armed posts, and made it unthinkable (literally, "taboo") for him to exit by the city gate. His cities which I had despoiled, I cut off from his land and gave them to Mitinti, king of Ashdod, Padi, king of Ekron, and Ṣilli-Bel, king of Gaza, and thus diminished his land. I imposed dues and gifts for my lordship upon him, in addition to the former tribute, their yearly payment.

55–58 He, Hezekiah, was overwhelmed by the awesome splendor of my lordship, and he sent me after my departure to Nineveh, my royal city, his elite troops (and) his best soldiers, which he had brought in as reinforcements to strengthen Jerusalem, his royal city, with 30 talents of gold, 800 talents of silver, choice antimony, large blocks of carnelian, beds (inlaid) with ivory, armchairs (inlaid) with ivory, elephant hides, ivory, ebony-wood, boxwood, multicolored garments, garments of linen, wool (dyed) red-purple and blue-purple, vessels of copper, iron, bronze and tin, iron, chariots, siege shields, lances, armor, daggers for the belt, bows and arrows, countless trappings and implements of war, together with his daughters, his palace women, his male and female singers. He (also) dispatched his messenger to deliver the tribute and to do obeisance.

* This translation updates and replaces the one I presented in *COS* 2.

32–35 **In my third campaign, I marched to Ḫatti**—Sennacherib's annals are numbered sequentially and not by the years of his reign as was the practice of Tiglath-pileser III and Sargon II. In this manner, the scribes were able to cover up the fact that the king did not undertake an annual campaign. The date of the third campaign, 701 BCE, is determined by the name of the eponym given in the colophon. Two campaigns preceded the present one, the First

Campaign to Babylon against Merodach-baladan, the Second Campaign to various kingdoms to the east and northeast of Assyria.

Ḫatti—That is, Syria, referring to the West; see note to Text no. 2.01, line 5.

Luli, king of Sidon. . . he fled overseas far-off—Luli was king of Tyre, and also bore the traditional title "king of Sidon," as did the earlier kings Hiram I and Ethbaal. He followed Metenna on the throne of Tyre (see Text no. 4.04, line 16′) and reigned for 36 years (c. 729–694 BCE). His relations with Assyria knew many ups and downs (see Katzenstein 1997:220–258) and his rebellion against Sennacherib led to his flight. Luli escaped capture and his whereabouts were unknown at the time of the composition of the Rassam Cylinder. The report inscribed on the Bull colossus (c. 696–694 BCE) updates the story; see Text no. 6.03. A relief in the palace of Sennacherib apparently depicts Luli's departure—the loading of his family on ships; see Barnett 1969: 6 and pl. 1. Josephus reports events from the early years of the reign of Luli (Elulaios), during which Tyre resisted Shalmaneser V (*Antiquities* 9.283–287).

Greater Sidon—Perhaps the fortified quarter of the city; also referred to in Josh 11:8; 19:28.

Little Sidon—This site is mentioned only here; it may refer to a particular quarter (the port area?) or to a suburb of the main city.

Bit-zitti—This toponym appears on a Phoenician seal בת זת (Beit Zeit) and might be the town Zayta, south of Sidon (so Greenfield 1985:132).

Ṣariptu—On the Mediterranean coast, 13 km south of Sidon. The ancient name is preserved in the nearby village of Sarafand. The prophet Elijah found food and shelter in the home of a woman from this town, Zarephath; see 1 Kgs 17:8–24.

Maḫaliba—Kh. el-Maḥālib; referred to in the inscriptions of Tiglath-pileser III (see Text no. 4.05, line 6). It is assigned to the tribe of Asher in Judg 1:31.

Ushu—The coastal quarter of Tyre, opposite Tyre island; see Text no. 9.02. Many identify it with Tell er-Rashidiyeh near Râs el-ᶜAyin. Some find the name in the biblical town Hosah in Josh 19:29, which is located 2.5 km east of Tell er-Rashidiyeh; but there are phonetic difficulties in this identification.

Achzib—Located on the seacoast at the mouth of Wadi ez-Zib, in the territory of the tribe of Asher (Josh 19:29; Judg 1:31), 3 km from the modern Israeli city of Nahariya.

Acco—The site of biblical Acco is at Tell el-Fuḥḥar, east of the old city of Acco; assigned to the tribe of Asher (Judg 1:31).

I installed Tubaʾlu on the his royal throne over them—With the flight of Luli and as punishment for Tyre's insurrection, Sidon was separated from Tyre and Tubaʾlu was appointed an independent vassal king. Tyre was not captured—Sennacherib had no navy to attack the island city—and apparently he reached an agreement with it some time later; see Katzenstein 1997:259–262.

36–38 **The kings of Amurru, all of them—Minuḫimmu of Samsimuruna, Tubaʾlu of Sidon, Abdiliʾti of Arvad, Urumilki of Byblos, Mitinti of Ashdod, Puduʾilu of Beth-Ammon, Chemosh-nadbi of Moab, Ayarammu of Edom**—This is a summary list of western vassal kings who submitted to Sennacherib without battle. It is nowhere stated that they had taken part in the revolt against his authority. Note that Tubaʾlu, who was set over Sidon in the course of the campaign, is included among the submissive. The placement of this list at this point in the narrative does not necessarily imply that a ceremony of submission took place at Ushu prior to the continued march of the Assyrian army along the coast towards Philistia (although the later Bull Inscription no. 4 does do so).

Minuḫimmu of Samsimuruna—Unidentified. Some suggest a location along the seacoast in the vicinity of the estuary of Nahr el-Kalb, just north of Beirut.

Puduʾilu of Beth-Ammon—He is also known from an Ammonite stamp seal (פדאל); see Avigad 1997:321, no. 857; 357, no. 965.

39–41 **As for Ṣidqa, king of Ashkelon, who had not submitted to my yoke**—Ṣidqa had apparently led an anti-Assyrian uprising in Ashkelon, during which he seized power and ousted (perhaps assassinated) Rukibti, who had been appointed by Tiglath-pileser III; see Text no. 4.10, line 10. Ṣidqa's lineage is not known; Tadmor suggested that he was the younger brother of Rukibti. His name appears on a seal of the servant of his son: "Belonging to Abd-eliab, son of Shibʾat, servant of Miti(n)ti, son of Ṣidqa" (Avigad 1997:399–400, no. 1066).

I set Sharru-lu-dari, son of Rukibti, their former king, over the people of Ashkelon—After the capture of Ashkelon, Sharru-lu-dari was appointed king over the city. His Assyrian name means: "May the king live forever." That a Philistine prince bore an Assyrian name is evidence of the pro-Assyrian stance taken by Ashkelon during Rukibti's reign. Whether Sharru-lu-dari had ever spent time as a "hostage" in Assyria, at which time he could have been given his new name, is unknown. Perhaps he received the Assyrian name when Sennacherib appointed him to the throne; Esarhaddon gave the same Assyrian name to one of his Egyptian vassals (see Text no. 9.01, line 90).

I deported and brought him to Assyria—No details are given as to how Ashkelon was taken, giving room for the speculation that after the conquest of Ṣidqa's cities north of the city, the rebels in Ashkelon surrendered without a battle.

In the course of my campaign, I surrounded and conquered Beth-Dagon, Joppa, Bene-berak, Azor, cities belonging to Ṣidqa—The enclave of cities that was subordinate to Ashkelon was centered on Joppa. Only Ashdod, which lay between them and Ashkelon, had not joined the rebellion.

Beth-dagon—Situated at the site of modern Bet Dagan (formerly Beit Dajan), 9 km southeast of Joppa, and not to be confused with the town of the same name, Beth-dagon, in the Judean Shephelah (Josh 15:41), some 40 km east of the battle area.

Joppa—The large mound overlooking the port of Old Jaffa (Tell Qal^{c}a).

Bene-berak—A Danite city according to Josh 19:45; identified with the former Arab village Ibn-Ibraq (Ḥeriya).

Azor—Located some 6 km east of Joppa, at the former Arab village of Jazur (nowadays Azor). This town appears in the Greek translation to Josh 19:45 in place of Hebrew *Yehud*.

42–48 **The officials, the nobles, and the people of Ekron who had thrown Padi, their king, (who was) under oath and obligation to Assyria, into iron fetters and handed him over in a hostile manner to Hezekiah, the Judean**—The major Philistine city of Ekron, Tel Miqne, near Kibbutz Revadim; it is listed among the Danite cities in Josh 19:43. The archaeological finds of late 8th century BCE Ekron were interpreted by its excavators Dothan and Gitin 1993 as indicating the relatively small size of the city; see Ussishkin 2006:339–343 for a suggested revision of site's chronology.

Padi, their king—This pro-Assyrian king is known from inscriptions discovered at Ekron; see Gitin, Dothan and Naveh 1997; Gitin and Cogan 1997.

(They) handed him over in a hostile manner to Hezekiah, the Judean—From this statement, it appears that Hezekiah took a leading role in the uprising against Assyria. According to 2 Kgs 18:8: "Hezekiah overran Philistia as far as Gaza and its border areas, from watchtower to fortified town"; this would have included the removal of Padi, the Assyrian protegé in Ekron.

The kings of Egypt, (and) the bowmen, chariot corps and cavalry of the king of Cush assembled a countless force and came to their (i.e., the Ekronites') aid—The Egyptian expeditionary force included Egyptians from the Delta and Cushites from Upper Egypt. The biblical source records that Tirhakah, king of Cush (2 Kgs 19:9; Isa 37:9), led these troops in battle. At the time, he was a young, twenty-year-old. This title, "king of Cush," given to him there, is anachronistic, as he did not come to the throne until 690 BCE; at the time of the present battles, Shabatka, his brother, ruled Egypt. For the chronological issues of the Egyptian kings at the end of the 8th century BCE, see the discussions of Kitchen 1973a:378–387; 1973b; Kahn 2001.

In the Assyrian annal report, the Egyptian force is associated solely with Ekron, when in fact, it supported all the anti-Assyrian kingdoms. This is known from the castigations of the prophet Isaiah against those who "go down to Egypt" to negotiate military support from its southern neighbor (cf. Isa 30:1–5; 31:1–3; also 2 Kgs 18:21). And indeed, Egyptian auxiliaries were stationed within Judean fortresses prior to the arrival of the Assyrian campaign as seen in the Lachish reliefs where Nubian soldiers are shown as being cruelly punished outside the walls of Lachish. See Fig. 17.

In the plain of Eltekeh, they drew up their ranks against me and sharpened their weapons—The battle against the Egyptians was waged in the coastal plain near Eltekeh, identified with Tell esh-Shallaf, about 3 km west of the city of Rehoboth; Eltekeh is a Danite city in Josh 19:44; 21:23.

I fought with them and inflicted a defeat upon them. The Egyptian charioteers and princes, together with the charioteers of the Cushites, I personally took alive in the midst of the battle—In 2 Kgs 19:9, the engagement with the Egyptians took place while negotiations were being

Fig. 17. Flaying of Nubian soldiers at Lachish (*Courtesy of the Trustees of the British Museum*).

undertaken in Jerusalem. The Assyrian annals dissociate the two actions. The Egyptian princes were likely held hostage in Nineveh until diplomatic relations with Egypt were resumed, which would allow for their release. Perhaps some of these high-ranking captives found their way to the court and other royal service; see Radner 2012.

I besieged and conquered Eltekeh and Timnah and carried off their spoil—Following the defeat of the Egyptian force, the Assyrians returned to the northern Shephelah and besieged Eltekeh and Timnah. Timnah, a Judean border town (Josh 15:10), is Tel Batash, on the western bank of Naḥal Sorek, 7 km west-northwest of Beth-shemesh.

I advanced to Ekron and slew its officials and nobles who had stirred up rebellion and hung their bodies on watchtowers all about the city—The harsh punishment inflicted on the rebels at Ekron is not uncommon in the manual of Assyrian warfare; the use of such tactics was likely aimed at striking terror among the re-conquered citizenry. This practice is graphically illustrated in the Lachish relief of Sennacherib, where the bodies of dead Judeans are shown impaled in front of the city gate. See *ANEP*, no. 373.

I freed Padi, their king, from Jerusalem and set him on the throne as king over them and imposed tribute for my lordship over him—The return of Padi to Ekron was likely negotiated at the end of the conflict, as part of the terms of surrender of Hezekiah. Its insertion at this point in the report is an example of "closing the narrative circle," which is often out of chronological sequence; for a biblical example of this literary technique, see Exod 16:35. Two years after Padi's reinstatement to the throne, he sent tribute to Nineveh, as evidenced by the bulla attached to the shipment that bore the inscription: "One talent (of silver) according to the light, royal (talent). From Pidi of Ekron. Month of Marcheshvan, day 23, eponym of Bel-sharrani (i.e., 699 BCE)" (SAA 11, no. 50, p. 42).

49–54 **As for Hezekiah, the Judean**—Later texts add the phrase: "who had not submitted to my yoke."

I besieged 46 of his fortified walled cities and surrounding smaller towns, which were without number—Cf. the summary statement in 2 Kgs 18:13: "Sennacherib, king of Assyria, marched against all the fortified towns of Judah and seized them."

Using packed-down ramps and applying battering rams, infantry attacks by mines, breeches, and siege machines (or perhaps: storm ladders), I conquered (them)—These assault techniques are illustrated on the Lachish relief (see further Text no. 6.02). For a discussion from a military point of view, see Yadin 1963:428–437; Eph^{c}al 2008. The destruction wrought by the Assyrian army informed Isaiah's diatribe: "Your land is a waste, your cities burnt down; before your eyes, the yield of your soil is consumed by strangers—A wasteland, like Sodom(!) overthrown. Fair Zion is left like a booth in a vineyard, like a hut in a cucumber field, like a city beleaguered" (Isa 1:7–8).

I took out 200,150 people, young and old, male and female, horses, mules, donkeys, camels, cattle, and sheep, without number, and counted them as spoil—The number of captives deported is extremely large and is at odds with the population estimates of the kingdom of Judah suggested by archaeologists, who set it at approximately 120,000; see Shiloh 1981; Broshi and Finkelstein 1992. The Assyrian scribes sought to enhance the king's victory by inflating the numbers; on this practice, see De Odorico 1995:172–174; for a different opinion, see Millard 1991.

He himself, I locked up within Jerusalem, his royal city, like a bird in a cage. I surrounded him with armed posts, and made it unthinkable (literally, "taboo") **for him to exit by the city gate**—The topography of Jerusalem did not easily permit the use of siege-wall technique, and so instead, fortified positions were erected to cut the city off from the outside world.

His cities which I had despoiled, I cut off from his land and gave them to Mitinti, king of Ashdod, Padi, king of Ekron, and Ṣilli-Bel, king of Gaza, and thus diminished his land—The kingdom of Judah was dismembered by the parcelling out of captured areas to nearby Philistine vassal city-states. In the somewhat later Bull Inscription, Ashkelon is included in this land division: "I gave it (i.e., his land) to the kings of Ashdod, Ashkelon, Ekron and Gaza" (Frahm 1997, no. 4), perhaps reflecting later arrangements in the Judean Shephelah. These circumstances are likely the background of the lament of the Judean prophet Micah in Mic 1:8–16; see Hallo 1999:40.

I imposed dues and gifts for my lordship upon him, in addition to the former tribute, their yearly payment—Hezekiah's prior vassalage is mentioned here for the first time; cf. 2 Kgs 18:7: "He rebelled against the king of Assyria and would not serve him."

55–58 **His elite troops (and) his best soldiers, which he had brought in as reinforcements to strengthen Jerusalem, his royal city**—Under the terms of surrender, Judah relinquished its skilled fighting force, which, if the precedent of Samaria was followed (see Text no. 5.02, col. iv, lines 25–49), was integrated into the Assyrian army. The term for "elite troops" (Akkadian *urbi*) is rarely used in the royal inscriptions, and is unrelated to the similar-sounding Akkadian name for Arabs (*Aribi*); see Cogan and Tadmor 1988:247, n. 2.

30 talents of gold, 800 talents of silver—Similar figures are given in 2 Kgs 18:14: "300 talents of silver and 30 talents of gold." It is further reported that in order to meet the heavy payment, Hezekiah stripped the precious metal overlays in the Temple that he himself had dedicated; see v. 16. But note that the similarity is deceiving, as the Assyrian and Judean talents were of different measures. The weight of a "light" talent, in use in Mesopotamia at the end of the 8th century BCE, was 30 kg; thus Hezekiah's payment was 900 kg of gold and 24,000 kg of silver. An enormous sum indeed!

Multicolored garments, garments of linen, wool (dyed) red-purple

and blue-purple, vessels of copper, iron, bronze and tin, chariots, siege shields, lances, armor, daggers for the belt, bows and arrows, countless trappings and implements of war—This part of the tribute list is omitted in later editions of Sennacherib's annals; it is replaced by the general phrase: "abundant treasure of all kind."

He (also) dispatched his messenger to deliver the tribute and to do obeisance—The tribute payment is said to have been made in Nineveh and received from the hands of a Judean delegation, implying Hezekiah's total surrender and his disablement from further rebellion.

No. 6.02—THE LACHISH RELIEF INSCRIPTIONS

A series of large slabs, depicting the assault and capture of the Judean city of Lachish, was set on the walls of room XXXVI in the southwest palace of Sennacherib at Nineveh. Their prominent position within the palace was apparently chosen so that "a visitor might justifiably conclude that

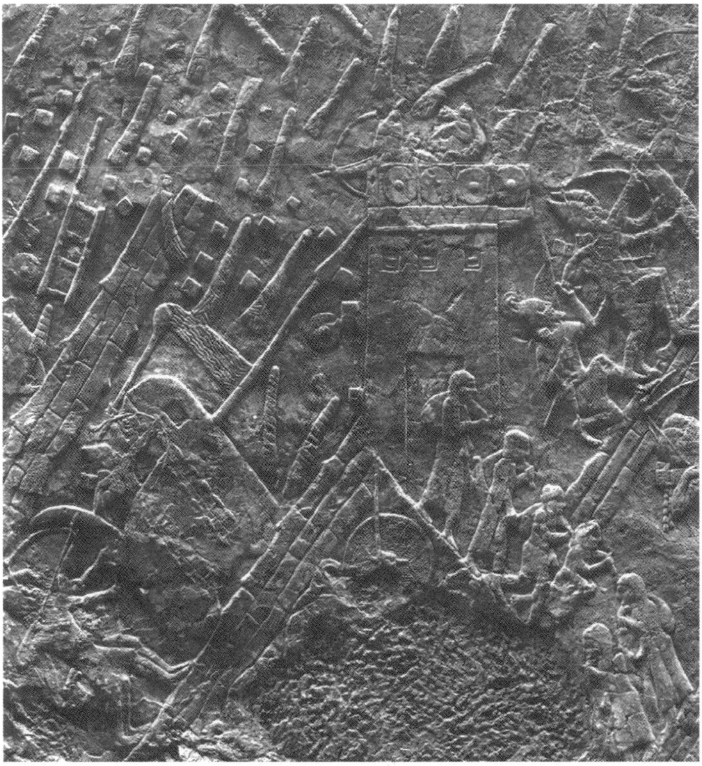

Fig. 18. The attack on Lachish, detail of relief from Sennacherib's Southwest Palace at Nineveh (*Courtesy of the Trustees of the British Museum*).

Fig. 19. Sennacherib receives booty and prisoners, from the Southwest Palace at Nineveh (*Courtesy of the Trustees of the British Museum*).

the surrender of Lachish was the high point of the western campaign" (Russell 1991:202–209, 252–257). The representation of the city follows the conventions of pictorial composition as practiced by Assyrian artists (Jacoby 1991; Uehlinger 2003), thus the identification of the location depends entirely on the epigraph inscribed on slab 12 to the left of the figure of the king, who is shown overseeing the attack and defeat of the city (Fig. 19). To the king's right is another epigraph identifying the royal tent (Fig. 20).

Though commemorated in this most outstanding fashion, the battle of Lachish was not referred to in the "official" annal account of the campaign to Judah in 701 BCE (see Text no. 6.01). On the other hand, Lachish is mentioned twice in the biblical accounts; it was one of the fortified cities of Judah attacked by the Assyrian army (2 Kgs 19:8) and was the site to which Hezekiah, suing for terms of surrender, sent his negotiators (2 Kgs 18:14). One suspects that the choice of Lachish to represent the battles in Judah was due to the fact that Sennacherib had set up his camp at the site and was on the scene personally supervising the events depicted in this grand relief.

Text edition: Grayson and Novotny 2014:110–112.
Translations: *ARAB* 2, §§489, 495; *DOTT* 70; *ANET* 288; *TPOA* 124; *TUAT* 1/4, 391; *COS* 2, 304; *HTAT* 334.
Illustrations: *ANEP*, nos. 371–374; Yadin 1963:428–437; Ussishkin 1982 passim.

Fig. 20. Royal tent pitched on wooded hill before Lachish, from the Southwest Palace at Nineveh (*Courtesy of the Trustees of the British Museum*).

Epigraph Fig. 19 Sennacherib, king of the universe, king of Assyria, seated upon an armchair; the spoils of Lachish passed before him.

Epigraph Fig. 20 The tent of Sennacherib, king of Assyria

Lachish—Tell ed-Duweir, located in the southeastern Shephelah, was a major link in the line of fortifications that protected the kingdom of Judah from attack from the West. The archaeological excavations at the site have clarified the methods of attack on the city as depicted on the Assyrian relief and uncovered defensive measures undertaken by the defenders (see Ussishkin 1982, 1992; Eph^{c}al 1984).

No. 6.03—CAMPAIGN TO THE WEST—THE BULL COLOSSI

Colossal stone figures representing bulls and lions with human heads were set at many of the entrances and doorways in Sennacherib's Southwest Palace at Nineveh where they served as protective genii. Many of them were embossed with summary inscriptions, relating up to six of the king's campaigns. Due to the circumstances of their discovery and their partial removal to the British Museum, there is much confusion concerning the original location of these colossi within the building and to which ones the texts, copied by the excavators, belong. The following excerpt, known as Bull Inscription 2, summarizes the events of the campaign to Judah that were reported in full in Sennacherib's annals. The text includes reports on five campaigns and can be dated to 696 BCE.

Text edition: Grayson and Novotny 2014:69.
Translations: *ARAB* 2, §§326–327; *DOTT* 68; *ANET* 288; *HTAT* 333–334.

17–22 Now Luli, king of Sidon, was afraid of doing battle with me, and he fled to Cyprus, which is in the midst of the sea, and took refuge. In that year, because of the terrifying appearance of the weapon of Ashur, my lord, he disappeared forever (i.e., died). I placed Tubaʾlu on the throne of his kingdom and imposed my royal tribute on him. I destroyed the wide district of Judah; the stubborn (and) mighty Hezekiah, its king, I had him bow down at my feet.

He fled to Cyprus—The early annal report of Luli's flight did not mention his place of refuge or his fate; see Text no. 6.01, lines 32–35. The death of Luli was first reported in the annal inscription of 697 BCE. While the circumstances of his demise are not given, his death is attributed to the god Ashur whose indomitable power reached even to the distant islands. On the Assyrian name for Cyprus—Yadnana, see Text no. 8.02, col. v, line 71.

I destroyed the wide district of Judah; the stubborn (and) mighty Hezekiah, its king, I had him bow down at my feet—The unusual description of Hezekiah's arrogance hints at the outcome of the campaign in 701 BCE that was not in conformity with Assyrian military or ideological standards. Rather than dethroning the king and dismantling his kingdom, Hezekiah was forced into submission and his kingdom destroyed. The symbolic act of kissing the overlord's feet is nowhere else reported of Hezekiah.

NO. 6.04—CONSTRUCTION WORK AT NINEVEH

Assyrian inscriptions typically conclude with a report of royal building works. In Sennacherib's case, his extensive undertakings at Nineveh—a new city-wall encompassing additional tracts of land, the refurbishing

Fig. 21. Taskmasters and slaves hauling on ropes to build the king's palace, detail of relief from Sennacherib's Southwest Palace at Nineveh (*Courtesy of the Trustees of the British Museum*).

of older palaces and the building of new ones, are highlighted (see Reade 1998–2001:399–416). These construction projects required the mobilization of a very large work force, which explains, in part, the vast population deportations from all corners of the empire undertaken during his reign. The following selection, which appears as the introduction to the final section of many annal inscriptions, describes the motivation of this enterprise and allows the reader to draw a map of the contemporary Assyrian empire that stretched from the Persian Gulf northwards to Mannea and eastern Anatolia, from there westward to the Mediterranean Sea, and then along the coast from Philistia in the southernmost corner north towards Phoenicia. This version is the one given in the Rassam cylinder (Text no. 6.01).

Text edition: Grayson and Novotny 2012:66–67; earlier Frahm 1997:55–56, lines 61–70.

1–30 At that time, Nineveh, the exalted cult center, the city beloved of Ishtar, wherein all the rites of the gods and goddesses are found; the eternal base of the ancient foundation, whose design had been drawn of old in accord with the heavenly writ; whose structure is clearly visible; the artistic place, the location of all secrets, where all the cults and hidden cosmic waters are brought together(?); indeed from former times, the earlier kings, my ancestors, who ruled over Assyria before me and exercised power over the subjects of Enlil, and therein received annually without interruption and immeasurable income, the tribute of the kings of the four quarters (of the world), not one of them paid attention or thought about the palace that was there, its shrine, its royal residence whose dimension had become too small, (and) not one of them considered or thought to straighten the city's streets and to widening (its) squares, to dig canals and plant trees; (until) I, Sennacherib, king of the universe, king of Assyria, considered and set my heart to undertaking this work by the command of the gods. The people of Babylon, the Arameans, and (people of) Mannea, Que and Cilicia, Philistia and the land of Tyre, who had not submitted to my yoke, I exiled them and had them carry the basket and make bricks. I cut down the canebrakes and reed marshes in Babylon and had their luxuriant reeds hauled by the enemy soldiers whom I captured for its (the palace) construction.

1–30 **The people of Babylon, the Arameans, and (people of) Mannea, Que and Cilicia, Philistia and the land of Tyre, who had submitted to my yoke**—From the order of geographic and ethnographic elements, it seems clear that the reference here is to the Aramean tribes who were settled in large numbers east of the Tigris and are attested for the first time in the inscriptions of Tiglath-pileser III; their origins are obscure (see Brinkman 1968:267–285).

Mannea—The mountainous territory northeast of Assyria, south of Lake Urmia; known from Assyrian sources from the mid-9th century BCE; its inhabitants were brought into the Assyrian orbit after Sargon II's campaign to the area in 716 BCE. The prophet Jeremiah joins Mannea (Hebrew מִנִּי) with Ararat and Ashkenaz, in referring to Babylon's enemies (Jer 51:27).

Que and Cilicia—The coastal region, the plain and its surrounding mountains, in southeastern Anatolia. The plain was known as Que (see Text no. 4.02); the mountainous perimeter, Cilicia (Akkadian *Ḫilakku*).

Philistia—The name refers to the southeast coast of the Land of Israel; similar usage is attested in biblical texts from the Neo-Assyrian period, cf. "Rejoice not, all Philistia, because the staff of him that beat you is broken" (Isa 14:29; also v. 31); "What is this that you are doing to Me, O Tyre, Sidon and all the districts of Philistia?" (Joel 4:4). Note that the Kingdom of Judah goes unmentioned, inasmuch as the places mentioned are points on the compass—East, North and West—and not a comprehensive list of subject kingdoms.

The land of Tyre—The venerable and leading commercial city, here representative of the entire Phoenician coast.

I exiled them and had them carry the basket and make bricks—These terms refer to corvée work imposed upon Assyrian subjects.

No. 6.05—THE MURDER OF SENNACHERIB

The murder of Sennacherib by his son(s) became a *cause célèbre* throughout the ancient Near East, remembered and discussed by generations after the event. The matter seems to have been silenced in Assyria—it goes unmentioned in the royal inscriptions; on the other hand, in Israel and Babylonia, both of which had suffered greatly at the hands of the Assyrian king, fuller reports of the event were recorded.

In Esarhaddon's apologia on his rise to the throne (Text no. 8.01), mention of the murder is clearly avoided. The text stresses Esarhaddon's legitimacy as opposed to the godless attempt of his brothers to prevent him—Sennacherib's chosen heir—from taking the throne. In the end, with the help of the gods and the army, Esarhaddon defeated his enemies to reign in Nineveh.

Biblical tradition is a bit fuller. The assassination of Sennacherib is recorded as the climax of the complex of stories concerning the Assyrian campaign to the West in 701 BCE (2 Kgs 18:13–19:37). The prophetic rendition of the events of that year told of Sennacherib's demand through the mission of the Assyrian high official, the Rabshakeh, that King Hezekiah of Judah surrender unconditionally. His words included blasphemous remarks against the God of Israel; in response, the prophet Isaiah declared that the Assyrian king would be punished: upon his return home, he would be cut down: "I myself will put a spirit in him, so that he shall hear a rumor and return to his own land; I will cause him to fall by the sword in his own land" (2 Kgs 19:7). The prophecy is later reported to have been fulfilled, as related in the chronicle-like statement:

> As he was worshiping in the house of his god Nisroch, his sons Adrammelech and Sharezer killed him with the sword, and they escaped into the land of Ararat. His son Esarhaddon succeeded him (2 Kgs 19:37).

Sennacherib had met his just desserts.

In Babylonia, the Babylonian Chronicle recorded, in its usual concise manner, the fact of Sennacherib's assassination by an unnamed son and noted that the "rebellion" continued for close to two months until Esarhaddon ascended the throne (Text no. 11.01, rev. iii:34–35). The observation that there was a rebellion in Assyria seems to suggest that the murder was associated with the question of the selection of Esarhaddon as the heir apparent; see Text no. 8.01.

Over a century and a half after the event, the assassination was treated in a text composed in the early years of Nabonidus, the last king of Babylon. Sennacherib's destruction of Babylon and its shrines, though undertaken because of Marduk's anger with his city, was carried out with "evil intent." As a result, the proud Assyrian was murdered by his son in an act of avengement for the wanton desecration.

Text edition: Schaudig 2001:515–516; earlier Langdon 1912:271–273, col. i, 1–41.
Translations: *ANET* 309; *TUAT* 1/4, 407.

col. i,

1–41 He (Sennacherib) planned evil; he thought out crimes [agai]nst the country; he had no mercy for the people [of Babylon]. With evil intentions he advanced on Babylon, he turned its sanctuaries to waste; he made the ground plan unrecognizable; he desecrated the cultic rites. He led the lord Marduk away and brought him to the city Ashur. In accord with the anger of the god, he acted (thus) against the country. The anger of lord Marduk was not eased. For 21 years, he established his residence in the city Ashur. (When) the days were fulfilled (and) the time arrived, the anger of the king of the gods, the lord of lords, calmed and he remembered (the temple) Esagil and Babylon, his lordly residence. The king of Subartu (Assyria), who in accord with Marduk's anger, had laid waste to the country, his very own son struck him down.

For 21 years, he established his residence in the city Ashur—The absence of Marduk's image from Babylon, is rationalized as the god's voluntary relocation to a foreign country. The twenty-one years are counted from 689, the year of the destruction of Babylon by Sennacherib, until the return of the image by Ashurbanipal in 668 BCE; see Text no. 11.01, col. iv, lines 34–36.

The king of Subartu (Assyria), who in accord with Marduk's anger, had laid waste to the country, his very own son struck him down—The affinity of the Babylonian view of the murder—avenging the destruction of their country by the Assyrian king—with the Israelite view expressed in 2 Kgs 19:6–7—avenging the blasphemy of YHWH uttered by Sennacherib, may stem from a reciprocal exchange of views between Judeans in Babylon and their neighbors; see Cogan 2009.

References

Avigad, Nahman
1997 *Corpus of West Semitic Stamp Seals*, Jerusalem.
Barnett, Richard D.
1969 Ezekiel and Tyre, *ErIsr* 9:6–13.
Brinkman, John A.
1968 *A Political History of Post-Kassite Babylonia 1158–722 B.C.*, Rome.
Broshi, Magen and Israel Finkelstein
1992 The Population of Palestine in Iron Age II, *BASOR* 287:47–60.
Cogan, Mordechai
2001 Sennacherib's Siege of Jerusalem. Once or Twice?, *BAR* 27:40–45, 69.
2009 Sennacherib and the Angry Gods of Babylon and Israel, *IEJ* 59:164–174.
2014 Cross-examining the Assyrian Witnesses to Sennacherib's Third Campaign: Assessing the Limits of Historical Reconstruction. Pp. 51–74 in I. Kalimi and S. Richardson (eds.), *Sennacherib at the Gate of Jerusalem (701 B.C.E.): Story, History and Historiography*, CHANE 71; Leiden.
Cogan, Mordechai and Hayim Tadmor
1988 *II Kings*, Anchor Bible 11, Garden City.
De Odorico, Marco
1995 *The Use of Numbers and Quantifications in the Assyrian Royal Inscriptions*, SAAS 3, Helsinki.

Dothan, Trude and Seymour Gitin

1993 Miqne, Tel (Ekron). Pp. 1051–1059 in vol. 3 of *NEAEHL*.

Eph^cal Israel

2008 *The City Besieged*, Jerusalem.

1984 The Assyrian Siege Ramp at Lachish: Military and Lexical Aspects, *Tel Aviv* 11:60–70.

Frahm, Eckart

1997 *Einleitung in die Sanherib-Inschriften*, AfO Beiheft 26, Wien.

Gallagher, W. R.

1999 *Sennacherib's Campaign to Judah. New Studies*, Leiden 91–142.

Galter, Hannes D., Louis D. Levine, Julian Reade

1986 The Colossi of Sennacherib's Palace and their Inscriptions, *ARRIM* 4:27–32.

Gitin, Seymour, Trude Dothan and Joseph Naveh

1997 A Royal Dedicatory Inscription from Ekron, *IEJ* 47:1–16.

Gitin, Seymour and Mordechai Cogan

1999 A New Type of Dedicatory Inscription from Ekron, *IEJ* 49:193–202.

Gonçalves, Francolino J.

1986 *L'expédition de Sennachérib en Palestine dans la littérature hébräique ancienne*, Paris.

Grayson, A. Kirk and Jamie Novotny

2012 *The Royal Inscriptions of Sennacherib, King of Assyria* (*704–681 BC*), Part 1, RINAP 3/1, Winona Lake, IL.

Greenfield, Jonas C.

1985 A Group of Phoenician City Seals, *IEJ* 35:129–134.

Hallo, William W.

1999 Jerusalem under Hezekiah: An Assyriological Perspective. Pp. 36–50 in L. I. Levine (ed.), *Jerusalem: Its Sanctity and Centrality to Judaism, Christianity, and Islam*, New York.

Jacoby, Ruth

1991 The Representation and Identification of Cities on Assyrian Reliefs, *IEJ* 41:112–131.

Kahn, Dan'el

2001 The Inscriptions of Sargon II at Tang-i Var and the Chronology of Dynasty 25, *Or* 70:1–18.

Katzenstein, H. Jacob

1997 *The History of Tyre*, 2nd ed., Beersheva.

Kitchen, Kenneth A.

1973a The Third Intermediate Period in Egypt (1100–650 BC), Warminster.

1973b Late Egyptian Chronology and the Hebrew Monarchy, *JANESCU* 5:225–231.

Laato, Antti

1995 Falsification of History in the Royal Inscriptions of Sennacherib, *VT* 45:198–226.

Langdon, Stephen

1912 *Die Neubabylonischen Königsinschriften*, VAB 4, Leipzig.

Millard, Alan R.

1991 Large Numbers in the Assyrian Royal Inscriptions. Pp. 213–222 in *Ah Assyria. . . Studies Tadmor*, Mordechai Cogan and Israel Eph^cal (eds.), *ScrHier* 33.

Radner, Karen

2012 After Eltekeh: Royal Hostages from Egypt at the Assyrian Court. Pp. 471–479 in H. Baker, K. Kaniuth, A. Otto (eds.), *Stories of Long Ago. Festschrift für Michael D. Raof*, AOAT 397.

Reade, Julian E.

1998–2001 Ninive (Nineveh). Pp. 388–433 in vol. 9 of *RlA*.

Russell, John M.

1991 *Sennacherib's Palace without Rival at Nineveh*, Chicago.

Schaudig, Hanspeter

2001 *Die Inschriften Nabonids von Babylon und Kyros' des Grossen*, AOAT 256, Münster.

Shiloh, Yigal

1981 The Population of Iron Age Palestine in the Light of Urban Plans, Areas and Population Density, *ErIsr* 15:274–282 (Hebrew).

Tadmor, Hayim

2011 Sennacherib's Campaign to Judah: Historical and Historiographical Considerations. Pp. 653–675 in idem, *"With my many Chariots I have gone up the heights of mountains": Historical and Literary Studies on Ancient Mesopotamia and Israel*, Mordechai Cogan (ed.), Jerusalem.

Uehlinger, Christoph

2003 Clio in a World of Pictures—Another Look at the Lachish Reliefs from Sennacherib's Southwest Palace at Nineveh. Pp. 221–305 in Lester L. Grabbe (ed.), *"Like a Bird in a Cage": The Invasion of Sennacherib in 701 BCE*, JSOTSup 363.

Ussishkin, David

1982 *The Conquest of Lachish by Sennacherib*, Tel Aviv.

1992 Lachish. Pp. 114–126 in vol. 4 of *ABD*.

2006 Sennacherib's Campaign to Philistia and Judah: Ekron, Lachish, and Jerusalem. Pp. 339–357 in Yairah Amit et al. (eds.), *Essays on Ancient Israel in its Near Eastern Context. A Tribute to Nadav Na'aman*, Winona Lake, IN.

Yadin, Yigael

1963 *The Art of Warfare in Biblical Lands in the Light of Archaeological Study*. Translated by M. Pearlman. 2 vols. New York.

Fig. 22. Boundary stone (*kudurru*) of Merodach-baladan, recording the king's grant of land to the governor of Babylon (*Vorderasiatisches Museum, Berlin*).

CHAPTER 7

MERODACH-BALADAN II

Merodach-baladan, chief of the (Bit-)Yakin tribe and intermittent king of Babylon, remains an elusive personality due to the paucity of sources on his thirty-plus years of political activity in southern Babylonia during the period of Assyria's rise to empire. Assyria's kings saw him as an adversary, and at the same time, there were circles in Babylon that recognized and supported his rule. At first, Merodach-baladan joined other Aramean chieftains in submission to Tiglath-pileser III, when the Assyrian king took Babylon in 729. But following the death of Shalmaneser V in 722, he broke with Assyria and assumed the throne in Babylon. He successfully withstood Sargon's attempt to remove him and continued to rule as king of Babylon for 12 years (721–710); see Text no. 11.01, col. i 33–ii 4. During the Assyrian campaigns against Babylon in 710 and 709, Merodach-baladan fled the capital and later also his familial fortress, Dur-Yakin. Following Sargon's death and Sennacherib's accession (705), Merodach-baladan again proclaimed himself king of Babylon. He escaped the advancing Assyrian forces during Sennacherib's campaign south in 703, and found safe haven in the vicinity of the Persian Gulf. During a final encounter with Assyria in 700, Merodach-baladan made off to Elam where he seems to have died sometime later. For a full review of the life of Merodach-baladan, see Brinkman 1964.

Merodach-baladan was also active on the international scene as is learned from the report of his dealings with Hezekiah, king of Judah. According to 2 Kgs 20:12–19, envoys of the Babylonian king visited Jerusalem, ostensibly bringing wishes of good health to the Judean king during his illness. While in Jerusalem, the Babylonians was treated to a private viewing of Hezekiah's immense wealth and armaments. Most readers agree that more than diplomatic protocol was behind this visit. More than likely the "'Get well!' greetings" were accompanied by an exchange of views on relations with Assyria, with whom both Babylon and Judah had strained relations; whether this included coordinated plans for joint rebellion against Assyria remains speculative. As to the date of the mission, considering Merodach-baladan's short reign at the start of Sennacherib's reign, the visit of the delegation is best assigned to the years 713–712 BCE; see further in Cogan and Tadmor 1988:260–263.

No. 7.01—THE RESTORATION OF THE EANNA TEMPLE IN URUK

The following excerpt is from the dedicatory inscription of Merodach-baladan, describing the repairs he made to Eanna, the temple of Ishtar in Uruk; it stems from the period of his first reign in Babylon. The text opens with a proclamation of the legitimacy of Merodach-baladan's rule, his having been chosen by Marduk to drive out the Assyrians from the land. Following the building section, it concludes with the traditional wish for blessings to be bestowed upon the king by the goddess. The barrel cylinder on which the text was inscribed was likely buried as a foundation deposit somewhere within the temple complex. It is, therefore, surprising that it was recovered in the ruins of Calah (Nimrud), the Assyrian capital. Furthermore, Sargon II, the arch-rival of Merodach-baladan, issued a similarly worded inscription, relating that he had undertaken the very same good work on the Eanna temple. It would appear that after his victory in the south in 709, Sargon had Merodach-baladan's inscription removed from Uruk and replaced it with his own reworked text, in which he, Sargon, proclaimed his legitimacy to rule Babylon. For a discussion of this "propaganda war," see Tadmor 1997:333–334.

Text edition: Frame 1995:136–138; earlier Gadd 1953.
Translations: Brinkman 1964:14 (lines 8–18).
Photograph: Mallowan 1966: 1, fig. 110.

1–7 To Ishtar, lady of the lands, exalted among the gods, valiant one, the Lady of Eanna, dwelling in Uruk, who is mistress of the cultic ordinances. Eanna, which Shulgi, a former king, had built, became old, and the shrine of Ningizzida, which Anam, an earlier king had built in it, this building, its walls fell down, its joints loosened, its parapet collapsed and disappeared. [None] of the kings who preceded (me) considered to do its (needed) work.

Fig 23. Stamped brick of Merodach-baladan from Uruk (*Courtesy of the Trustees of the British Museum*). The Sumerian inscription reads:

"For the lady, Inanna, lady of the lands, his lady, Merodach-baladan, king of Babylon, offspring of Eriba-Marduk, king of Babylon, Eanna, her beloved temple, built."

7-18 At that time, the great lord Marduk had become angry with Akkad and [*for seven years*] the wicked enemy, the Subarian, ruled over the land of Akkad, [until] the days were complete and the appointed time arrived. The great lord Marduk became reconciled with Akkad, with which he had been angry. He looked upon Merodach-baladan, king of Babylon, the prince who reveres him, his own appointment, the true eldest son of Eriba-Marduk, king of Babylon, who established the foundation of the land. Asari, king of the gods, truly pronounced his name for shepherding the land of Sumer and Akkad, (and) he said with the utterance of his mouth, thus: "Behold, the shepherd, who gathers the scattered (flock)." With the might of the great lord Marduk and of the hero of the gods, the god Utulu, he inflicted a defeat on the vast army of Subartu; he shattered their weapons. He overthrew them and thus barred them from the soil of Akkad.

Shulgi, a former king—The second ruler of the Third Dynasty of Ur (2094–2047 BCE).

Anam, an earlier king—King of Uruk in the late Old Babylonian Period.

the Subarian—The term Subartu is known as early as the third millennium BCE and in Babylonian tradition refers to the foreigners of the North, from the Tigris east to the Zagros Mountains; in later times, this archaic ethnicon stands for Assyria.

[*for seven years*] the wicked enemy, the Subarian, ruled over the land of Akkad—The reference is to the seven-year Assyrian rule of Babylon, the two years of Tiglath-pileser III and the five years of Shalmaneser V (see 11.01, obv. col. 24–32).

Merodach-baladan, king of Babylon—The Babylonian name was Marduk-apla-iddina, "Marduk has granted an offspring." In Hebrew transcription, the name appears in several garbled forms, due to miscopying, cf. 2 Kgs 20:12; Isa 39:1.

Eriba-Marduk, king of Babylon—The dates of his rule, c. 769–761, more than likely makes him the grandfather of Merodach-baladan.

Asari, king of the gods—Marduk, the chief god of Babylon, in his manifestation as "giver of arable land"; cf. *Enuma elish*, vii, 1–2.

Utulu—A name or form of the god Ninurta.

he inflicted a defeat on the vast army of Subartu—The reference seems to be to the battle of Der in 720, see no. 11.01, col. i, lines 33–35.

References

Brinkman, John A.
1964 Merodach-Baladan II. Pp. 6–53 in *Studies Presented to A. Leo Oppenheim*, Chicago.

Cogan, Mordechai and Hayim Tadmor
1988 *II Kings*, Anchor Bible 11, Garden City.

Frame, Grant

1995 *Rulers of Babylonia: From the Second Dynasty of Isin to the End of Assyrian Domination (1157–612 BC)*, Toronto

Gadd, C. J.

1955 Inscribed Barrel Cylinder of Marduk-apla-iddina II, *Iraq* 15:123–134.

Mallowan, Max Edgar Lucien

1966 *Nimrud and its Remains*, 2 vols., London.

Tadmor, Hayim

1997 Propaganda, Literature and Historiography: Cracking the Code of the Assyrian Royal Inscriptions. Pp. 325–338 in S. Parpola and R. M. Whiting (eds.), *Assyria 1995*, Helsinki (= idem, pp. 3–24 in *"With my many chariots I have gone up the heights of mountains." Historical and Literary Studies on Ancient Mesopotamia and Israel*, M. Cogan [ed.], Jerusalem 2011).

Fig. 24. The Zenjirli Stela of Esarhaddon (*Staatliche Museen zu Berlin*).

CHAPTER 8

Esarhaddon

After the assassination of Sennacherib, the crown prince Esarhaddon (681–669 BCE) ascended the throne with the support of the army. The opposition to his accession was overcome, but the murderer escaped and found refuge in Urartu (cf. 2 Kgs 19:37). Esarhaddon's tenure was marked by renewed Egyptian meddling in the affairs of Phoenicia and the Land of Israel under the vigorous King Tirhakah. His response was repeated campaigning in the West, accompanied by severe punishment of those who rebelled against Assyria. This area also served as a forward base for Assyria's campaigns to Egypt that had become, for the first time, a military objective. The attempt to invade the Nile Valley in 674 failed (Text no. 11.01, col. iv, 16), and though a second campaign in 671 was crowned with success, Assyria's dominion over Egypt proved to be short-lived (see Text nos. 8.03; 9.01).

Most of the extant inscriptions of Esarhaddon are summary inscriptions, although a number of them are numbered according to campaigns, as is the case with those of Sennacherib.

The long-reigning Manasseh, king of Judah (698–642 BCE) is referred to twice in the lists of Esarhaddon's western vassals who were summoned to render corvée on imperial construction projects and to provide troops for the Assyrian campaigns in Egypt. These small bits of information complement the biblical report on Manasseh's reign, which concentrates solely on the king's cultic apostasy (cf. 2 Kgs 21:1–18). The picture that emerges from the extant Assyrian texts is that the kingdom of Judah remained submissive during all of Esarhaddon's reign; see further remarks on Text no. 8.04, line 35.

No. 8.01—THE ACCESSION OF ESARHADDON—PRISM NINEVEH A

The violent circumstances surrounding the ascent of Esarhaddon to the kingship of Assyria are related in a royal inscription from the king's seventh year. That these events served as the opening section of an inscription that surveys in typical fashion Esarhaddon's military campaigns and the construction of the armory at Nineveh points to the ongoing friction between the king and his court over the issue of monarchic succession. The inscription was composed in 673 BCE, a year following Assyria's defeat in Egypt (see Text no. 11.01, col. iv, 16) and just months before Esarhaddon arranged for the succession of his sons Ashurbanipal and Shamash-shum-ukin to the thrones in Assyria and Babylonia, respectively. It appears that the question of transfer of rule weighed heavy on the king, so much so that he had the official, apologetic story of his own rise to power promulgated. According to this construction, Sennacherib, supported by the gods, had chosen Esarhaddon, a younger son, to succeed him, but his sinful brothers fomented intrigue at court between himself and his father. Esarhaddon was forced to seek asylum outside the capital because of this hostility; the murder of Sennacherib by those opposed to the named heir followed shortly thereafter. In the end, Esarhaddon won the day; he returned, and with the support of the army defeated his enemies and ascended the throne.

But more than rivalry for the throne between competing siblings may have been involved. This emerges from the sharp shift from Sennacherib's hard line towards the south to Esarhaddon's kid-gloves approach. Violence often accompanies diplomatic changes of direction and the issue of how Assyria would handle its decades-long Babylonian problem may have abetted the patricide by the disgruntled brother who was passed over for the throne. See further Brinkman 1984:67–84.

Text edition: Leichty 2011:11–14; earlier Borger 1956:40–45, Nin. A, Ep. 2.
Translations: *ARAB* 2, §§ 500–506; *ANET* 289–290; *TUAT*, 393–395.

Col. i,

1–7 The Palace of Esarhaddon, great king, mighty king, king of the world, king of Assyria, governor of Babylon, king of Sumer and Akkad, king of the four quarters (of the world), true shepherd, favorite of the great gods, whom from his youth, Ashur, Shamash, Bel, Nabu, Ishtar of Nineveh, (and) Ishtar of Arbela had named for kingship over Assyria.

8–22 Though I am younger than my older brothers, my father, my begetter, duly chose me out of all my brothers on the command of Ashur, Sin, Shamash, Bel and Nabu, Ishtar of Nineveh (and) Ishtar of Arbela, saying: "This is the son, my successor." (Then) he inquired of Shamash and Adad by means of extispicy and they answered him with a firm "yes," saying: "He is your replacement." He strictly observed their important command and so he assembled together the people of Assyria, young (and) old, (as well as) my brothers, my father's offspring; he had them swear a solemn oath to protect my succession in front of (the images of) Ashur, Sin, Shamash, Nabu (and) Marduk, the gods of Assyria, the gods who live in heaven and earth. In a favorable month, on a day of acceptance (of prayers), in accord with their august command, I joyfully entered the Succession Palace, the august place where those appointed to kingship stay.

23–31 *Pursuit and jealousy* fell over my brothers and they abandoned (the will of) the gods, put their trust in insolent ways (and) and plotted evil. They made up evil rumors, slander (and) lies against me of which the gods disapprove, and spread lies, incorrect and hostile, behind my back; they alienated the friendly heart of my father from me, against the will of the gods, though inwardly his heart had compassion and his view was set that I should be king.

32–40 I thought and considered (the matter), as follows: "Their ways are insolent and they trust (only) their own judgment. What will they (not) do against the will of the gods?" To Ashur, king of the gods (and) merciful Marduk, for whom malice is an abomination, with blessings, supplications and gestures of humility, I prayed, and they accepted my words. In accord with the judgment of the great gods, my lords, considering the(se) evil deeds, they had me stay in a hidden place and they spread their good shadow over me and protected me for the kingship.

41–52 Afterwards, my brothers went out of their minds; they did everything that was inappropriate for gods and man and plotted evil. They girded weapons; in the midst of Nineveh, they butted each other like kids (for the right) to exercise kingship in ungodly fashion. Ashur, Sin, Shamash, Bel, Nabu, Ishtar of Nineveh, (and) Ishtar of Arbela looked unfavorably upon the deeds of the rebels that were done against the will of the gods and they did not side with them. They changed their strength to weakness and caused them to submit to me. The people of Assyria, who had sworn a loyalty oath by the great gods by oil and water to protect my kingship, did not come to their help.

53–79 I, Esarhaddon, who, trusting in the great gods, my lords, never turns back in battle, quickly heard of their evil deeds and I cried: "Woe!" I tore my princely garment and cried out in mourning. I raged like a lion and my mood was furious. I beat my hands together out of concern for exercising the kingship of my father's house. I raised my hands to Ashur, Sin, Shamash, Bel, Nabu and Nergal, Ishtar of Nineveh (and) Ishtar of Arbela, and they accepted my words. With a firm "yes" they continually sent omens of confidence: "Go, do not hold back! We will go at your side and we will kill your enemies!" I did not delay one day or two days; I did not wait for my troops, nor did I look for the rear guard. I did not muster contingents of horses broken to the yoke, or battle equipment; I did not prepare provisions for my campaign. I was not afraid of the snow and the cold of the month of Shevat, the hardest one of winter. Like a flying eagle, I spread my wings to overthrow my enemies. I proceeded on the road to Nineveh despite its difficulty; but ahead of me, in the land of Ḫanigalbat, all their elite troops had seized the road and were sharpening their weapons. The fear of the great gods, my lords, overwhelmed them, and when they saw my strong attack, they went mad. Ishtar, mistress of war and battle, who loves my priesthood, stood at my side; she broke their bow(s) and dispersed their battle formation. Among their hosts, it was said: "This is our king!" By her exalted command, they all came over to my side and fell in behind me; like lambs they gamboled and prayed to my lordship.

Col. i, 80–ii, 11

The people of Assyria, who had sworn a loyalty oath by the great gods on my behalf, came towards me and kissed my feet. When the rebels, who had stirred up revolt and rebellion, heard of the advance of my campaign, they deserted their trusted troops and fled to an unknown land. I reached the banks of the Tigris, (and) by the command of Sin (and) Shamash, gods of the river-bank, I had all of my troops jump across the wide Tigris as if it were a ditch. In the month of Adar, a favorable month, on the 8th day, the day of Nabu's festival, I joyfully entered Nineveh, my lordly city, and sat happily on the throne of my father. The south wind, the breath of Ea, blew upon me a wind whose blowing is a good sign for exercising kingship. Favorable signs in heaven and earth came in good time to me. Oracles of the ecstatics, the messages of the gods and goddesses, they (the gods) continuously sent me and made my heart confident. I sought out the guilty persons, to the last one, who had plotted evil with my brothers to gain the kingship of Assyria; I severely punished them and wiped out their descendants.

Fig. 25. Assyrian hieroglyphs generally interpreted as representing Esarhaddon's name and titles; see Leichty 2011:238–243, no. 115 (*Courtesy of the Trustees of the British Museum*).

Col i, 8–40

my father, my begetter, duly chose me out of all my brothers on the command of Ashur . . .—Speculation on the circumstances surrounding Esarhaddon's rise includes the suggestion that Zakutu/Naqiʾa, the mother of Esarhaddon, had a hand in the choice.

they had me stay in a hidden place—The location of his refuge is unknown. Considering Esarhaddon's statement that he crossed Ḫanigalbat—the term for the area to the west of Nineveh—on the way back to the capital to engage the rebels, one may venture a guess that he had been staying in Harran, the major center in north Syria (Leichty 2007).

41–52 **Afterwards, my brothers went out of their minds; they did everything that was inappropriate for gods and man and plotted evil. They rebelled (with) weapons**—Most strikingly, no mention is made of the murder of Sennacherib. The subject of the patricide is entirely absent from Assyrian inscriptions; see Text no. 6.05.

who had sworn a loyalty oath by the great gods by oil and water—The ceremonious use of oil and water in treaty-making is mentioned in Esarhaddon's treaty concerning the succession of Ashurbanipal; see Cogan 2013, Text No. 3.01, §94.

53–79 **I beat my hands together**—A gesture of concern and dissatisfaction.

I was not afraid of the snow and the cold of the month of Shevat, the hardest one of winter—Esarhaddon's boast that the harsh weather conditions did not delay him contrasts with the admission of Sennacherib that because of the "bitter cold (that) set in and a severe rainstorm," he abandoned his thrust into Elam (Grayson and Novotny 2012:181, lines 6–11a).

Col. i, 80–ii, 11

The people of Assyria, who had sworn a loyalty oath by the great gods on my behalf—The imposition of a loyalty oath by Sennacherib to protect Esarhaddon's succession is not known from elsewhere; a fragmentary *adê* text from his reign may belong to this act. For the *adê* oath, see Cogan 2013:55–56.

they deserted their trusted troops and fled to an unknown land—According to the report in 2 Kgs 19:37 the king's assassins fled to Urartu. The question of their extradition may have been the object of the campaign to Shubria in 673 BCE (Leichty 1991:56–57).

No. 8.02—CAMPAIGNS IN THE WEST—PRISM NINEVEH A

The following excerpts from the continuation of Text no. 8.01 tell of Esarhaddon's battles at Tyre and Arza and the service imposed on the king's western vassals. The style of the text is that of a summary inscription and is referred to in scholarly literature as the "Nineveh" text after the closing sections of the text that commemorate construction projects at Nineveh. The text, written on a large six-sided prism, was first composed in 676 BCE and was updated in later recensions until 673 (the recensions are distinguished by the sigla A, B, C, D). Only recension D is organized according to campaigns—"In my first campaign, ... in my second campaign," etc.

Text edition: Leichty 2011:16–18, 22–24; earlier Borger 1956:48–49, Nin. A, Ep. 5; 50, Ep. 7; 59–60, Ep. 21.

Translations: *ARAB* 2, §§511–512, 515, 690; *TGI* 70; *ANET* 290–291; *TPOA* 126–129; *TUAT* 1/4, 393–397; *HTAT* 339–342.

Col. ii, 65–82

Abdi-milkutti, king of Sidon, who did not fear my lordship, did not heed the utterance of my lips, who trusted in the rolling sea, threw off the yoke of the god Ashur. Sidon, his supply city, which lies in the midst of the sea, I swept over like a flood. I uprooted its wall and its foundations and threw them into the sea, and its site I destroyed. Abdi-milkutti, its king, who had fled before my weapons into the midst of the sea, by the command of the god Ashur, my lord, I caught him like a fish in the sea (and) cut off his head. His wife, his sons and his daughters, the persons of his palace, gold, silver, property and possessions, precious stones, multicolored linen garments, elephant hides, ivory, ebony and boxwood, everything in his palace treasuries—I carried off in great quantity as spoil. His people, from far and wide, without number, cattle and sheep and asses, I led away to Assyria. I gathered all the kings of Ḫatti and the seacoast, and had them build a city in another place; and I named it Kar-Esarhaddon.

Col. iii, 1–19

In the cities in the environs of Sidon—Bit-Ṣupuri, Shikku, Giʾ, Inimme, Ḫildua, Qartimme, Biʾru, Kilme, Bitirume, Sagu, Ampa, Bit-Gisimeia, Birgiʾ, Gambulu, Dalaimme, Isiḫimme—a place of pasture and water, his supply base, which I had taken with my own hand with the support of the god Ashur, my lord, I settled people, captives of my bow, from the mountains and the sea of the East, and I annexed (it) to Assyria. I reorganized that district; I appointed my eunuch over them as governor. I again imposed upon them tax and tribute, more than previously. From among these cities, I assigned Maʾarubbu and Ṣariptu to Baal, king of Tyre. To the earlier tax, a yearly due, I added a lordly tribute and imposed it upon him.

39–42 The city Arza, which is on the border of the Wadi of Egypt, I despoiled and Asuḫili, its king, I placed in fetters and brought him to Assyria. I placed him, tied, near the gate in the center of Nineveh with a bear, a dog and a pig.

Col. v, 40–vi, 1

At that time, the armory of Nineveh, which the kings, my ancestors, who preceded me, had built, in order to prepare the troops and review the war horses, mules, chariots, weapons, war material, enemy booty of all kinds, which the god Ashur, king of the gods, had granted me as a royal gift—that place became too small for me for the galloping of the horses and parading of the chariots. Therefore I ordered the people of the lands, the captives of my bow, to carry the hoe and the basket and they made bricks. That small palace I tore down completely and I added to it a large plot of land that I detached from the fields as an augmentation. I laid its foundation with limestone, a hard mountain stone, and filled in the terrace.

I mobilized the kings of Ḫatti and "Beyond-the-River": Baal, king of Tyre; Manasseh, king of Judah; Qaus-gabri, king of Edom; Muṣuri, king of Moab; Ṣilli-Bel, king of Gaza; Mitinti, king of Ashkelon; Ikausu, king of Ekron; Milki-ashapa, king of Byblos; Mattan-Baʾal, king of Arvad; Abi-Baʾal, king of Samsimuruna; Puduʾilu, king of Beth-Ammon; Aḫimilki, king of Ashdod—twelve kings of the seacoast; Ekishtura, king of Edil; Pilagura, king of Kitrusi; Kisu, king of Silua; Ituandar, king of Pappa; Eresu, king of Silli; Damasu, king of Kuri; Admesu, king of Tamesi; Damusi, king of Qarti-ḫadashti; Unusagusu, king of Lidir; Buṣusu, king of Nuria—ten kings of Cyprus, in the midst of the sea—a total of twenty-two kings of Ḫatti, the seacoast (and) the midst of the sea. I gave orders for all of them to drag to Nineveh, my lordly city, with exertion and difficulty, large timbers, long beams, (and) thin boards of cedar and cyprus, the product of Mount Sirara and Mount Lebanon, that from olden days grew exceedingly thick and long; (also) bull colossi of granite, *lamassu* and *apsasatu* figures, thresholds and building stone of alabaster and granite, colored (?) marble, *alallu* and *girinḫilba* stone, the products of the mountains.

Col. ii, 65–82

At the beginning of the paragraph, recension D adds: "In my second campaign." According to the Babylonian Chronicle, this campaign took place in Esarhaddon's fourth year, 677/76 BCE (Text no. 11.01, col. iv, lines 3–4).

Abdi-milkutti, king of Sidon—Apparently Abdi-milkutti followed Ethbaal as king of Sidon, who had been appointed by Sennacherib as king of Sidon (Text no. 6.01, lines 32–35). Sanduarri, king of Kundu and Sissu, cities in the Taurus Mountains in southern Turkey, had joined Sidon in rebellion against Esarhaddon.

I cut off his head—The Babylonian Chronicle also recorded this decapitation

(Text no. 11.01, col. iv, lines 6–8), but there it is dated to Esarhaddon's 5th year (676/75 BCE). This is an error, inasmuch as the punishment was carried out a year earlier and was recorded in the Nineveh prism composed in 677/76.

Everything in his palace treasuries—Two alabaster vases for oil and perfume were discovered in the city Ashur and bore an inscription stating that they were part "of the treasure of the palace of Abdi-milkutti, king of Sidon" (see *ARAB* 2, §721).

I gathered all the kings of Ḫatti and the seacoast—A complete list of these western vassals is given further ahead in the inscription with reference to the construction work at Nineveh.

I had them build a city in another place; and I named it Kar-Esarhaddon—The name means: "Port Esarhaddon." The new city replaced Sidon and became the capital and seat of the governor of the province founded in the area. Bel-Ḫarran-shadua, governor of Kar-Esarhaddon, was eponym in 650 BCE.

Col. iii, 1–19

In the cities in the environs of Sidon . . . I settled people, captives of my bow—Not many of these towns and villages can be identified; see the full discussion by Dussaud 1927.

Ḫildua—Perhaps Ḥalda, south of Beirut.

Dalaimme, Isiḫimme—The ancient names are preserved in those of the towns Dalhum and Sheḥim, about 10 km northeast of Sidon (Dussaud 1927:39).

I reorganized that district; I appointed my eunuch over them as governor—The boundaries of the new province are nowhere given; it may be suggested that in the south, the border was the River Zaharani and in the north, in the vicinity of Byblos.

I assigned Maʾarubbu and Ṣariptu to Baal, king of Tyre—Baal's position was strengthened by the annexation of these two towns to his territory.

Maʾarubbu and Ṣariptu—Ṣariptu, modern Sarafand, on the coast south of Sidon (see Text no. 6.01, lines 32–35); Maʾarubbu may be Adlun, 6 km farther south (see Forrer 1920:65–66).

39–42 **The city Arza, which is on the border of the Wadi of Egypt**—Arza has been identified with Iursa mentioned in the inscription of Thutmose III (*ANET* 235), possibly Tell Jemmeh on the banks of Naḥal Besor, c. 13 km south of Gaza (so Mazar 1952). But this identification is problematic. The distance between Tell Jemmeh and the Wadi of Egypt (Wadi el-^{c}Arish) is c. 25 km, and it would seem better to look for Arza in the vicinity of el-^{c}Arish, perhaps at Rhinocorura, a Hellenistic site, 3 km from the mouth of the wadi (so Alt 1964).

A Babylonian Chronicle devoted to the reign of Esarhaddon (Grayson 1975:125, no. 14, lines 7–8) records that Arza was captured in the king's second year, i.e., 679/78 BCE. If this notation is accurate, Esarhaddon reached the border of Egypt in northern Sinai at a relatively early date in his reign, likely as a show of Assyrian power in answer to the renewed Egyptian activity in Philistia under Tirhakah. But inasmuch as in the present inscription Arza is mentioned in conjunction with the conquest of Sidon, it has been suggested that Arza was taken as part of the preparations for the campaign to Egypt and its capture took place several years later than the date given in the Chronicle (so Eph^{c}al 1982:53–54). See, too, Text no. 4.07, line 18.

Near the gate in the center of Nineveh I placed him—The place of Asuḫili's embarrassing incarceration was at the center of Assyrian rule on the acropolis of Nineveh, today Tell Kuyunjik, the location of the royal palace and the temples. Ashurbanipal inflicted a similar punishment upon Uate$^{\supset}$ of Kedar; see Text no. 9.05, col. ix, 90–114.

Col. v, 40–vi, 1

At that time, the armory of Nineveh . . . that place became too small—The closing section of the Nineveh inscription describes in detail the refurbishing of the city's armory.

I mobilized the kings of Ḫatti and "Beyond-the-River"—These two terms are somewhat coterminous. Ḫatti is the established term used when referring to the West, more specifically northern Syria (see Text no. 2.01, line 5), while "Beyond-the-River" (*Eber nāri*) is a Neo-Assyrian neologism that delimits all the territory west of the Euphrates, from the Mediterranean in the north and to Philistia in the south. It became standard in administrative parlance and passed on to the Persians; cf. the use of *Eber nāri* in biblical Aramaic עֲבַר נַהֲרָה (Ezra 4:11; 5:6). See Rainey 1969. The description of King Solomon's realm: "He held sway over all 'Beyond-the-River,' from Tiphsah to Gaza, over all the kings of 'Beyond-the-River'" (1 Kgs 5:1), uses this late term and is surely anachronistic.

Manasseh, king of Judah—Besides the present instance, Manasseh is referred to in an inscription of Ashurbanipal (Text no. 9.01), and he is also included by extension in those cases where the general formula "kings of Ḫatti and the seacoast" or "kings of the seacoast" is used. If the order of the kings reflects their rank (as is the case of the list of states allied against Shalmaneser III [Text no. 1.01]), Manasseh's position near the head of the list would indicate his influential political standing in the West.

Qaus-gabri, king of Edom—For bullae of seals belonging to Qaus-gabri קוסג[בר] מלך א[דם], see Avigad 1997:387–388, nos. 1048, 1049.

Mitinti, king of Ashkelon— Mitinti was the son of Ṣidqa and had been deported, together with his father by Sennacherib (Text 6.01, lines 39–41), and after a period of 're-education' in Assyria, returned to the throne of Ashkelon as a loyal vassal. The king's name appears on a seal of one of his servants in the form: "Mattat, son of Ṣidqa᾽ (מתת בן צדקא)" (Avigad 1997:399–400, no. 1066).

Ikausu, king of Ekron—A dedicatory inscription of Ikausu was discovered at Ekron in which his genealogy is given: "Ikausu, son of Padi, son of *Ysd*, son of Ada᾽, son of Ya᾽ir, ruler of Ekron" (see Gitin, Dothan, and Naveh 1997:9–11). The name can be explained as derived from the Greek ᾽Αχαιός, the "Achean," that is, Greek. The name appears in biblical Hebrew in the form אָכִישׁ, Achish, borne by the king of Gath at the time of David (cf. 1 Sam 21:11–16); this vocalization is of late origin.

Pudu᾽ilu, king of Beth-Ammon—The Ammonite king was noted by Sennacherib as being his loyal vassal (see Text no. 6.01).

Ten kings of Cyprus, in the midst of the sea—The kings of Cyprus were interested in a commercial agreement with Assyria considering that it was master of the Phoenician coast. Earlier, seven kings of Cyprus had sent gifts to Sargon II for a similar reason (Fuchs 1994:232, lines 145–146). Esarhaddon's claim that the Cypriots were mobilized for corvée may be somewhat of an exaggeration, though it can be expected that the islanders sent gifts on the occasion of the armory's inauguration.

Only a few of the Cypriote cities can be identified with any certainty. For a detailed discussion, see Lipiński 1991.

Ekishtura, king of Edil—Identified with Idalion, presently Dhali, 25 km northwest of Larnaka.

Pilagura, king of Kitrusi—Chytroi, Kythrea, 10 km northeast of Nicosia.

Ituandar, king of Pappa—Paphos, in the southwest near Kouklia.

Admesu, king of Tamesi—Tamasso, now Politiko.

Damusi, king of Qarti-ḫadashti—The Phoenician name means "New town"; Neapolis in the Roman period; today Limossol.

Unusagusu, king of Lidir—Ledra, present-day Nicosia.

No. 8.03—THE EGYPTIAN CAMPAIGN—ZENJIRLI STELA

On his return from Egypt, Esarhaddon erected a large stela (3.20 m high) at the gate of the city of Samʾal (Zenjirli in southwest Turkey near the Syrian border) commemorating his victory in the land of the Nile. After the opening invocation and praises of the gods and the king, the inscription gives a relatively full account of the battles in Egypt against Tirhakah, king of Egypt, in 671 BCE; for other reports, see Text nos. 8.04, 8.05, 11.01; also Onasch 1994:24–43. On the face of the stela is a relief showing the Assyrian king holding two miniaturized persons on a leash; their attire helps in their identification: the kneeling figure with negroid features is captive son of Tirhakah and the bearded person with pointed hat is Baal, king of Tyre, who had been party to the rebellion against Assyria (see Fig. 24; Text no. 8.05 for the battle at Tyre).

Text edition: Leichty 2011:185–186; earlier Borger 1956:98–99, §65.
Translations: *ARAB* 2, §§573–581; *ANET* 293.
Photograph: *ANEP*, no. 447.

Rev. 37–50

As for Tirhakah, king of Egypt and Cush, cursed of their great godhood, I inflicted a great defeat upon him from Ishḫupri to Memphis, his royal city, a distance of 15 days, daily without let-up. I struck him five times with arrow after arrow, a blow for which there is no healing. I laid siege to Memphis, his royal city, and captured (it) in half-a-day by means of tunneling, breaches (in the walls), and ladders. I destroyed, I devastated, I set (it) on fire. His wife, the women of his palace, Ushanaḫuru, the crown prince, and the rest of his sons and his daughters, his property and his possessions, his horses, his cattle, his sheep, without number, I took as spoil to Assyria. I tore out the root of Cush from Egypt and did not leave (anyone) to praise (me). I appointed anew over all of Egypt kings, governors, officers, port inspectors, overseers, controllers. I established (the payment of) regular offerings and contributions to the god Ashur and the great gods, my lords, and I imposed on them tax and tribute, (payable) yearly, unceasingly.

Rev. 37–50

As for Tirhakah, king of Egypt and Cush—Tirhakah, scion of the 25th dynasty, ruled Upper and Lower Egypt (690–664 BCE). Before ascending to the throne, he had fought against Sennacherib in Philistia in 701 BCE (see Text no. 6.01).

From Ishḫupri to Memphis, his royal city—Ishḫupri is unidentified. Memphis, some 13 km south of Cairo on the western bank of the Nile, served as capital of Egypt in various periods.

I struck him five times with arrow after arrow, a blow for which there is no healing—The fatal blow described here is a bit of scribal hyperbole. Tirhakah recovered from his wounds and continued to harass the Assyrian presence in Egypt for at least seven more years.

I laid siege to Memphis, his royal city, and captured (it) in half-a-day—The battle is briefly reported in the Babylonian Chronicle; see Text no. 11.01, rev. iv, lines 25–28. The victory in Egypt was depicted on painted wall tiles at Calah, fragments of which have been recovered; see Nadali 2006.

His wife—The Akkadian term for the wife of first rank is *ša ekalli*, literally, "the woman of the palace." This term entered Hebrew in the Neo-Assyrian period in the form שֵׁגָל, and is often translated as "consort"; cf. Ps 45:10; Dan 5:2, 3, 23; Neh 2:6.

I tore out the root of Cush from Egypt—After ousting the Cushites from the Delta area, Esarhaddon based his rule of Egypt on the integration of local rulers within the Assyrian administration, a practice that was to prove unreliable (see Text no. 9.01).

I appointed anew over all of Egypt kings—The names of the Egyptian kings that were reinstated by Esarhaddon are preserved in an inscription of

Ashurbanipal; see Text no. 9.01, col. i, lines 90–117.

Governors, officers, port inspectors, overseers, controllers—Assyrian officials served as supervisors, e.g., port inspectors, over the native workers who were familiar with local conditions.

I established (the payment of) regular offerings and contributions to the god Ashur and the great gods, my lords—These taxes were directed to the temples in Assyria. Assyrian cults were not initiated in Egypt, but at the same time, it cannot be ruled out that the native Assyrians continued to honor their gods even during their service in Egypt.

No. 8.04—THE EGYPTIAN CAMPAIGN—NAHR EL-KALB INSCRIPTION

North of Beirut, on an outcrop facing the sea near the mouth of Nahr el-Kalb, Esarhaddon had an inscription incised telling of his victories in Egypt in the campaign of 671 BCE. The inscription was set alongside those of earlier conquerors (e.g., Ramses II and several Assyrian kings) who had also chosen to be immortalized at this impressive site. Though the text is severely worn, it is still possible to get an impression of the vast booty taken from Egypt.

Text edition: Leichty 2011:191; earlier Borger 1956:101–102, §67.
Translations: *ARAB* 2, §§582–585; *ANET* 293.

1–3 [The gods Ashur, Anu, Enlil,] Ea, Sin, Shamash, Adad, Marduk, [Ishtar, Sibitti, the great gods], all of them, who determine fate, who grant [the king,] their [favorite,] power and strength.

4–7 [Esarhaddon, great king], mighty [king], king of Assyria, governor of Babylon, [king of Sumer and Akkad], king of Karduniash, all of them (i.e., these lands), king of the kings [of Egypt and Pathros and] Cush, king of the four quarters of the world, son of Sennacherib, [great king, migh]ty [king], king of the world, king of Assyria.

7–35 In happiness and rejoicing, [I entered] Memphis, his royal city. *x x x x x* [up] on ... inlaid with gold, I sat [down] joyfully. ... weapons ... [ ] *x x* gold and silver. ... Afterwards, *x x x* ... [I ent]ered [...] *x* his palace, the gods and the goddesses of Tirhakah, king of Cush, together with their property [I counted] as spoil. His wife, [the women of] his palace, Ushanaḫuru, his heir-apparent, [. . .] *x x x x* his courtiers, . . . property and possessions, [. . .] gold(?), lapis lazuli, ivory, wooden *x* [that were in]laid with gold [. . .] their openings (?) [ ] DITTO, utensils of gold, silver and stone of all kinds, [be]fitting a palace, without [*number* (?)] [. . .] artistically crafted. Their [ ], I opened and [ ] their chests. [ ] his royal [ ], *x x* [. . .] . . . the king . . . they left them, together with 15 cro[wns . . .] 30 crowns for the king's wives, DITTO [ ] fine [ ] of baked bric[k . . . in] great quantity, [. . .] treasures, gold, silver, koh[l, . . .] fine linen garments, [ ] like *x x x x x x x* [. . .] bronze, tin, lead, ivory, [. . .] *x x x x x x x* [poss]essions of the Sutu, [. . .] *x x x x x* his [ ], his sons-in-law, his family [. . .] *x x x* his [ ], the princes [. . .] *x x* [ ] *x x* [ ] physicians, diviners, [. . .] *x x* [. . .] goldsmiths, metalworkers, . . . after 2 lines . . . son of Binzuqi [the city of] Ashkelon [ ] which Tirhakah [*had made ?*] as their strongholds, [. . .] Tyre [. . .] twenty-two kings [. . .] *x x x*

1–3 The symbols of the gods mentioned by name are depicted above the head of the king as was customary on royal stela. An example of this feature can be seen on the stela from Tell al-Rimaḥ; see Fig. 7.

4–7 **Governor of Babylon, [king of Sumer and Akkad], king of Karduniash**—Esarhaddon held the traditional titles of Babylonian kings. The terms Sumer and Akkad were in use in the early 2nd millennium BCE; Karduniash is the name for Babylonia introduced during the Kassite rule in the mid-2nd millennium.

King of the kings [of Egypt and Pathros and] Cush—This title reflects the Assyrian policy of rule in Egypt. After the eviction of the Cushite invaders, the local Egyptian kings of the Delta were allowed to continue in their roles under Assyrian overseers (see Text no. 8.03). These same three divisions of the Nile Valley appear in Isaiah's vision of future redemption in Isa 11:11: "On that day, My Lord will extend His hand yet a second time to redeem the rest that will remain of His people from Assyria, from Egypt, from Pathros, from Cush, from Elam, from Shinar, from Hamath and the coastlands."

Pathros—The Egyptian name for Upper Egypt, meaning "southern land." Ezekiel refers to "the land of Pathros, the land of their (the Egyptians') origin" (Ezek 29:14).

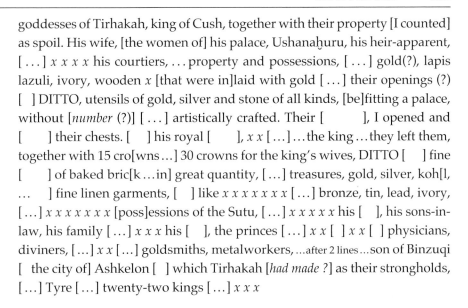

7–35 **Together with 15 cro[wns . . .] 30 crowns for the king's wives, DITTO**—It was scribal practice to use a shorthand when preparing lists; in the present instance, the copyist noted that next item was the same as the one he had just written by using the cuneiform sign KIMIN, equivalent to the Latin "ditto."

Physicians, diviners, [. . .] ***x x*** **[. . .] goldsmiths, metalworkers**—In addition to the members of the Egyptian royal court, artisans of all sorts—even soothsayers—were deported to Assyria where they contributed to the economy and cultural life of the capital. A further tablet fragment lists other skilled laborers that were exiled (see *ANET* 293b). The Babylonian king Nebuchadnezzar dealt similarly with Jerusalem, deporting "the craftsmen and the smiths" (2 Kgs 24:14, 16).

[poss]essions of the Sutu . . . son of Binzuqi—An unidentified person.

The city of] Ashkelon [ ] which Tirhakah [*had made ?*] as their strongholds, [. . .] Tyre [. . .] twenty-two kings—The poor state of preservation of the inscription does not permit reconstruction of these lines; all that is left is the name of two cities and the formulaic "twenty-two kings," i.e, Assyria's vassals in the West that were somehow associated with Tirhakah. The reference might be to the conspiracy between the Phoenician and Philistine cities and Tirhakah that precipitated the attack on Egypt. This is certainly true of Ashkelon, for there is evidence of its hostility towards Assyria and association with Egypt. Among the questions placed by Assyrian diviners before Shamash, the god of divination, are several that inquired about the possible outcome of war by Esarhaddon against Ashkelon and Egyptian auxiliary troops that would be sent against him (see SAA 4, nos. 81, 82). Given these circumstances, it would have been necessary for Esarhaddon to protect his rear prior to his advance on Egypt by subduing these rebels, and once he emerged victorious from his campaign against Tirhakah, he attended to restoring their former vassal status.

Some have suggested that the imprisonment of Manasseh, king of Judah, by "the army officers of the king of Assyria, who took Manasseh captive in manacles, bound in fetters, and led him off to Babylon," reported in 2 Chr 33:11, was associated with this uprising against Esarhaddon (so Hirschberg 1932:61–72), but this remains speculative.

No. 8.05—THE EGYPTIAN CAMPAIGN—NINEVEH TABLET FRAGMENT

Inscribed on a large clay tablet, of which only three fragments are extant, was a report on Esarhaddon's military activities, including a lengthy description of the Egyptian campaign. This tablet may have been a draft for a text, parts of which survive on a broken octagonal prism (see Eph^{c}al 2005:104–105). The text is one of the few examples from the king's reign in which his campaigns are numbered consecutively, following the example of the inscriptions of Sennacherib (see introductory remarks to Text no. 8.02). Most unique are the description of the northern Sinai Peninsula and the crossing of the desert by the Assyrian army with the help of the local nomads, impressed into service by Esarhaddon.

Text edition: Leichty 2011:87–88; earlier Borger 1956:111–112, § 76.
Translations: *ARAB* 2, §§553–559; *ANET* 292–293; *TPOA* 129–130; *TUAT* 1/4, 398–399.

Obv. 6–18

In my tenth campaign, the god Ashur [*encouraged me*...] I set my face towards the land of Makan(?) [*and Meluḫḫa*], that in popular parlance are c[alled] Cush and Egypt. I mobilized the vast troops of Assyria that were in [...]. In the month of Nisan, the first month, I set out from my city Ashur. I crossed the Tigris and the Euphrates in [their] flood. I advanced like a wild bull over difficult mountains. In the course of my campaign, I surrounded with armed posts Baal, king of Tyre, who put his trust in his friend Tirhakah, king of Cush, and threw off the yoke of the god Ashur, my lord, (and) answered me with insolence. I withheld (from them) food and water that sustains life. I broke camp from Egypt and headed straight to Meluḫḫa—a distance of thirty double-hours from Aphek that is in the district of Same(ri)n[a] to Raphia by the side of the Wadi of Egypt, a place where there is no river. I gave drink to my army, drawing water from wells by means of ropes, chains (and) buckets.

Rev. 1–19

In accord with the command of the god Ashur, my lord, I had in my mind and considered (the following): I mob[ilized] camels from all the Arab kings and I had them [*carry water-skins*(?)]. Twenty(?) (or 30?) double-hours, a distance of 15 days, through great sand dunes, I advanced. Four (?) (or 14 ?)

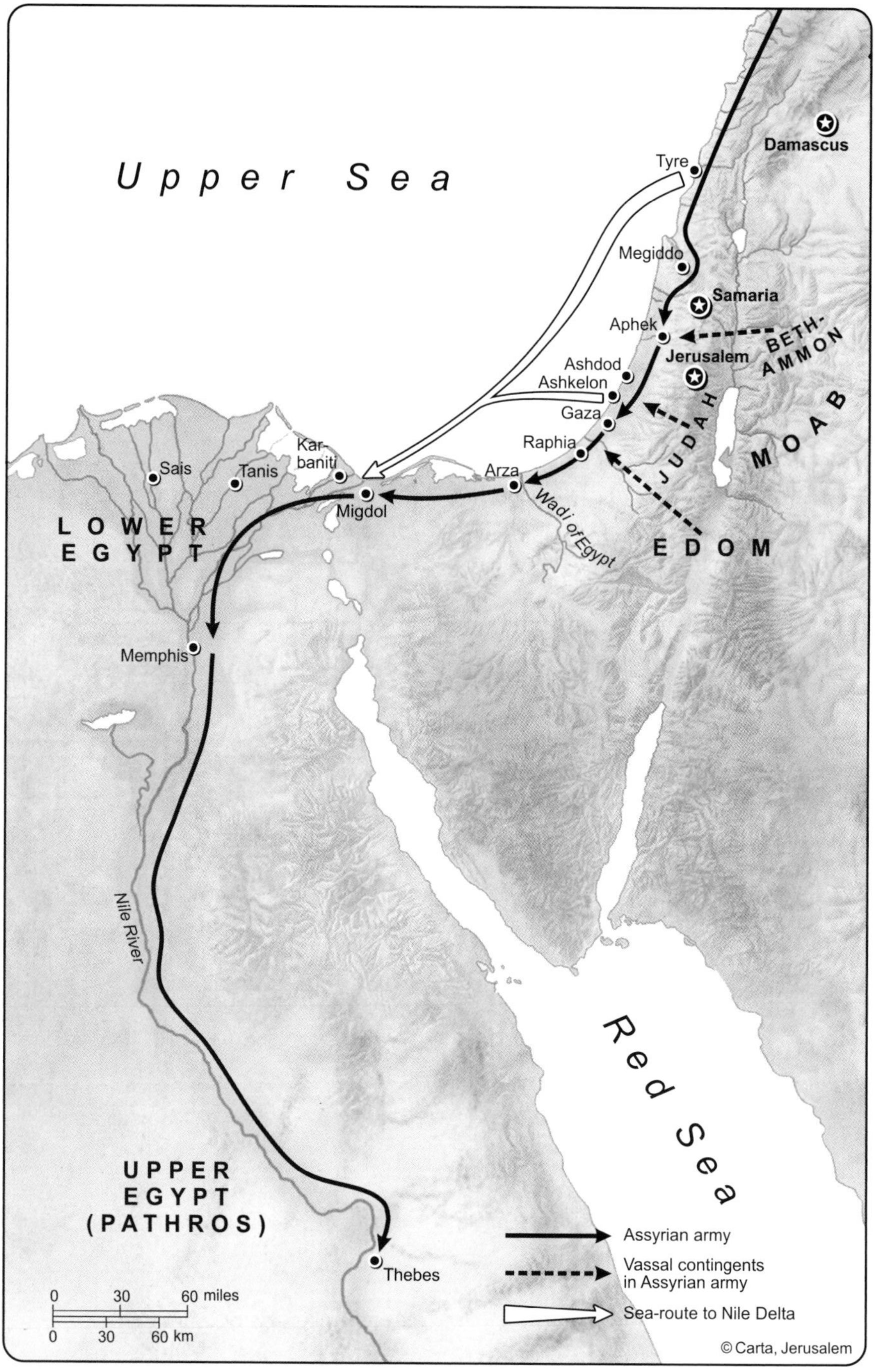

THE ASSYRIAN CAMPAIGNS TO EGYPT, 671–663 BCE

double-hours, through (an area of) alum stone and [ ] I marched. Four double-hours, a distance of 2 days, I trampled on two-headed snakes, whose [ ] was death, and I moved on. Four double-hours, a distance of [2 days], (there were) yellow-green [*snakes* ?] whose wings flutter. Four double-hours, a distance of 2 da[ys, . . .] Fifteen double-hours, a distance of 8 days, I moved on. [...] *x x x* The god Marduk, the great lord, came to my aid, [...], he kept my troops alive. Twenty days, 7 [...] the border of Eg[ypt] *x x x* I spent the night. From the city Migdol to the city [...] a distance of 40 double-hours, I advanced. That area, like [ ] stone, like the point of an arrow [...] blood and pus *x*[...] the stubborn enemy, to [...] to the city Ishḫup[ri] [...] *x x* [...]

Obv. 6–18

In my tenth campaign—671 BCE; the year is determined by the date of the campaign given in the Babylonian Chronicle (see Text no. 11.01, rev. iv, lines 23–28).

The land of Makan(?) [*and Meluḫḫa*]—If the reading is correct, the reference is to Egypt. See further, Text no. 9.01, col. i, line 52.

I crossed the Tigris and the Euphrates in [their] flood. I advanced like a wild bull over difficult mountains—This description of Esarhaddon's bravery and his feats of valor were part of Assyrian historiographical rhetoric; cf. the similar motif in Shalmaneser III's Kurkh monument, Text no. 1.01.

I surrounded with armed posts Baal, king of Tyre, who put his trust in his friend Tirhakah, king of Cush, and threw off the yoke of the god Ashur—Baal had violated his vassalage by aligning himself with Tirhakah, both of whom sought to unseat Assyria from its dominant position in the Mediterranean coastal cities. Esarhaddon's unsuccessful attempt to invade Egypt in 673 BCE may have prompted this alliance. Other cities may have joined the rebels; see Text no. 8.04.

I withheld (from them) food and water that sustains life—Tyre on the island was dependent on vital supplies from the mainland; these sources were impounded by the Assyrian troops, thus bringing the city under siege. Ashurbanipal used the same tactic in his siege of Tyre; see Text no. 9.01. Tyre's submission is not recorded, but it seems that the siege continued at the same time as the main army proceeded to Egypt. Another inscription sums up the battle in this manner: "I captured Tyre that is in the midst of the sea; Baal, its king, who trusted in Tirhakah, king of Cush, I took away from him all his cities and his property" (Leichty 2011:135, lines 7–8; Borger 1956:86, §57; *ARAB* 2, §710).

I broke camp from Egypt and headed straight to Meluḫḫa—A difficult phrase, considering that the Assyrian army was still camped in the coastal plain of Israel. If this is not a scribal error, perhaps it refers to the Egyptian influence in Philistia.

A distance of thirty double-hours from Aphek that is in the district of Same(ri)n[a] to Raphia by the side of the Wadi of Egypt, a place where there is no river—The army encamped at Aphek, classical Antipatris, near the headwaters of the River Yarkon at Rosh Ha^{c}ayin; Aphek was part of the province of Samerina. On his return from Egypt, Esarhaddon erected a victory stela in the Sharon plain, a fragment of which was discovered in the ruins of the village Qaqun, 13 km east of Netanya. It contains further details of his crossing the Sinai desert; see Appendix. The "double hour" (Akkadian *bēru*) is a Mesopotamian measure of length, over 10 kilometers, used in descriptions of long distances.

Rev. 1–19

I mob[ilized] camels from all the Arab kings and I had them [*carry water-skins*(?)]—Esarhaddon was the first king to undertake an attack on Egypt by crossing the northern Sinai. Modern calculations show that 200 camels were needed to provide a three-day water supply for 1,000 men; for details, see Eph^{c}al 1982:137–142.

Twenty (?) (or 30 ?) double-hours, a distance of 15 days, through great sand dunes, I advanced—The following section of the text imitates the itinerary style that is identifiable in some royal inscriptions, in which the advance of the army is noted from station to station, marked by the distance covered each day; see, in detail, Baruchi-Unna 2008:60–61.

I trampled on two-headed snakes, whose [ ] was death, and I moved on... (there were) yellow [*snakes* ?] whose wings flutter—In addition to overcoming the natural obstacles of the great desert, Esarhaddon encounters monstrous death-dealing creatures that threaten to thwart his advance.

The frightfulness of the Sinai desert is also recalled in the account of the biblical Exodus: "the great and terrible wilderness with its fiery (or: *seraph*) serpents and scorpions, a parched land with no water in it" (Deut 8:15); cf. Isaiah's description of the Negeb desert: "Through a land of distress and hardship, of lion and roaring king of beasts, of viper and flying fiery serpent (or *seraph*)" (Isa 30:6).

From the city Migdol to the city [...]—The Semitic noun *migdal*, "watchtower," entered the Egyptian language and there are several fortresses in the eastern Delta of the Nile with that name; this makes it difficult to identify with certainty the Migdol referred to here. For the suggestion to identify it with the site T21 (Tell Qaduʾa), near Tell el-Ḥeir, c. 20 km northeast of Qantara, see Oren 1984; also Redford 1993:360, n. 199.

Migdol is mentioned as a camp stop of the Israelites who left Egypt (cf. Exod 14:2; Num 33:7). The city was also the home to groups of exiles from Judah after 586 BCE (Jer 44:1; 46:14; also Ezek 29:10).

To the city Ishḫup[ri]—Perhaps in the eastern Delta, but of unsure identification; also mentioned in Text no. 8.03.

References

Alt, Albrecht
1964 Neue assyrische Nachrichten über Palästina. Pp. 226–234 in idem, *Kleine Schriften zur Geschichte des Volkes Israel*, 2, München.

Avigad, Nahman
1997 *Corpus of West Semitic Stamp Seals*, Jerusalem.

Baruchi-Unna, Amitai
2008 Crossing the Boundaries: Literary Allusions to the Epic of Gilgameš in the Account of Esarhaddon's Egyptian Campaign. Pp. 54–65 in M. Cogan and D. Kahn (eds.), *Treasures on Camels' Humps. Historical and Literary Studies from the Ancient Near East Presented to Israel Ephʿal*, Jerusalem.

Borger, Rykle
1956 *Die Inschriften Asarhaddons Königs von Assyrien*, AfO Beiheft 9, Graz.

Brinkman, John A.
1984 *Prelude to Empire. Babylonian Society and Politics, 747–626 B.C.*, Philadelphia.

Cogan, Mordechai
2013 *Bound for Exile*, Jerusalem.

Dussaud, R.
1927 *Topographie historique de la Syrie antique et médiévale*, Paris.

Eph^cal, Israel

1982 *The Ancient Arabs*, Jerusalem.

2005 Esarhaddon, Egypt, and Shubria: Politics and Propaganda, *JCS* 57:99–111.

Forrer, Emil

1920 *Provinzeinteilungen des assyrischen Reiches*, Leipzig.

Fuchs, Andreas

1994 *Die Inschriften Sargons II. aus Khorsabad*, Göttingen.

Gitin, Seymour, Trude Dothan and Jospeh Naveh

1997 A Royal Dedicatory Inscription from Ekron, *IEJ* 47:1–16.

Grayson, A. Kirk

1975 *Assyrian and Babylonian Chronicles*, Locust Valley.

Grayson, A. Kirk and Jamie Novotny

2012 *The Royal Inscriptions of Sennacherib, King of Assyria (704–681 BC), Part 1*, RINAP 3/1, Winona Lake, IL.

Hirschberg, Hans

1932 *Studien zur Geschichte Esarhaddons König von Assyrien (681–669)*, Ohlau.

Leichty, Erle V.

1991 Esarhaddon's "Letter to the Gods". Pp. 52–57 in Mordechai Cogan and Israel Eph^cal (eds.), *Ah Assyria. . . Studies in Assyrian History and Ancient Near Eastern Historiography Presented to Hayim Tadmor*, Scripta Hierosolymitana 33, Jerusalem.

2007 Esarhaddon's Exile: Some Speculative History. Pp. 189–191 in M. Roth, et al. (eds.), *Studies Presented to Robert D. Biggs, June 4, 2004*, AS 27, Chicago.

2011 *The Royal Inscriptions of Esarhaddon, King of Assyria (680–669 BC)*, RINAP 4, Winona Lake, IL.

Lipiński, Edward

1991 The Cypriot Vassals of Esarhaddon. Pp. 58–64 in Mordechai Cogan and Israel Eph^cal (eds.), *Ah Assyria... Studies in Assyrian History and Ancient Near Eastern Historiography Presented to Hayim Tadmor*, *ScrHier* 33.

Mazar, Benjamin

1952 Yurza. The Identification of Tell Jemmeh, *PEQ* 84:48–51.

Nadali, Davide

2006 Esarhaddon's Glazed Bricks from Nimrud: The Egyptian Campaign Depicted, *Iraq* 68:109–120.

Onasch, Hans-Ulrich

1994 *Die assyrischen Eroberungen Ägyptens*, ÄAT 27, Wiesbaden.

Oren, Eliezer D.

1984 Migdol: A New Fortress on the Edge of the Eastern Nile Delta, *BASOR* 256:7–44.

Rainey, Anson F.

1969 The Satrapy "Beyond the River," *Australian Journal of Biblical Archaeology* 1:5–78.

Redford, Donald B.

1993 *Egypt, Canaan, and Israel in Ancient Times*, Princeton.

Spalinger, Anthony

1974 Esarhaddon and Egypt: An Analysis of the First Invasion of Egypt, *Or* 43:295–326.

Tadmor, Hayim

1983 Autobiographical Apology in the Royal Assyrian Literature. Pp. 36–57 in H. Tadmor and M. Weinfeld (eds.), *History, Historiography and Interpretation, Studies in Biblical and Cuneiform Literatures*, Jerusalem 1983 (= Pp. 63–85 in H. Tadmor, *"With my many chariots I have gone up the heights of mountains": Historical and Literary Studies on Ancient Mesopotamia and Israel*, M. Cogan [ed.], Jerusalem 2011).

Fig. 26. Ashurbanipal in his chariot shooting at lions (*Courtesy of the Trustees of the British Museum*).

CHAPTER 9

ASHURBANIPAL

During Ashurbanipal's long reign (669–627 BCE), Assyria underwent consolidation and entrenchment in the traditional areas under its control. In accord with the testament of Esarhaddon, rule of Assyria passed to Ashurbanipal, with Babylon assigned to his brother Shamash-shum-ukin. Much of the king's first decade was taken up with the question of retaining Egypt within the empire. In the end, this proved beyond Assyria's means and ability and Egypt was set free, under terms that go unreported in the sources. By the mid-seventh century, much effort had to be expended on the war that broke out against Ashurbanipal in Babylon, which with its would-be ally Elam, threatened the unity of the empire. In addition, the mountain peoples to the north and east of Assyria remained an always-present threat.

The king's military activities were summarized in a large number of annals and summary inscriptions, almost all from his first years and from the third decade of his rule. The order of presentation in the annals is principally geographic, and the king's victories are set out beginning with Egypt in the southwest corner of the empire, then continue north along the Mediterranean coast to Tyre and Anatolia, and conclude with the clashes in Babylonia and Elam, and the desert-dwelling Arab tribes. The annals of Ashurbanipal underwent at least six major editorial revisions, the distinguishing marks of each edition being their omissions and additions of reported battles and the dedicated constructions.

No. 9.01—THE CAMPAIGNS TO EGYPT—EDITION A

During the closing days of Esarhaddon's reign, a revolt broke out in Egypt against the Assyrian rule, and on the way to putting down the insurrection, Esarhaddon died. The decision whether to continue to pursue this challenge to imperial goals fell to Ashurbanipal. In 667 BCE, a new military campaign was undertaken, aimed at bringing Egypt under Assyrian dominion once again. Among the forces recruited for the Assyrian army were contingents from the vassal kingdoms in the West, including the kingdom of Judah. Despite the claimed victory, Assyrian objectives were only partially attained, seemingly because of the lingering influence of the Cushite Tirhakah in the Delta. Thus, two years after the first campaign, it was necessary for Ashurbanipal to organize a further military operation to Egypt, this time against Tanutamon, who had succeeded Tirhakah.

The following excerpt from the annals of Ashurbanipal is from edition A (also known as the Rassam Cylinder), one of the latest editions of the annals, dated to 643 BCE. The differences that are detectable in this edition as compared with the earlier reports reflect, in part, the state of affairs at the time of its composition; see Spalinger 1974.

Text edition: Borger 1996:17–26; earlier, Streck 1916:6–13.
Translations: *ARAB* 2, §§770–778; *ANET* 294–295.

Col. i, 52–67

In my first campaign, I marched to Makan and Meluḫḫa. Tirhakah, king of Egypt and Cush, whom Esarhaddon, king of Assyria, my father, my begetter, had defeated and ruled his land, he, Tirhakah, forgot the might of the god Ashur, the god Ishtar and the great gods, my lords, and trusted in his own strength. He marched against the kings and the supervisors whom my my father, my begetter, had appointed in Egypt, in order to kill, plunder and seize Egypt. He attacked them and took up residence in Memphis, the city that my father, my begetter, had captured and added to the territory of Assyria. A swift courier came to Nineveh and informed me. My heart was furious because of these deeds and my innards were enraged. I raised my hands (and) prayed to the god Ashur and the Assyrian Ishtar. I mobilized my outstanding troops that Ashur and Ishtar had handed me and I made straight for Egypt.

68–89 In the course of my campaign, twenty-two kings of the seacoast, (the islands) in the midst of the sea, and the mainland—servants, my subjects, brought their rich gifts before me and kissed my feet. Those kings, together with their forces, (on) their ships, by sea and by land, together with my troops, I set them on the road. I proceeded quickly in order to bring urgent aid to the kings (and) the supervisors in Egypt, servants, my subjects. I marched to Kar-baniti. Tirhakah, king of Egypt and Cush, in Memphis, heard of the march of my campaign and he mobilized his troops, his fighters, to do battle and wage war against me. With the support of Ashur, Bel and Nabu, the great gods, my lords, who go at my side, I defeated his troops in a battle in the open field. Tirhakah, in Memphis, heard of the defeat of his troops; the splendor of Ashur and Ishtar overwhelmed him and he went mad. My royal radiance, with which the gods of heaven and earth had adorned me, covered him. He abandoned Memphis and fled to Thebes to save his life. I captured that city; I had my troops enter it and take up positions in it.

90–117 Neco, king of Memphis and Sais; Sharru-lu-dari, king of Ṣiʾnu; Pishanḫuru, king of Natḫu; Paqruru, king of Pishaptu; Bukunaniʾpi, king of Athribis; Naḫke, king of Ḫininshi; Puṭubishti, king of Tanis; Unamunu, king of Natḫu; Ḫarsieshu, king of Ṣabnuti; Puiyama, king of Piṭiṭi; Shishak, king of Busiris; Tapnaḫti, king of Punubu; Bukunaniʾpi, king of Aḫni; Iptiḫarṭieshu, king of Piḫattiḫurunpiki; Naḫtiḫuruansini, king of Pishapdiʾa; Bukurninip, king of Paḫnuti; Ṣiḫa, king of Shiautu; Lamintu, king of Ḫimuni; Ishpimaṭu, king of Tayani; Mantimeanḫe, king of Thebes—these kings, governors, (and) supervisors whom my father, my begetter, had appointed in Egypt and who had left their posts because of Tirhakah's attack and had filled the steppe, I returned them to their positions and (re)appointed them in their residences. I reorganized Egypt (and) Cush that my father, my begetter, had captured. I strengthened the forts more than before and made binding agreements (with them). With many prisoners and much spoil, I returned safely to Nineveh.

i, 118–ii, 4

Afterwards, all the kings whom I had appointed sinned against my loyalty oath; they did not heed the sanctions of the great gods. They forgot the good I had done them and they plotted evil. They spoke seditious words and came to an unfortunate decision: "(Here) Tirhakah has been driven out of Egypt, how can we, ourselves, remain?" They sent their mounted messengers to Tirhakah, king of Cush, to establish a treaty of loyalty and peace: "Let there be peace between us, and let us come to an agreement among ourselves. We will divide the country between us and no other shall be ruler among us." They plotted evil against the Assyrian troops, my lordly force, that I had stationed (in Egypt) for their support. My officials heard about these matters; they seized their mounted messengers with their messages and learned about their seditious activities. They seized these kings and put their hands and feet in iron fetters and cuffs. The sanctions of Ashur, king of the gods, overtook them because they sinned against the loyalty oath of the great gods. I called them to account for the good, which I had done in (their) favor. The people of Sais, Piṭiṭi (and) Ṣiʾnu and the rest of the cities that had joined them (and) plotted evil, young and old, they struck down with the sword. No one among them escaped. They hung their corpses from stakes; they flayed their skins and covered the city-wall (with them).

ii, 5–19 Those kings, who had plotted evil against the Assyrian troops, they brought alive before me to Nineveh. As for Neco, out of all of them, I had mercy on him and spared his life. I made a loyalty oath with him, more stringent than the former one. I dressed him in a multicolored garment; I placed upon him a golden *chain* (?), a symbol of his kingship; I put gold rings on his hands; I gave him an iron dagger for his girdle (on which) I wrote my name. I presented him with chariots, horses (and) mules for his lordly riding. I sent my officers (as) governors with him to aid him. Sais, the place where my father, my begetter, had appointed him king, as residence I returned to him. Nabu-shezibani, his son, I appointed in Athribis; I showed him greater good and favor than my father, my begetter.

20–27 (Meanwhile), the awesomeness of the weapon of Ashur, my lord, overwhelmed Tirhakah in the place to which he had fled and he passed away. Tanutamon, son of Shabaka (var. son of his sister), ascended his royal throne. He made Thebes and Heliopolis his strongholds; he gathered his forces. He opened the attack to strike the Assyrian troops that were in Memphis. He encircled these men and seized their exits. A swift messenger came to Nineveh and told me about this.

28–48 In my second campaign, I made straight for Egypt and Cush. Tanutamon heard of the march of my campaign (and) that I had crossed the border of Egypt. He abandoned Memphis and in order to save his life, he fled to Thebes. The kings, governors and supervisors whom I had appointed in Egypt came to meet me and kissed my feet. I set out after Tanutamon and marched as far as Thebes, his fortress. He saw my strong onslaught and so abandoned (it) and fled to Kipkipi. That city (i.e., Thebes) and its environs, I myself captured with the support of Ashur and Ishtar. Silver, gold, precious stones, the property of his palace, as much as there was, multicolored linen garments, large horses, the people—male and female, two tall obelisks cast of shining silver alloy, whose weight was 2,500 talents (and) stood by the gate of the temple, I uprooted from their positions and took to Assyria. I

Fig. 27. Battle in an Egyptian city—Cushite soldiers taken captive by Assyrian army; relief from the palace of Ashurbanipal at Nineveh (*Courtesy of the Trustees of the British Museum*).

took away from Thebes heavy spoil, that was uncountable. I fought bitterly against Egypt and Cush and I established victory (over them). With full hands, I returned safely to Nineveh, my lordly city.

Col. i, 52–67

In my first campaign, I marched to Makan and Meluḫḫa—These geographical names stem from Sumerian and Akkadian tradition of the 3rd millennium BCE in which they indicated the ends of the known world, seemingly east Arabia and India. In the first millennium, they had become literary terms and were as designations of distant Egypt and Cush.

Tirhakah, king of Egypt and Cush—He is known from the inscriptions of Esarhaddon as the bitter rival of Assyria in the kingdoms along the Mediterranean coast; see Text nos. 8.03, 8.04, 8.05.

I mobilized my outstanding troops that Ashur and Ishtar had handed me and I made straight for Egypt—In the earlier editions of the annals, it was reported that the commander-in-chief (*turtānu*) led the army to Egypt, which consisted of forces stationed in the Assyrian provinces and vassal states; the king himself did not participate in the campaign. In edition A, the victory is credited to Ashurbanipal, a "historical correction" that is not unusual in Assyrian history writing.

58–89 **In the course of my campaign, twenty-two kings of the seacoast, (the islands) in the midst of the sea, and the mainland**—In the earlier annals, edition C, a list of the twenty-two kings is given at this point (Borger 1996:18–19; *ANET* 294). It is the same list recorded in Esarhaddon's inscriptions (see Text no. 8.02, col. v, lines 40ff.), except for two names: Yakinlu, king of Arvad and Aminadab, king of Beth-Ammon. About five to six years had elapsed between the record from Esarhaddon's reign and the list from the time of Ashurbanipal's Egyptian campaign; the list of the reigning kings was updated accordingly. Aminadab is the name of several Ammonite kings; see Aḥituv 2008:363. As for the kingdom of Judah, Manasseh is mentioned as still reigning in Judah in the Ashurbanipal list.

Those kings, together with their forces, (on) their ships, by sea and by land, together with my troops, I set them on the road—The quickest way to reach Egypt was by sea, and the Phoenician cites and Cyprus provided ships for the transport of the troops. This experience by the Judean soldiers in Ashurbanipal's army is likely echoed in the warning to those Israelites who might break the covenant: "The Lord will send you back to Egypt in ships, by a route I told you you would not see again" (Deut 28:68).

I marched to Kar-baniti—This city has not been identified, but is apparently to be sought in the eastern Delta of the Nile, at the entrance to Egypt, perhaps Pelusium (so Onasch 1994:33). The name is Assyrian and means "The quay of the goddess Banit." This city, along with many others in Lower Egypt, had been renamed by Esarhaddon as part of his policy of subordination of the conquered areas to his rule; for a partial list of these new "Assyrian" cities in Egypt, see *ANET* 293–294.

He abandoned Memphis and fled to Thebes—Situated in Upper Egypt on both banks of the Nile about 700 km from the sea, at modern Luxor and Karnak. Thebes served as the capital during the Cushite rule of Egypt (25th dynasty). In the Hebrew Bible, the name of the city is No-amon, "the city (of the god) Amon" (Nah 3:8); in its shortened form: No (Jer 46:25; Ezek 30:14).

90–117 The list of the Egyptian rulers is given in the two late recensions of the annals, editions C and A, with C presenting only the first six names. For a discussion of their Egyptian equivalents, see Onasch 1994:36–43, 151–152.

Neco, king of Memphis and Sais—Neco's rule over two major cities points to his senior position among the Egyptian kings listed.

Sharru-lu-dari, king of Ṣiʾnu—The king's Assyrian name means "May the king live for ever." Names of this sort were often given to royal hostages in Assyria, where they were "re-educated," and later returned to their homelands as loyal vassals. Sharru-lu-dari, an Egyptian, may have been deported by Esarhaddon at the time of his reorganization of the Nile Valley. For the same name borne by a Philistine vassal, cf. Sharru-lu-dari of Ashkelon in Text no. 6.01, lines 39–41. Ṣiʾnu is biblical "Sin, stronghold of Egypt" (Ezek 30:15), classical Pelusium, at Tell Farama, in the northeastern Nile Delta, 2.5 km from the Mediterranean.

Puṭubishti, king of Tanis—Biblical Zoan (cf. Isa 19:11, 13; Ps 78:12, 43), in the northeastern Nile Delta, now San el-Hagar, near the southern coast of Lake Manzala.

With many prisoners and much spoil, I returned safely to Nineveh—Further information on the looting is had from a fragmentary text that speaks of dark-skinned royal captives and large amounts of booty taken from [Me]mphis(?); see Lambert 1982.

Col. i, 118–ii, 4

They sent their mounted messengers to Tirhakah, king of Cush, to establish a treaty of loyalty and peace—Assyrian rule turned out to be more onerous than that of the Cushites.

They hung their corpses from stakes; they flayed their skins and covered the wall(s) of the city with them)—The harsh punishments meted out to the rebels is not unheard of in the annals of Assyrian warfare; see, for example, Text no. 6.01, lines 42–48.

Col. ii, 5–19

As for Neco, out of all of them, I had mercy on him and spared his life. I made a loyalty oath with him, more stringent than the former one—It seems that Ashurbanipal sought to create in the Delta a counterbalance to Tirhakah who continued to pose a threat from his southern stronghold. Perhaps he had come to the realization that Egypt could not be ruled without the genuine cooperation of native rulers. Neco I and his son were pardoned; the other Egyptian kings were executed. See Spalinger 1974:323. The pardon of King Manasseh of Judah and his return to the throne in Jerusalem, after a period of imprisonment by the Assyrians (2 Chr 33:11–13), has sometimes been compared to Ashurbanipal's treatment of Neco (e.g., Japhet 1993:1003); but this remains highly speculative.

Nabu-shezibani, his son, I appointed in Athribis; I showed him greater good and favor than my father, my begetter—His Akkadian name means, "Nabu, save me!" He is better known by his Egyptian name, Psammetichus, and later ruled all of Egypt (664–610 BCE).

20–27 **(Meanwhile), the awesomeness of the weapon of Ashur, my lord, overwhelmed Tirhakah in the place to which he had fled and he passed away**—The Cushite had escaped the powerful Assyrian army, but divine punishment was able to reach him in his refuge.

Tanutamon, son of Shabaka (var. son of his sister), ascended his royal throne—He was either the son of Shabaka or the nephew of Tirhakah, and was the last king of the 25th dynasty who reigned c. 664–656 BCE.

He opened the attack to strike the Assyrian troops that were in Memphis—A stela of Tanutamon tells of this invasion of Lower Egypt and his avenging the cooperation with Assyria; it was probably at this time that Neco I lost his life and was succeeded by Psammetichus I. See Breastead 1906:467–473.

28–48 **In my second campaign, I made straight for Egypt and Cush**—About two years separate the two campaigns. In annal edition F, the "first campaign" is completely omitted and the present campaign becomes the "first" military undertaking of Ashurbanipal.

He fled to Kipkipi—The city has yet to be identified; perhaps it is to be sought in the vicinity of Aswan in Upper Egypt or farther south within Cush.

That city (i.e., Thebes) and its environs, I myself captured with the support of Ashur and Ishtar—This fabled city finally fell to the Assyrians and was thoroughly looted. Another text mentions several species of apes among the spoil carried off to Nineveh. A palace relief at Nineveh depicts the breakthrough of the walls of Thebes and a line of captives leaving the city; see Fig. 27.

The conquest of Thebes lived on in the memory of the Judeans who had fought in Egypt, as evidenced by the reference to the event in the prophecy of Nahum. The prophet compared the fall of the illustrious Egyptian capital to the impending collapse of Nineveh: "Are you better than Thebes that sat by the Nile, with water around her, her rampart a sea, water her wall? Cush was her strength, Egypt too, and that without limit; Put and the Libyans—they were her helpers. Yet even she was exiled, she went into captivity" (Nah 3:8–10).

Two tall obelisks cast of shining silver alloy, whose weight was 2,500 talents (and) stood by the gate of the temple—The two columns stood in the temple at Karnak and their weight was c. 75 tons.

I fought bitterly against Egypt and Cush and I established victory (over them)—This rhetorical close to the Egyptian campaign in no way reflects the later history of Assyria's rule over the Nile Valley and certainly not the situation in the late 640s when edition A was composed. About a decade earlier, in the mid-650s, Egypt had regained its independence, under Psammetichus I, who, with the aid of Lydian mercenaries, took control of Egypt.

No. 9.02—THE EARLY CAMPAIGN TO TYRE—EDITION B

Baal, king of Tyre, who had submitted to Esarhaddon in the course of the Assyrian campaign to Egypt in 671 BCE, remained loyal to his overlord and did not join in the further revolt against Assyria instigated by Tirhakah. Moreover, when Ashurbanipal undertook to suppress the Egyptian uprising, Baal provided him with ships, allowing for the speedy transfer of troops and supplies to the Delta; see Text no. 9.01. But towards the end of the first decade of Ashurbanipal's rule, Baal revolted against Assyria under circumstances that are not at all clear. Following Baal's surrender, an Assyrian province was apparently established on the coast facing island Tyre; evidence for this step can be found in the service of Bel-Ḫarran-shadua, the governor of Kar-Esarhaddon, as governor of Tyre as well; he was eponym in 650 BCE.

The first report on the operations against Tyre was given in annal edition B, composed in 649 BCE.

Text edition: Borger 1996:28–29; earlier, Piepkorn 1933:40–45.
Translations: *ARAB* 2, §§847–848; *ANET* 295–296; *TUAT* 1/4, 399–400; *TPOA* 133–134.

Col. ii, 41–70

In my third campaign, I marched against Baal, king of Tyre, who lives in the midst of the sea, because he did not heed my royal word (and) did not obey my orders. I surrounded him with armed posts and I strengthened the guard so that his people could not exit. I seized his roads on sea and on land; I cut off his way. Water and food, that keep them alive, I made scarce. I confined him within a strong enclosure (from which) there was no escaping. I restricted and shortened their lives, (and thus) brought him into submission to my yoke. He brought his daughter, the issue of his loins, and the daughters of his brother before me to serve as palace women. His son, who had never crossed the seas, he brought before me to serve me. I received his daughters and the daughters of his brother with the large dowry. I had pity on him and returned his son, the issue of his loins, to him. I removed the armed posts with which I had surrounded him and I opened all the roads on land and seas that I had seized. I received his rich tribute. I returned safely to Nineveh, my lordly city. The kings in the midst of the sea and the kings who dwell in high mountains saw these mighty deeds of mine and they respected my lordship.

Col. ii, 41–70

In my third campaign, I marched against Baal, king of Tyre, who lives in the midst of the sea, because he did not heed my royal word (and) did not obey my orders—Baal's revolt is not reported in the inscriptions of Ashurbanipal's first decade, which suggests that it was unrelated to the events in Egypt (otherwise Katzenstein 1997:287–292). At the same, it is well to remember that Esarhaddon imposed a restrictive commercial treaty upon Baal (see Cogan 2013:91–99), which likely continued under Ashurbanipal. Thus Baal had good reason to seize whatever opportunity presented itself in order to throw off the imperial yoke.

I surrounded him with armed posts and I strengthened the guard so that his people could not exit. I seized his roads on sea and on land; I

cut off his way—The Assyrian army deployed on the coast opposite Tyre that was situated on an island some 600–750 m from the coast; in this way they prevented the transfer of supplies to the islanders. Only three centuries later, in 332 BCE, was Tyre joined to the mainland by a runway that was built during the siege of the city conducted by Alexander.

His son, who had never crossed the seas, he brought before me to serve me—In edition A, his name is given as Aḫimilki, and from the description given here, he seems to have been a minor at the time.

No. 9.03—THE LATE CAMPAIGN TO TYRE—EDITION A

The leading commercial position of the city of Tyre, "that sits at the gateway of the sea, that trades with the peoples on many coastlands" (Ezek 27:3), was not lost on Ashurbanipal. For almost two decades, after his first campaign against Tyre in the late sixties of the seventh century BCE (see Text no. 9.02), relations between Tyre and Assyria seem to have been conducted in an orderly fashion. A report that appears only in the late annals, edition A (643 BCE), tells of a punitive action taken against Tyre in support of the local administration loyal to Assyria.

This is the latest evidence in Assyrian sources for military action in Phoenicia and in the West in general. Ashurbanipal reigned for another sixteen years and the question of when Assyria's position in the area weakened is disputed.

Text edition: Borger 1996:69; earlier Streck 1916:80–83.
Translations: *ARAB* 2, §779; *ANET* 300; *TUAT* 1/4, 401; *HTAT* 347.

Col. ix, 115–128

On my return, I captured Ushu that is situated on the seacoast. I slew the people of Ushu who were disobedient to their governors (and) did not deliver their tribute, their yearly due. I executed judgment against the people who had not been submissive. I carried off their gods (and) their people to Assyria as spoil. I slaughtered the unsubmissive people of Acco; I hung their corpses on stakes around the city. Their remainder I took to Assyria. I organized (them) into a contingent and added (them) to the large forces that the god Ashur granted me.

Col. ix, 115–128

On my return—This incident at Tyre is the concluding battle in the king's "ninth campaign" that was devoted to encounters with the Arab tribes in western reaches of the Assyrian empire which had posed a threat to areas from Jebel Bishri to Damascus. The expression "on my return" is a formulaic editorial term linking compositional units and should not be taken literally. A local Assyrian force may have operated against Tyre.

I captured Ushu that is situated on the seacoast—The name refers to Old Tyre (*Palaityros*) on the coast opposite island Tyre; it was the source of water for the residents of the island. See Text no. 6.01, lines 32–35.

I hung their corpses on stakes around the city—This punishment is not unusual in the manual of Assyrian warfare; the unsubmissive were made an object lesson for all those who survived. Sennacherib impaled the rebels of Ekron in this same manner; see Text no. 6.01, lines 42–48.

No. 9.04—THE EARLY CAMPAIGNS AGAINST ARAB TRIBES—EDITION B

The inscriptions of Ashurbanipal present some of the most extensive accounts of the efforts expended in restraining the nomads of the Syrian desert and bringing some order to the relations between them and the empire. Military operations focused on two fronts: in the south against the Arab tribes who supported the rebellion of Shamash-shum-ukin in Babylon, and in the West against the raiding bands who harassed the frontier kingdoms that were Assyrian vassals. The early description in edition B (from 649 BCE, preceding the events in Babylon) tells of Assyrian activity in Transjordan and southern Syria. For full analysis, see Eph^{c}al 1982:142–169; Gerardi 1992.

The present narration is separated from the one preceding it by a line drawn on the prism, but it is not numbered as a separate campaign as are the campaigns against the Arabs in later editions, thus, e.g., in edition A, parts of the report in edition B are given under the rubric: "In my ninth campaign...."

Text edition: Borger 1996:113–114; earlier Piepkorn 1933:80–85.
Translation: *ARAB* 2, §§869–870.

Col. vii, 93-viii, 30

Yautaʾ, son of Ḫazaʾil, king of Kedar, who was my servant, appealed to me concerning his gods and he implored my kingship. I had him take an oath by the great gods and I gave him back the god Atarsamaʾin. Afterwards, he transgressed my loyalty oath and did not uphold the alliance (that I had made with him); he threw off my lordly yoke. He kept from coming to inquire of my welfare and withheld his gifts. He incited the people of Arabia to revolt with him and they continually raided the land of Amurru. My troops, which were stationed on the border of his land, I sent out against him. They defeated them; the people of Arabia, all those who had gone up against me, they beat down with weapons. They set fire to their tents, their dwellings; they consigned (them) to the flames. Cattle, sheep, asses, camels and people, without number, they carried off as spoil. The entire extent of the land (of Assyria), round about, they filled. I divided camels like sheep (and) I distributed (them) to the people of Assyria. In my country, a camel was sold for one shekel (or) half-shekel, according to the market price. The tavern maid as a gift, the brewer for a pitcher, the gardener for a bundle (of greens)—they received camels and people.

The rest of the Arabs, who had fled before my weapons, the god Erra, the hero, struck down. Famine broke out among them and in their hunger, they ate the flesh of their children. All the curses, according to what was written in their loyalty oath, the gods Ashur, Sin, Shamash, Bel, Nabu, Ishtar of Nineveh, Ishtar of Arbaʾil, the great gods, my lords, brought upon them.

viii, 31–38

(As for) Yautaʾ, evil befell him and he fled alone (to the land of Nebaioth). Abiyate, son of Teʾri, came to Nineveh and kissed my feet. I had him take a loyalty oath, to serve me; I made him king in place of Yautaʾ. I imposed upon him as yearly tribute: gold, "eye stones," *pappardillu*-stones, kohl, camels, (and) prime quality asses.

39–50 Ammuladin, king of Kedar, who, like him, became hostile (to Assyria) (and) continually raided the land of Amurru, by invoking my name, which the gods Ashur, Sin, Shamash, Bel, Nabu, Ishtar of Nineveh (and) Ishtar of Arbaʾil had made great, Kamasḫalta, king of Moab, a servant of mine, inflicted upon him a defeat in an open field battle. With his own hands, he captured Ammuladin (and) the rest of the people who escaped from the battle; he put them, hand and foot, in iron fetters and sent them to me to Nineveh.

51–63 Natnu, king of Nebaioth, whose place is far off, heard of the might of Ashur (and) Marduk who supported me; while in the past he did not send his messenger to the kings, my fathers, (and) did not inquire of their welfare, now sent his messenger of welfare and he kissed my feet. He implored my lordship to establish a loyalty oath of peace and servitude. I looked upon him with joy and I was favorably disposed towards him. I imposed a yearly tax and tribute upon him.

Col. vii, 93–viii, 30

Yautaʾ, son of Ḫazaʾil, king of Kedar—Sennacherib had fought against Ḫazaʾil, Yautaʾ's father, in the area of Wadi Sirhan (Ephʿal 1982:118–119, 124). The scene of the present encounter was the eastern fringes of Transjordan.

Kedar—Assyrian contacts with the Kedarites were first established in the eighth century, during the reign of Tiglath-pileser III; see Text no. 4.03.

Appealed to me concerning his gods—The capture and removal of the divine images to Assyria had taken place during the reign of Esarhaddon, but is known only from the inscriptions of Ashurbanipal.

I gave him back the god Atarsamaʾin—The name of the Arabian deity is transcribed in its Aramaic form and means: "Aṯtar of the Heavens." Other divine names contain the element *samaʾin*: בעל שמם (in Phoenician) and בעלשמין (in Aramaic).

My troops, which were stationed on the border of his land, I sent out against him. They defeated them; the people of Arabia, all those who had gone up against me, they beat down with weapons—The later edition A includes a list of stations where Assyrian forces were posted, among them: Edom, Yabrud Pass, Beth-Ammon and Moab (Borger 1996:61, col. vii, lines 108–114; see Ephʿal 1982:149, n. 514).

I divided camels like sheep (and) I distributed (them) to the people of Assyria—The country was flooded with the spoils of war so that the market price of these goods dropped to extremely low levels. So great was the victory over the Arabs!

Famine broke out among them and in their hunger, they ate the flesh of their children. All the curses, according to what was written in their loyalty oath . . . the great gods, my lords, brought upon them—Among the curses

Fig. 28. Assyrian forces fighting Arab tribesmen, from the palace of Ashurbanipal at Nineveh (*Courtesy of the Trustees of the British Museum*).

recorded in the loyalty oath that guaranteed Ashurbanipal's succession to the throne is one anticipating the circumstances described here: "May Adad, the canal inspector of heaven and earth, cut off the rain of heaven from your land and deprive your meadows of [grain]. . . . May a mother bar the door to her daughter. In your hunger, eat the flesh of your sons! In want and famine may one man eat the flesh of another" (Cogan 2013:77–78, lines 440–441, 448–450). Similar maledictions are known from biblical sources, e.g., "You shall eat your own issue, the flesh of your sons and your daughters that the Lord your God has given you, because of the desperate straits to which your enemy shall reduce you" (Deut 28:53; cf., too, Lev 26:29). Whether the said cannibalism is a depiction of reality or merely a literary motif is a moot question.

viii, 31–38

(As for) Yautaʾ, evil befell him and he fled alone (to the land of Nebaioth). Abiyate, son of Teʾri, came to Nineveh and kissed my feet. I had him take a loyalty oath, to serve me—A fragment of the treaty between Ashurbanipal and the Kedarites (with Abiyate?) survives, and besides swearing loyalty to the Assyrian overlord, it obligates them to disassociate themselves from all association with the renegade Yautaʾ; see Cogan 2013:99–101.

39–50 **Kamasḫalta, king of Moab, a servant of mine, inflicted upon him a defeat in an open field battle**—In the later editions of the annals, this victory by the king of Moab is credited to Ashurbanipal.

51–63 **Natnu, king of Nebaioth, whose place is far off**—Apparently this "far-off place" was south of Wadi Sirhan. In biblical genealogy, Nebaioth is the first-born of Ishmael (cf. Gen 25:13; Isa 60:7). Despite the phonological similarity between the names Nebaioth and the Nabateans, the two peoples should be kept separate; the consonants of the names are different and the Nabateans do not appear in historical sources before the late 4th century BCE (Ephʿal 1982:221–223).

No. 9.05—THE LATE CAMPAIGNS AGAINST ARAB TRIBES—EDITION A

The military actions against the Arab tribes in the Palmyra–Jebel Bishri–Damascus salient are reported for the first time in Edition A (Rassam Prism) of the annals of Ashurbanipal, composed in 643 BCE. The campaigns in this area were undertaken in the mid-640s, after the completion of the major campaigns against Babylon and Elam that had engaged the Assyrian army for the first half of the decade; their goal was to return order to this vital area through which the important trade routes connecting Assyria and the West passed. The military reports given in this section are particularly rich in visual imagery and make use of a number of genres, exemplifying the literary talents of the author of Prism A (Cogan 2014).

Text edition: Borger 1996:63–69.
Translations: *ARAB* 2, §§ 822–829; *ANET* 299–300.

col. viii, 65–72

But Abiyate, son of Teʾri, did not regard the good (done for him) (and) did not keep the oaths of the great gods; he spoke rebellious words against me and came to an agreement with Natnu, king of Nebaioth. They mobilized their forces for an evil attack against my border.

viii, 73–119

At the command of Ashur, Sin, Shamash, Adad, Bel, Nabu, Ishtar of Nineveh, the Queen of Kidmuri, Ishtar of Arbela, Ninurta, Nergal (and) Nusku, I mobilized my troops and they took the direct road against Abiyate. They crossed the Tigris and Euphrates safely in their flood state. They took a distant road; they climbed up high mountains (and) wound their way through forests with deep shadows. Through tall trees, thorn bushes, and brambles, on a road (full of) thorny shrubs, they advanced safely. In a desert, a place of parching thirst, where the birds of heaven do not fly (and) wild donkeys or gazelles do not graze, one hundred double- hours from Nineveh, the city beloved of Ishtar, wife of Enlil, they thrust ahead against Uateʾ, king of the Arabs and Abiyate, who marched with the forces of Nebaioth.

In the month of Sivan, the month of the god Sin, the first-born of Enlil, the preeminent, on the 25th day, (the day of) the procession of Belet-Babili (lit. Lady of Babylon), the most prominent among the great gods, I set out from Ḫadatta and I pitched camp in Laribda, a fortress with stone walls, by the water cisterns. My troops drew water for their refreshment. They marched on to a region of thirst, a parched place, to Ḫurarina. Between the towns of Yarki and Azalla, in the desert, a distant place, a place where there are no wild animals and the birds of heaven do not build nests, I defeated the Isammeʾ, a confederation of the god Atarsamaʾin, and Nebaioth. I plundered people, donkeys, camels and sheep, without number. For eight double-hours my troops marched about victoriously and they returned safely and in Azalla drank water to their fill.

viii, 120–ix, 8

From Azalla to Quraṣiti, a distance of six double-hours, a place of parching thirst, they marched forward. I surrounded the confederation of Atarsamaʾin and the Kedarites under Uateʾ, son of Bir-Dada, king of the Arabs. His gods, his mother, his sisters, his wife, his family, all the people of Kedar, donkeys, camels and sheep—all that I captured with the support of Ashur and Ishtar, my lords, I set on the road to Damascus.

ix, 9–24

In the month of Ab, the month of the Bow Star, the heroic daughter of Sin, on day 3, the evening of the festival of the king of the gods, Marduk, I set out from Damascus, a distance of six double-hours. The entire night I marched forward to Ḫulḫuliti. On Mount Ḫukkuruna, an inaccessible mountain, I reached the confederation of Abiyate, son of Teʾri (and) the Kedarites. I inflicted a defeat upon them and took away their spoil. At the command of Ashur and Ishtar, my lords, I myself captured alive Abiyate (and) Ayammu, the son(s) of Teʾri, in the midst of battle. I put iron fetters on (their) hands and feet, and together with the spoil of their land, I took them to Assyria.

ix, 25–52

Those who escaped my weapons fled; in their fear, they took to Mount Ḫukkuruna, an inaccessible mountain. I stationed guards at the water sources and springs, as many as there were, in the towns of Manḫabbi, Apparu, Tenuquri, Ṣayuran, Marqana, Saratein, Enzikarme, Taʾna, Saraqa. I withheld water that keeps them alive; I made drink scarce from their mouths. Through parching thirst they lay down their lives. Those remaining cut open the camels, their mounts; in their thirst they drank blood and filthy water. Those who went up the mountain (and) entered (its region) to take refuge, none escaped; no one slipped out of my hand. I myself caught them in their refuges.

I carried off as spoil to Assyria people—male and female—donkeys, camels, oxen and sheep, without number. The entire extent of my land that Ashur gave me, round about, they filled. I divided camels like sheep (and) I distributed (them) to the people of Assyria. In my country, a camel was sold for one shekel (or) half-shekel, according to the market price. The tavern maid as a gift, the brewer for a pitcher, the gardener for a bundle (of greens)—they received camels and people.

ix, 53–74

Uateʾ, together with his troops, who had not kept my loyalty oaths and had fled before the weapons of Ashur, my lord (and) escaped to Natnu, the god Erra, the hero, struck them down. Famine broke out among them and in their hunger, they ate the flesh of their children. All the curses, according to what was written in their loyalty oath, the gods Ashur, Sin, Shamash, Bel, Nabu, Ishtar of Nineveh, Sharrat Kidmuri, Ishtar of Arbaʾil, Ninurta, Nergal, Nusku, brought upon them. Camel foals, donkey foals, calves (and) lambs, at (the udders of) seven nursing ewes could not be sated with milk. The people of Arabia asked each other: "On what account have these events befallen Arabia?" (They answered:) "Because we did not keep the great loyalty oath of Ashur. We have sinned against the goodness (shown by) Ashurbanipal, the king, the beloved of Enlil."

ix, 75–89

Mullissu, the wild cow, the supreme goddess, most heroic among the goddesses, who, together with Anu and Enlil, holds a pre-eminent position, gores my enemies with her mighty horns. Ishtar, who resides in Arbela, clad in (divine) fire, bearing divine splendor, rains down flames on Arabia. Erra, the hero, organized for battle, smites my enemies. Ninurta, the arrow, the great hero, son of the mighty Enlil, slit the throats of my enemies with his sharp arrow. Nusku, the attentive minister, who proclaims lordship, who, at the command of Ashur, Mullissu, and the valiant Lady of Arbela, walks at my side (and) protects my kingship, takes the lead of my troops and throws down my enemies.

ix, 90–114

The troops of Uateʾ experienced the onslaught of the weapons of Ashur and the great gods, my lords, who had come to my assistance during the battle, and so defected from him. He, himself, was frightened and left the house where he had taken refuge. Trusting in Ashur, Sin, Shamash, Adad, Bel, Nabu, Ishtar of Nineveh, the Queen of Kidmuri, Ishtar of Arbela, Ninurta, Nergal and Nusku, I myself captured him and brought him to Assyria. By reason of my prayer concerning the capture of my enemies that I constantly directed to Ashur and Mullissu, I pierced his jaw with *a piece of wood from a chariot* that I held in my hand; I put a rope through his jaw. I put a dog collar on him and at the east gate of Nineveh (that is) named "The Entrance for Inspection of the World," (and) had him guard the bolt. I had mercy on him and kept him alive in order to praise the glory of Ashur, Ishtar and the great gods, my lords.

---

col. viii, 65–72

Natnu, king of Nebaioth—Natnu is referred to in the earlier campaign; see Text no. 9.04, vii, 51–63.

viii, 73–119

They crossed the Tigris and Euphrates safely in their flood state—For this common trope, denoting the heroic actions of the Assyrian army, cf. Text no. 1.01, ii, 81–87.

one hundred double-hours from Nineveh—Approximately 1,000 kilometers. For this measure, see Text no. 8.05, obv. 6–18.

In the month of Sivan . . . on the 25th day . . . I set out for Ḫadatta—The campaign began in the early summer and lasted at least three months—the second stage began on the 3rd of Ab (see ahead)—in the height of summer. It proceeded in three stages, from Ḫadatta to Azalla, from Azalla to Quraṣiti, and from Damascus to Mount Ḫukkurina. The location of these sites is still obscure; see the proposals and discussion in Ephᶜal 1982:161–164.

They marched on to a region of thirst, a parched place, to Ḫurarina. Between the towns of Yarki and Azalla, in the desert, a distant place, a place where there are no wild animals and the birds of heaven do not build nests—Crossing inhospitable desert areas, ascending steep mountains and penetrating thick forests are frequent topoi in Assyrian royal inscriptions; cf. Text no. 8.05, rev. 1–1; *ARAB* 2, §520 (Esarhaddon); *ARAB* 2, §358 (Sennacherib).

viii, 120–ix, 8

From Azalla to Quraṣiti, a distance of six double-hours, a place of parching thirst, they marched forward—For the itinerary style of this passage, see Text no. 8.05, rev. 1–19.

ix, 9–24

I marched forward to Ḫulḫuliti—Perhaps the village of Ḥulḥuleh in the northeastern part of the al-Leja region in southern Syria.

ix, 25–52

the towns of Manḫabbi, Apparu, Tenuquri, Ṣayuran, Marqana, Saratein, Enzikarme, Taʾna, Saraqa—None of these sites can be identified, but they were likely to the east of Ḥulḥuleh.

The entire extent of my land that Ashur gave me, round about, they filled. I divided camels like sheep (and) I distributed (them) to the people of Assyria—This same description appeared in the earlier Edition B (see Text no. 9.04, vii, 93–viii, 30) with reference to Yautaʾ, son of Ḫazaʾil. Here, in Edition A, it describes the outcome of the late campaign against Abiyate. Such free movement of literary units to different settings is an example of the editorial license available to the authors of the royal annals.

ix, 53–74

Famine broke out among them and in their hunger, they ate the flesh of their children—These acts of cannibalism also appear with reference to Yautaʾ in Edition B; see Text no. 9.04, vii, 93–viii, 30.

Camel foals, donkey foals, calves (and) lambs, at (the udders of) seven nursing ewes could not be sated with milk—This divine punishment is the mirror image of a curse that often appears among treaty imprecations. For example, the Aramaic treaty from Sefire (mid-7th century BCE) includes a curse against violators of the treaty: "Seven mares shall suckle a colt, and it shall not be s[ated. Seven] cows shall suckle a calf, and it shall not be sated. Seven ewes shall suckle a lamb, and [it shall not be s]ated" (*ANET* 659).

The people of Arabia asked each other: "On what account have these events befallen Arabia?" (They answered:) "Because we did not keep the great loyalty oath of Ashur. We have sinned against the goodness (shown by) Ashurbanipal, the king, the beloved of Enlil"—Biblical tradition knows this same question-answer motif, but assigns the exchange to the foreign onlookers, who observed Israel's suffering and destruction: "All nations will ask, 'Why did the Lord do thus to this land? Wherefore that awful wrath?' They will be told, 'Because they forsook the covenant that the Lord, God of their fathers, made with them when He freed them from the land of Egypt'" (Deut 29:23–24; cf. Jer 22:8–9).

ix, 75–89

Mullissu, the wild cow . . . gores my enemies with her mighty horns. Ishtar, who resides in Arbela, clad in (divine) fire, . . . rains down flames

on Arabia...—These lines and those that follow continue the punishments meted out by the divine witnesses to the loyalty oaths already begun in the preceding paragraph. Each god is referred to by a familiar epithet. Compare the invocation of gods in the first series of curses of Esarhaddon's treaty for the accession of Ashurbanipal, e.g., "May Ninurta, the foremost among the gods, fell you with his fierce arrow." See further, Cogan 2013, Text no. 3.01, §§38–56.

ix, 90–114

I pierced his jaw with *a piece of wood from a chariot* that I held in my hand; I put a rope through his jaw—A similar humiliation had been inflicted by Esarhaddon on the king of Arza; see Text 8.02, iii, 39–42. This typically Assyrian practice is incorporated, in ironic fashion, in Isaiah's diatribe against Sennacherib: "I will put my hook in your nose and my bridle through your lips, and turn you back on the very road by which you came" (2 Kgs 19:28; cf. Ezek 29:4; 2 Chr 33:11).

References

Aḥituv, Shmuel
2008 *Echoes from the Past*, Jerusalem.
Borger, Rykle
1996 *Beiträge zum Inschriftenwerk Assurbanipals*, Wiesbaden.
Breastead, James Henry
1906 *Ancient Records of Egypt*, vol. 4, Chicago.
Cogan, Mordechai
2013 *Bound for Exile*, Jerusalem.
2014 The Author of Ashurbanipal Prism A (Rassam): An Inquiry into his Plan and Purpose, with a note on his Persona, *Orient* 49:69–83.
Elayi, Josette
1983 Les cités phéniciennes et l'empire assyrien a l'époque d'Assurbanipal, *RA* 77:45–48.
Eph^{c}al, Israel
1982 *The Ancient Arabs*, Jerusalem.
Gerardi, Pamela
1992 The Arab Campaigns of Assurbanipal: Scribal Reconstruction of the Past, *SAAB* 6:67–103.
Japhet, Sara
1993 *I & II Chronicles*, Louisville.

Katzenstein, H. Jacob
1997 *The History of Tyre*, 2nd ed., Beer-sheva.

Lambert, Wilfred George
1982 Booty from Egypt? *JJS* 33:61–70.

Onasch, Hans-Ulrich
1994 Die assyrischen Eroberungen Ägyptens, ÄAT 27, Wiesbaden.

Piepkorn, Arthur Carl
1933 *Historical Prism Inscriptions of Ashurbanipal*, Chicago.

Spalinger, Anthony
1974 Assurbanipal and Egypt: A Source Study, *JAOS* 94:316–328.

Streck, Maximlian
1916 *Assurbanipal und die letzten assyrischen Könige bis zum Untergange Nineveh's*, 3 vols., Leipzig.

Verreth, Herbert
1999 The Egyptian Eastern Border Region in Assyrian Sources, *JAOS* 119:234–247.

Weippert, Manfred
1973 Die Kämpfe des assyrichen Königs Assurbanipal gegen die Araber, *WO* 7:39–85.

Fig. 29. The lot (*pūru*) of Yaḫalu (*Yale Babylonian Collection*). The text reads:

"O Ashur, great lord! O Adad, great lord! (This is) the lot of Yaḫalu, the chief treasurer of Shalmaneser (III), king of Assyria, the governor of Kipshuni, Qumeni, Meḫrani, Uqi, the Cedar Mountain, customs officer. May the harvest of the land of Ashur prosper during his eponymy, his lot; may his lot come up before Ashur and Adad."

CHAPTER 10

The Assyrian Eponym Chronicle

Assyrian calendar years were counted according to eponyms (Akkadian *limmu/līmu*, literally, "circle, turn"), i.e., each year was named after a high-ranking official in the Assyrian administration; the king himself served as eponym at the beginning of his reign. The eponym system is attested from the beginning of Assyrian history in the early second millennium BCE until the fall of Nineveh in 612 BCE. The choice of eponym was evidently determined by the casting of lots (Akkadian *pūru*; Hebrew פור). One such lot has been discovered, that of Yaḫalu, who was the administrator of the royal household under Shalmaneser III; he served as eponym in the years 833, 824, 821 BCE (see Fig. 29). In the course of time, a more or less fixed order of eponyms was established; during the first millennium, after the king's year—usually his second year—came those of the commander-in-chief (*turtānu*), the palace herald, the chief cupbearer (*rab šāqê*), the chief treasurer, and various senior provincial governors (Zawadski 1997). In the seventh century, the circle of eponyms widened to include governors who served in distant areas of the empire, e.g., Nabu-kena-uṣur, governor of Samaria (690 BCE); Issi-Adad-anenu, governor of Megiddo (679 BCE); Shamash-kashid-ayyabi, governor of Ashdod (669 BCE); and Nabu-shar-aḫḫeshu, governor of Samaria (646 BCE). In the last decades of the empire, palace officials close to the king entered the ranks of the eponyms for the first time (Matilla 2009).

Effective and efficient management of government and business dealings required the recording of the names of the eponyms in the order of their term of office, and in time, titles were added to the names in the eponym lists so as to distinguish between persons who bore the same personal name. The longest, uninterrupted list of eponyms begins with the year 910 BCE (Adad-nerari II) and continues down to 649 (in the middle years of Ashurbanipal). The names of the eponyms from 648 until 612 are known from royal and private documents—there are even more eponym names than years!—and several reconstructions of their order have been suggested (see Whiting

1994; Reade 1998). This surfeit of names may indicate that during the strife in the years following the death of Ashurbanipal there were several rival administrative centers, each with its eponym appointees.

The eponym calendar was in use in all areas of Assyrian rule and on the administrative documents discovered in Israel, the eponym dates help establish the historical context of these texts. From Gezer, two documents are dated to 651 and 649; from Tel Ḥadid, 698 and 664; see Horowitz and Oshima 2006:55–59; 61–64; Cogan 2013:24–29.

An expanded form of the eponym lists, the Eponym Chronicle, is known from the reign of Shalmaneser III (858–824 BCE) onward. Characteristic of this text is the extra column alongside those of the eponyms and their titles; in this column, a central event is recorded for each year, generally the name of a city or country that was the goal of the year's campaigning. Beginning with the year 745, there is a noticeable expansion in the information recorded in the last column of the Eponym Chronicle, resulting in its spread across the other columns; in style, it approaches that of the Babylonian Chronicles. But while this late form of record-keeping may have been influenced by Babylonian chronistic practice (so Weissert 1992), it cannot be overlooked that an Eponym Chronicle had been produced in the early 2nd millennium; fragments of such a text from the days of the Assyrian kings at the kingdom of Mari (18th century BCE) have been recovered (Glassner 2004: no. 8). Copies of the Neo-Assyrian Eponym Chronicle for years after 700 BCE have not yet surfaced.

Absolute dates can be established by means of the Eponym Chronicle owing to the note recorded for the eponymate of Bur-saggale, governor of Gozan: "Revolt in the city of Ashur; in Sivan, there was an eclipse of the sun." Astronomical calculations set the date at June 15th, 763 BCE. This date is the cornerstone for much of the chronological framework of the first half of the first millennium BCE in the ancient Near East.

No. 10.01—THE EPONYM CHRONICLE

The tablets of the Eponym Chronicle are ruled with vertical lines that divide the tablets into four columns. In the first column, the formula "In the (year of the) eponym" (Akkadian *ina limme*) appears. On some tablets, the copyists added a horizontal line before the eponym year of the king, and two manuscripts summarize the total years of the reign of each king thus divided. Copies of the Eponym Chronicle have been discovered in the imperial centers of Nineveh and Ashur, and at Sultantepe (ancient Ḫuzirina), 16 km southeast of Urfa in Turkey, not far from the provincial capital of Harran.

The following translation of the Eponym Chronicle is based on an eclectic text and reflects all the extant manuscripts (following the edition of Millard 1994). The formulaic first column is omitted and Julian calendar dates are added.

Text edition: Millard 1994; earlier Ungnad 1938.
Translations: *ARAB* 2, §1198; *ANET* 274; *COS* 1, 465–466; Glassner 2004:164–177, no. 9; *TUAT* NF II, 33–34 (extracts); *HTAT* 273–274, 288.

Name of Eponym	Title	Event	Year
Adad-nerari (III)	King of Assyria	To Media	809
Nergal-ilaya	Commander-in-chief	To Gozan	808
Bel-dan	Palace herald	To Mannea	807
Ṣilli-Bel	Chief cupbearer	To Mannea	806
Ashur-taklak	Chief treasurer	To Arpad	805
Ilu-issiya	Governor of Ashur	To Ḫazazu	804
Nergal-eresh	(Governor) of Raṣappa	To Baʾalu	803
Ashur-balti-ekurri	(Governor) of Arrapḫa	To the sea; plague	802
Ninurta-ilaya	(Governor) of Aḫizuḫina	To Ḫubushkia	801
Shep-Ishtar	(Governor) of Niṣibin	To Media (var. Mannea)	800
Marduk-ishmanni	(Governor) of Amedi	To Media (var. Mannea)	799
Mutakkil-Marduk	Chief eunuch	To Lushia	798
Bel-tarṣi-iluma	(Governor) of Calah (var. Kilizi)	To Namri	797
Ashur-bel-uṣur	(Governor) of Ḫabruri	To Manṣuate	796
Marduk-shaduni	(Governor) of Raqmat	To Der	795
Mukin-abua	(Governor) of Tushḫan	To Der	794
Mannu-ki-Ashur	(Governor) of Gozan	To Media (var. Der)	793
Mushallim-Ninurta	(Governor) of Tille	To Media	792
Bel-iqishanni	(Governor) of Shibḫinish	To Ḫubushkia	791
Shep-Shamash	(Governor) of Isana	To Ituʾa	790
Ninurta-mukin-aḫi	(Governor) of Nineveh	To Media	789
Adad-mushammer	(Governor) of Kilizi	To Media.	788
The foundations of the Nabu temple	in Nineveh	laid	
Ṣilli-Ishtar	Governor of Arbela	To Media.	787
Nabu	the new temple	entered	
Nabu-sharra-uṣur	(Governor) of Talmusa	To Kiski	786
Adad-uballiṭ	Governor of Tamnunna	To Ḫubushkia	785
The Great God	to Der	went	
Marduk-sharra-uṣur	Governor of Arbela	To Ḫubushkia	784

Name of Eponym	Title	Event	Year
Ninurta-naṣir	(Governor) of [Maz]amua	To Ituʾa	783
Iluma-leʾi	(Governor) of [Niṣ]ibin	To Ituʾa	782
	[2]8 years, [Adad-nerari], king of Assyria		
Shalmaneser (IV)	King of Assyria	To Urartu	781
Shamshi-ilu	Commander-in-chief	To Urartu	780
Marduk-remanni	Chief cupbearer	To Urartu	779
Bel-lesher	Palace herald	To Urartu	778
Nabu-ishdeya-kaʾʾin	Chief treasurer	To Ituʾa	777
Pan-Ashur-lamur	Governor of Ashur	To Urartu	776
Nergal-eresh	Governor of Raṣappa	To the Cedar Mountain	775
Ishtar-duri	Governor of Niṣibin	To Urartu; Namri	774
Mannu-ki-Adad	Governor of Raqmat	To Damascus	773
Ashur-bel-uṣur	Governor of Calah	To Hadrach	772
	[10] years, Shalmaneser, king of Assyria		
Ashur-dan (III)	King of Assyria	To Gananati	771
Shamshi-ilu	Commander-in-chief	To Marad	770
Bel-ilaya	(Governor) of Arrapḫa	To Ituʾa	769
Aplaya	(Governor) of [Ma]zamua	In the land	768
Qurdi-Ashur	(Governor) of [Aḫi]zuḫina	To Gananati	767
Mushallim-Ninurta	(Governor) of Tille	To Media	766
Ninurta-mukin-nishi	(Governor) of Ḫabruri	To Hadrach; plague	765
Ṣidqi-ilu	(Governor) of Tushḫan	In the land	764
Bur-saggale	(Governor) of Gozan.	Revolt in Ashur. In Sivan, there was an eclipse of the sun	763
Ṭab-belu	(Governor) of Amedi	Revolt in Ashur	762
Nabu-mukin-aḫi	(Governor) of Nineveh	Revolt in Arrapḫa	761
La-qipu	(Governor) of Kilizi	Revolt in Arrapḫa	760
Pan-Ashur-lamur	(Governor) of Arbela	Revolt in Gozan; plague	759
Ana-beli-taklak	(Governor) of Isana	To Gozan; peace in the land	758
Ninurta-iddin	(Governor) of Kurbaʾil	In the land	757
Bel-shadua	(Governor) of Tamnunna	In the land	756
Iqisu	(Governor) of Shibḫinish	To Hadrach	755
Ninurta-shezibanni	(Governor) of Talmusa	To Arpad; return from Ashur	754
	[ ]		
Ashur-nerari (V)	King of Assyria	In the land	753

Name of Eponym	Title	Event	Year
Shamshi-ilu	Commander-in-chief	In the land	752
Marduk-shallimanni	Palace herald	In the land	751
Bel-dan	Chief cupbearer	In the land	750
Shamash-kenu-dugul	Chief treasurer	To Namri	749
Adad-bela-kaʾʾin	Governor of Ashur	To Namri	748
Sin-shallimanni	(Governor) of Raṣappa	In the land	747
Nergal-naṣir	(Governor) of Niṣibin	Revolt in Calah	746

Nabu-bela-uṣur	(Governor) of Arrapḫa	In the month Iyyar, day 13,	745
	Tiglath-pileser	took the throne.	
	[In the month] Tishri, to Between-the-River(s)	he marched.	
Bel-dan	(Governor) of Calah	To Namri	744
	10 years, [Ashur-nerari], king of Assyria		

Tiglath-pileser (III)	King of Assyria	In Arpad,	743
	a defeat on Urartu	was inflicted.	
Nabu-daʾʾinanni	Commander-in-chief	To Arpad	742
Bel-Ḫarran-bela-uṣur	Palace herald	To DITTO; captured after three years	741
Nabu-eṭeranni	Chief cupbearer	To Arpad	740
Sin-taklak	Chief treasurer To Ulluba;	Birtu taken	739
Adad-bela-kaʾʾin	Governor of Ashur	Calneh captured	738
Bel-emuranni	(Governor) of Raṣappa	To Media	737
Ninurta-ilaya	(Governor) of Niṣibin	To the foot of Mount Nal	736
Ashur-shallimanni	(Governor) of Arrapḫa	To Urartu	735
Bel-dan	(Governor) of Calah	To Philistia	734
Ashur-daʾʾinanni	(Governor) of Mazamua	To Damascus	733
Nabu-bela-uṣur	(Governor) of Siʾimme	To Damascus	732
Nergal-uballiṭ	(Governor) of Aḫizuḫina	To Shapiya	731
Bel-lu-dari	(Governor) of Tille	In the land	730
Lipḫur-ilu	(Governor) of Ḫabruri	The king took the hand of Bel	729
Dur-Ashur	(Governor) of Tushḫan. The king	took the hand of Bel; the city of Ḫi[ ]	728

Bel-Ḫarran-bela-uṣur	(Governor) of [Go]zan	To [ ]	727
	[Shalman]eser	[ascend]ed the t[hrone]	
Marduk-bela-uṣur	(Governor) [of Ame]di	I[n *the land* ?]	726
Maḫde	(Governor) of Nineveh	To [ ]	725
Ashur-ishmanni	(Governor) [of Kili]zi	To [ ]	724
	[ ] years		

Name of Eponym	Title	Event	Year
Shalmaneser (V)	King of [Assyria]	T[o]	723
Ninurta-ilaya	[	]	722
Nabu-tariṣ	[	-t]i	721
Ashur-nirka-daʾʾin	[	]	720
	[ye]ars		
Sargon (II)	King of [Assyria]	[en]tered	719
Zeru-ibni	Governor of Ra[ṣappa]	[To Ta]bal	718
Ṭab-shar-Ashur	Chief treasurer		717
	[*The foundations of*	Dur-Sharru]kin laid	
Ṭab-ṣil-Esharra	Governor of Ashur	[To] Mannea	716
Taklak-ana-beli	Governor of Niṣibin	[ ] governors appointed	715
Ishtar-duri	Governor of Arrapḫa	[To Ur]artu; Muṣaṣir; (the god) Ḫaldia	714
Ashur-bani	Governor of Calah	[the no]bles in Ellipi.	713
	[*The god X*]	entered his new tem[ple].	
		[T]o Muṣaṣir	
Sharru-emuranni	Governor of Mazamu[a]	In the land	712
Ninurta-alik-pani	Governor of Siʾimme	To Marʾash	711
Shamash-bela-uṣur	Governor of Ar[zuḫina]	To Bit-zeri. The king stayed the night in Kish	710
Mannu-ki-Ashur-leʾi	Governor of Tille	Sargon took the hand of Bel	709
Shamash-upaḫḫir	Governor of Ḫab[ru]ri	Kummuḫ captured; a governor appointed (var. Nobles against Kummuḫ *x x*)	708
Sha-Ashur-dubbu	Governor of Tushḫan	The king returned from Babylon.	707
	The administrator, the nobles, [the boo]ty	of Dur-Yakin carried off.	
	[ ]	Dur-Yakin destroyed	
The month Tishri, day 22,	the gods of Dur-Sharrukin	[entered their] temples.	
Mutakkil-Ashur	Governor of Gozan	The nobles	706
	The king in the land	[in Karalla.]	
The month Iyyar, day 6,	Dur-Sharrukin	the king [ ] received.	
Nasḫur-bel	Governor of Amedi	The king [ ]	705
against Gurdi	the Kulummaean;	[ ]	
the king was killed;	the camp of the king of Assyria	[ ]	
In the month Ab, day 12,	Sennacherib, so[n *of*	*Sargon became king* ?]	
Nabu-deni-epush	Governor of Nineveh	T[o]	704

Name of Eponym	Title	Event	Year
Larak,	Sarabanu	[ ];	
the palace of Kilizi was built; … [ ]		[ ]	
the nobles against [ ]		[ ]	
Nuḫshaya	Governor of Kilizi	[ ]	703
Nabu-leʾi	Governor of Arbela	[ ]	702
Ḫananu	Governor of Til-Barsip	From Ḫalzi *x* [ ]	701
Mitunu	Governor of Isana	[ ]	700
[Ash]ur-nadin-shumi, son of [Sennacherib		]	
of the palace in the city [		]	
great cedar beams [		]	
alabaster	in Mount	]	
in Kapar-dargil[i		]	
to [		]	
[ ] the king … [		]	

805–796 BCE—During this decade, Adad-nerari III was mostly engaged in re-establishing Assyria's presence in the West as is indicated by the objectives listed in the Chronicle and the summary descriptions on the royal monuments; see Text nos. 2.01, 2.02, 2.03.

786–784 BCE—There is a different order of eponyms for these three years on the Sultantepe tablet. One of the Nineveh manuscripts has Balaṭu as eponym for 786; this has sometimes been explained by positing Balaṭu's death early in the year, after which Nabu-sharra-uṣur took the post. If so, it would seem that the office of eponym was not merely an honorary title, but carried certain state (and ritual?) duties, requiring the position to be filled on the demise of the eponym.

775, 774–772 BCE—Assyria returned to the West after an absence of several decades; see Text no. 3.01.

745 BCE—According to the Chronicle, Tiglath-pileser III took the throne in the second month (Iyyar) and so 743, his second full year, was the year of his eponymate. Contrariwise, the authors of the royal inscriptions counted 745 as his "first year."

742–740 BCE—The extended three-year siege of Arpad sought to root out the influence of Urartu in northern Syria and to reassert Assyrian hegemony in this area. The note concerning the capture of Arpad, written in the line for 741, belongs to 740.

738 BCE—The fragmentary annal report of the engagement with Azriyau and the list of tributaries in the annals relate to this year; see Text nos. 4.01, 4.02, 4.03. Calneh, Kullania in Neo-Assyrian, is identified with Tell Ta^{c}yinat in Unqi (Patina).

734–732 BCE—The Assyrian campaigns to Philistia and Damascus are treated in the Summary Inscriptions, Text nos. 4.05–4.08, annal fragments, Text nos. 4.09–4.10, and in the Bible, 2 Kgs 15:29, 16:7–9. In actuality, there was a single, extended campaign during these three years. In 734, after securing control of the coast down to the border with Egypt at the Wadi of Egypt, the Assyrian army moved north to Damascus to beset the city for two years (733–732), during which they marched against the Israelite Galilee and Transjordan.

729 BCE—Tiglath-pileser III participated in the Babylonian New Year's ceremony, a sign of recognition by the local priesthood of the legitimacy of his rule; cf. entry for year 709. For the expression "took the hand of Bel," see Text no. 11.05, obv. line 14.

727 BCE—There are no signs preserved after the word "To"; therefore the early restored reading: "To Da[mascus]" (see *ARAB* 2, §1198) has no basis and should not be utilized in historical studies as is still sometimes done.

723 BCE—The delay by Shalmaneser V in assuming the eponymate is most unusual; perhaps this was due to his protracted stay in the West on campaign; see Finkel and Reade 1998:253.

712 BCE—The note that Sargon was "in the land" should be compared to the claim put forward in his inscriptions that he personally led the campaign to Ashdod; see Text nos. 5.01, 5.08.

705 BCE—The Anatolian name of Sargon's enemy, Gurdi, confirms the suggestion that the king found his death in the campaign to Tabal referred to in the Babylonian Chronicle.

700 BCE—Ashur-nadin-shumi, Sennacherib's eldest son, was appointed king in Babylonia after the final ouster of Merodach-baladan. He reigned for six years until 694, when hostilities between Assyria and the Chaldeans broke out once again, during which some Babylonians handed him over to the king of Elam. His fate in Elamite hands is unknown.

References

Cogan, Mordechai
2013 *Bound for Exile*, Jerusalem.

Finkel, Irving L. and Julian E. Reade
1998 Assyrian Eponyms, 873–649 BC, *Or* 67:250–254.

Horowitz, Wayne and Takayoshi Oshima
2006 *Cuneiform in Canaan: Cuneiform Sources from the Land of Israel in Ancient Times*, Jerusalem.

Matilla, Raija
2000 *The King's Magnates: A Study of the Highest Officials of the Neo-Assyrian Empire*, SAAS 11, Helsinki.
2009 The Chief Singer and Other Late Eponyms. Pp. 159-166 in Mikko Luukko et al. (eds.), *Of God(s), Trees, Kings, and Scholars. Neo-Assyrian and Related Studies in Honour of Simo Parpola*, Studia Orientalia 106, Helsinki.

Millard, Alan
1994 *The Eponyms of the Assyrian Empire 910–612 BC*, SAAS 2, Helsinki.

Reade, Julian E.
1998 Assyrian Eponyms, Kings and Pretenders, 648–605 BC, *Or* 67:255–265.

Ungnad, Arthur
1938 Eponymen. Pp. 412–457 in vol. 2 of *RlA*.

Weissert, Elnatan
1992 Interrelated Chronographic Patterns in the Assyrian Eponym Chronicle and the "Babylonian Chronicle": A Comparative View. Pp. 273–281 in D. Charpin and F. Joannès (eds.), *La circulation des biens, des personnes et des idées dans le Proche-Orient ancien*, Paris.

Whiting, Robert
1994 The Post-Canonical and Extra-Canonical Eponyms. Pp. 72–78 in Alan Millard, *The Eponyms of the Assyrian Empire 910–612 BC*, SAAS 2, Helsinki.

Zawadski, Stefan
1997 The Question of the King's Eponymate in the Latter Half of the 8th Century and the 7th Century BC. Pp. 383–389 in S. Parpola and R. M. Whiting (eds.), *ASSYRIA 1995. Proceedings of the 10th Anniversary Symposium of the Neo-Assyrian Text Corpus Project Helsinki, September 7–11, 1995*, Helsinki.

Fig. 30. Babylonian Chronicle tablet (*Courtesy of the Trustees of the British Museum*).

CHAPTER 11

NEO-BABYLONIAN CHRONICLES

The essential characteristic of the chronicle texts is their orderly arrangement according to the regnal years; this chronological principle is upheld even in those instances where certain years or an entire reign are skipped over. The literary style of the chronicles is, as a rule, succinct and straightforward, and in many cases, three to four lines summarize an entire year, though examples of fuller reports are also known. The topics most often recorded include: battle reports (both victories and defeats), state affairs and cultic matters. The reports contain no argumentation or justification and so the impression of objectivity, that is, the events are presented "as they truly happened," is overriding. At the same time, it is certain that scribes selected from a large source of data those events they considered significant for inclusion in their chronicles. Chronistic writing was at home in Babylonia, where it appears most developed, though there are indications that this genre was also known in Assyria, though it did not take root there. See further in Introduction.

The interest in recording of near-contemporary history as evidenced in the Neo-Babylonian Chronicles has been traced to the mid-eighth century BCE, to the reign of Nabonassar, traditionally seen an age of innovation in a number of intellectual pursuits (Hallo 1988). Apparently it continued through the Persian and Hellenistic periods, though there are great gaps in our sources; see the collections of Grayson 1975; Finkel and van der Speck 2004.

NO. 11.01—THE REIGNS OF NABONASSAR TO SHAMASH-SHUM-UKIN

This chronicle text surveys events in Babylonia from the reign of Nabonassar (747–734 BCE) until the accession of Shamash-shum-ukin (668–648 BCE). The years during which kings of Assyria served as kings of Babylon are also included. In a number of instances, events in Elam, Babylon's neighbor to the east and its support in the struggle against Assyria, is also noted.

Three copies of this chronicle are extant, the fullest being a very large tablet from Babylon (193 mm long × 158 mm wide) divided into four columns, two on each side. The size of the tablet and its arrangement, as well as the note in the colophon that it was "the first section" of a series, point to the tablet's being a library copy, that is, a reference text. Its date: "The [+]6th day of [the month of . . .], the twenty-second year of Darius, king of Babylon and all the lands" (499 BCE).

Three selections follow: the first one summarizes in a few lines the reigns of Tiglath-pileser III and Shalmaneser V, the second tells of Sargon's rule as king of Babylon, and the third covers, year by year, the period from the murder of Sennacherib until the accession of Ashurbanipal.

Text edition: Grayson 1975:69–87, No. 1.
Translations: *TGI* 60; *ANET* 301–303; *TPOA* 105–106, 126; *TUAT* 1 / 4, 401–402; *COS* 1, 467; Glassner 2004:193–207; *TUAT* NF II, 35-40; *HTAT* 300–301, 335.
Photographs: Grayson 1975, plates xii–xiii.

Obv. col. i

Year 3. Mukin-zeri. Tiglath-pileser
when he went down to Akkad
he destroyed Bit-Amukani and captured Mukin-zeri.
Three years Mukin-zeri ruled Babylon.
Tiglath-pileser ascended the throne in Babylon.

Year 2. Tiglath-pileser in the month Tebeth (went to his) fate.
‹Eighteen years› Tiglath-pileser ruled Akkad
and Assyria. Two years he ruled Akkad.
(In) the month Tebeth, day 25, Shalmaneser in Assyria
‹and Akkad› ascended the throne. He destroyed Samaria.

Year 5. Shalmaneser in the month Tebeth (went to his) fate.
Five years Shalmaneser ruled Akkad and Assyria.
(In) the month Tebeth, day 12, Sargon ascended the throne in Assyria.
In the month Nisan, Merodach-baladan ascended the throne in Babylon.

Year 2. Merodach-baladan. Ummanigash, king of Elam, in the district of Der, engaged Sargon, king of Assyria, in battle and caused the Assyrians to retreat; he inflicted a great defeat upon them. Merodach-baladan and his troops, who to the aid of the king of Elam had marched, did not reach the battle (in time), and he withdrew.

Obv. col. ii

Year 12. Merodach-baladan. Sargon went down [to Akkad] and engaged [Merodach-bal]adan in battle. Merodach-baladan [retreated] before him; he escaped to Elam. Twelve years [Merodach-balad]an ruled Babylon. Sargon ascended the throne in Babylon.

Year 13. Sargon to[ok] the hand of Bel. He captu[red] Dur-Yakin.

Year 14. The king (stayed) in [the land].

Year 15. The month Tishri, day 22, the gods of the Sealand [to] their [*shrines*] returned. There was plague in Assyria.

[Year *17*. Sarg]on to Tabal [marched].

Rev. col. iii

Year 8. There was no king in Babylon. The month Tammuz, day 3, the gods of Uruk (went) from [Assyr]ia (and) entered Uruk. In the month Tishri, day 23, Ḫumban-[ḫal]tash, king of Elam, at midday, was paralyzed and died at sunset. Eight years Ḫumban-ḫaltash ruled Elam. Ḫumban-ḫaltash the Second, his [son] ascended the throne. The month Tebeth, day 20, Sennacherib, king of Assyria, his son killed him in a rebellion. [Twenty-four] years Sennacherib ruled Assyria. From day 20 of the month Tebeth until day 2 of the month Adar, the rebellion continued.

The month Adar, day [1]8 (or [2]8), Esarhaddon his son, ascended the throne in Assyria.

Year 1. Esarhaddon. Zer-kitti-lishir, governor of the Sealand, when he went upstream, he encamped against Ur; he did no[t *take*] the city. He fled from the officers of Assyria and [*entered*] Elam. In Elam, the king of Elam captured him and killed him by the sword. An unknown month. In Nippur, the governor [ ] In the month Elul, Ishtaran and the gods [of Der] went [from] to Der. *x x* [ ] went to Dur-Sharrukin [ ] In the month Adar *x x x x* [ ]

[Year 2.] The chief steward [ ] *x* [ ] *x* [ ]

Col. iv

[Year 3. -aḫ]ḫe-Shullim, the governor (of Nippur) [(and) Shamash-ibni, son of Dakk]uri, were taken to Assyria and in Assyria were killed.

[Year 4.] Sidon was captured and plundered. [In the sa]me [year,] the chief steward raised a levy in Akkad.

Year 5. The month Tishri, day 5, the army of Assyria captured Bazza. In the month Tishri, the head of the king of Sidon was cut off and brought to Assyria. In the month Adar, the head of the king of Kundu and Sissu was cut off and brought to Assyria.

Year 6. The king of Elam entered Sippar. There was a slaughter. Shamash did not go out of (the temple) Ebabbarra. Assyria ‹marched› to Melid. (The month) Elul, (day) 7, Ḫumban-ḫaltash, king of Elam, without being ill, died in his palace. For five years Ḫumban-ḫaltash ruled Elam. Urtaku, his brother, ascended the throne in Elam.

In an unknown month, Shuma-iddina, the governor (of Nippur)
and Kudurru, son of Dakkuri, were brought to Assyria.

Year 7. (In) the month Adar, day 5, the army of Assyria was defeated in Egypt.
In the month Adar, Ishtar of Agade and the gods of Agade
went from Elam and in the month of Adar, day 10, entered Agade.

Year 8. Esarhaddon. The month Tebeth, day [broken]
Shubria was captured and plundered.
In the month Kislev, its booty reached Uruk.
(In) the month Adar, day 5, the wife of the king died.

Year 10. (In) the month Nisan, the army of Assyria marched to Egypt. [broken]
The month Tammuz, day 3, day 16, day 18,
Three times, there was a slaughter in Egypt.
Day 22, Memphis, the royal city, was taken.
Its king saved himself; his son and his bro[ther were cap]tured.
It was plundered; its people were taken captive, its property carried off.

Year 11. In Assyria, the king executed a large number of his nobles.

Year 12. The king of Assyria marched to Egypt.
On the way, he became ill and in the month Marcheshvan, day 10, (went to his) fate.
Twelve years Esarhaddon ruled Assyria.
Shamash-shum-ukin in Babylon and Ashurbanipal in Assyria, his two sons, ascended the throne.

The accession year. Shamash-shum-ukin. In the month Iyyar
Bel and the gods of Akkad from the city Ashur
went out and in the month Iyyar, day [14/24 ?] entered Babylon.
(In) the same year, Qirbit was tak[en,] its king captured.
(In) the month Tebeth, day 20, Bel-eṭir, judge of Babylon, was captured and killed.

Col. i,

19 **Year 3 (of) Mukin-zeri**—729 BCE. Nabu-mukin-zeri, a member of the Bit-Amukani tribe of Chaldeans, seized the throne in Babylon and ruled for three years (732–729 BCE), until he was ousted by Tiglath-pileser III.

24 **Year 2**—727 BCE. The years are counted according to the number of years Tiglath-pileser reigned in Babylon.

25–26 **‹Eighteen years› Tiglath-pileser ruled Akkad and Assyria**—The number is missing for some unknowable reason. The scribe generally indicated that his source text was faulty by writing "broken" at the break (see, for example, rev. col. iv, lines 19, 23); he did not do so in the present instance. Perhaps the source had a blank at this point and the scribe considered coming back later to fill it in after he had checked another text, but forgot to do so.

28 **He destroyed Samaria**—The text gives the Babylonian form of the name *Šamaraʾin*; for the Assyrian form, see Text no. 5.01, line 25. The major event of the five-year rule of Shalmaneser V was the conquest of Samaria. This is the only historical datum from cuneiform sources associated with Shalmaneser, as no royal inscriptions from his reign have been recovered. The year in which Samaria fell cannot be determined because the scribe did not indicate the year of the event; he simply included it between the lines that separated the years of Shalmaneser V from those of his predecessor and his successor (so Becking 1992:22–25; for a different view, see Na'aman 1990).

The submission of Israel to Shalmaneser, followed by its rebellion and the capture of Samaria, reported in 2 Kgs 17:3–6a, are likely to have taken place during the time that the Assyrian king conducted an extended campaign against Tyre, information for which comes from Josephus (*Antiquities* 9.283–287).

29 **Year 5**—722 BCE.

31 **(In) the month Tebeth, day 12, Sargon ascended the throne in Assyria**—The accession year of Sargon II lasted two and a half months, after which his first regnal year was counted.

32 **In the month Nisan, Merodach-baladan ascended the throne in Babylon**—Merodach-baladan (Akkadian *Marduk-apla-iddina*) took control of Babylon for twelve years, until he was ousted by Sargon; cf. below, col ii, lines 1–5 and Text no. 5.01. Merodach-baladan is reported to have sent "get-well wishes" to Hezekiah, king of Judah (cf. 2 Kgs 20:12–13), an act that may have

had wider, conspiratorial connotations. For his biography, see the study of Brinkman 1964.

33 **Year 2**—720 BCE. The years are counted from the accession of Merodach-baladan.

33–35 **Merodach-baladan. Ummanigash, king of Elam, in the district of Der, engaged Sargon, king of Assyria, in battle and caused Assyria's retreat; he inflicted a great defeat upon them**—In Sargon's inscriptions, victory belongs to the Assyrians; see Text no. 5.01, lines 23–27, and discussion there.

36–37 **Merodach-baladan and his troops, who to the aid of the king of Elam had marched, did not reach the battle (in time), and he withdrew**—The same phrase is used in a later chronicle with reference to the attack on the city of Ashur; see Text no. 11.03, line 28.

Obv. col. ii

1 **Year 12**—710 BCE.

Sargon drove Merodach-baladan from Babylon, having failed to do so at the battle of Der in 720. But the Chaldean continued to be a thorn in the side of Assyria for at least another decade until he was driven from Babylonia for the last time by Sennacherib in 700.

6 **Year 13**—709 BCE.

Sargon to[ok] the hand of Bel—The entry in the Eponym Chronicle (Text no. 10.01) for this year records the same ritual act, on which see Text no. 11.05, line 14.

7 **Year 14**—708 BCE.

The king (stayed) in [the land]—That is, Babylonia. The Eponym Chronicle for 707 notes that Sargon returned to Assyria in that year.

11 **[Year *17*]**—705 BCE.

Sarg]on to Tabal [marched]—According to the Eponym Chronicle for 706, the king stayed home; it is not unusual for the Babylonian Chronicle to skip over a year (or years) of inactivity or inconsequence. The year 705 was Sargon's last regnal year, the one in which he lost his life.

Rev. iii,

28 **Year 8**—681 BCE.

There was no king in Babylon—After capturing and destroying Babylon in 689 BCE, Sennacherib did not assume the title "king of Babylon" and in effect abolished the monarchy in Babylonia.

28–29 **The month Tammuz, day 3, the gods of Uruk (went) from [Assyr]ia (and) entered Uruk**—Uruk, modern Warka, Erech in biblical sources (e.g., Gen 10:10), lies some 200 km southeast of Babylon. The divine images had been removed from Uruk in 693 BCE as a punitive measure against this Babylonian city that had rebelled against Sennacherib. The immediate cause for their return after twelve years of "exile" is not clear.

34–35 **The month Tebeth, day 20, Sennacherib, king of Assyria, his son killed him in a rebellion**—A complementary statement concerning the assassination is given in 2 Kgs 19:37: "As he was worshiping in the house of his god Nisroch, his sons Adrammelech and Sharezer killed him with the sword, and they escaped into the land of Ararat. His son Esarhaddon succeeded him." The identity of the murderer, as disclosed by a letter sent to Esarhaddon, was Arda-Mullissu; see the full exposition by Parpola 1980; also the discussion in Text no. 6.05.

39 **Year 1**—680 BCE.

Esarhaddon—There is a duplicate of the text from this point on that is known as the "Esarhaddon Chronicle" (Grayson 1975:125–128, No. 14). Its variant readings are noted in the following comments.

39–42 **Zer-kitti-lishir, governor of the Sealand**—Nabu-zer-kitti-lishir was the son of Merodach-baladan and leader of the Bit-Yakin tribe that resided near the Persian Gulf (here "the Sealand"). He did not recognize Esarhaddon's rule in Babylon and threatened the city of Ur (Tell al-Muqayyar in southern Babylonia). He fled to Elam in the hope of finding refuge, but Ḫumban-ḫaltash, king of Elam, had him killed.

44 **In the month Elul, Ishtaran and the gods [of Der] went [from] to Der**—The images of the city of Der had been held in Assyria since their seizure by Shamshi-Adad V at the end of the ninth century.

46 **Went to Dur-Sharrukin [ ]**—Perhaps the city is Dur-Sharruku, a Babylonian city northeast of Sippar.

48 **[Year 2]**—679 BCE.

Col. iv,

1 **[Year 3]**—678 BCE.

1–2 **[-aḫ]ḫe-Shullim, the governor (of Nippur) [(and) Shamash-ibni, son of Dakk]uri, were taken to Assyria and in Assyria were killed**—Shamash-ibni, the leader of the Bit-Dakkuri tribe in southern Babylonia, was executed together with the governor of Nippur for having confiscated land and stirring up disturbances in the vicinity of Babylon and Borsippa; see Frame 1992:79–81.

3 **[Year 4]**—677 BCE.

Sidon was captured and plundered—The capture of Sidon is reported in several of Esarhaddon's inscriptions; see Text no. 8.02, col. ii, 65–82.

5 **Year 5**—676 BCE.

5–6 **The month Tishri, day 5, the army of Assyria captured Bazza**—The location of the land of Bazza is unknown; perhaps it should be sought in the northeast Arabian desert, west of the Persian Gulf; so Eph^{c}al 1982:130–137. The biblical Buz (cf. Gen 22:21; Jer 25:23) is of other origin.

In the month Tishri, the head of the king of Sidon was cut off... In the month Adar, the head of the king of Kundu and Sissu was cut off—It is possible that the assignment of the report to Year 5 is erroneous; in Esarhaddon's inscriptions dated to 677, the decapitation is already recorded (see Eph^{c}al 1982:54). The beheaded were Abdi-milkutti, king of Sidon, and Sanduarri, king of Kundu and Sissu; see Text no. 8.02, col. ii, lines 65–82. The cities Kundu and Sissu were situated north of Que. Tadmor (2004:269–270) speculated that the severing of the heads was part of a victory celebration at the *Akitu* festivities of the months of Tishri and Nisan.

9–10 **Year 6**—675 BCE.

The king of Elam entered Sippar. There was a slaughter. Shamash did not go out of (the temple) Ebabbarra—The Elamite attack on Sippar and the accompanying massacre contradicts other information that points to good relations between Assyria and Elam at this time. Note is taken of the disruption of the cult of Shamash. This event is not reported in the "Esarhaddon Chronicle."

12 **For five years Ḫumban-ḫaltash ruled Elam**—The scribe erred in his copying because Ḫumban-ḫaltash had reigned six years, having taken the throne in Esarhaddon's accession year (see above, col. iii, line 33); the parallel chronicle

text indeed records "six years" at this point (Grayson 1975:126, No. 14, line 17).

14–15 **Shuma-iddina, the governor (of Nippur) and Kudurru, son of Dakkuri, were brought to Assyria**—Their incarceration in Assyria was apparently followed by their execution; see Grayson 1975:126, No. 14, line 19. Their crime is unknown; cf. above the entry for 678 BCE and what may have been similar circumstances.

16 **Year 7**—674 BCE.

(In) the month Adar, day 5, the army of Assyria was defeated in Egypt—This first Assyrian attempt to invade Egypt is not reported in any Assyrian source; the so-called "Esarhaddon Chronicle" (see above, note to col. iii, line 39) skips over this defeat and in its place records: "(In) the month Adar, day 8, the Assyrian army [marched] to Sha-amile" in southern Babylonia (Grayson 1975:126, No. 14, line 20). It has been suggested that prior to this unsuccessful invasion of the Delta, the Assyrian army engaged an Egyptian force in Philistia, near Ashkelon; see note to Text no. 8.04, lines 7–35; Spalinger 1974:298–302; for this encounter see, too, Tadmor 1966:99–100; Kahn 2004:110, and n. 19.

17–18 **Ishtar of Agade and the gods of Agade went from Elam and . . . entered Agade**—The return of the images to Agade likely took place after an accord had been reached between Esarhaddon and Urtaku, the new Elamite king.

19 **Year 8**—673 BCE.

The month Tebeth, day broken—The scribe indicated that the text he was copying was broken at this point and that he was unable to complete the gap.

20 **Shubria was captured and plundered**—Located southwest of Lake Van.

21–22 **In the month Kislev, its booty reached Uruk**—An error in calculation or copying. The spoil from Shubria reached Uruk a month before the fall of the city—Kislev is the ninth month, Tebeth, the tenth month in the Babylonian calendar. Note should also be taken that a Babylonian city and not one in Assyria was the benefactor of the booty, evidence of Esarhaddon's policy of reconciliation with Babylon (Brinkman 1984:71–84).

[Year 9]—672 BCE. The ninth year is not noted and no summary of events is given; the source text may have been faulty at this point, but the scribe did not indicate this. This year is also missing from the parallel "Esarhaddon Chronicle," suggesting that both chronicles depended on the same source.

23 **Year 10**—671 BCE.

25 **Three times, there was a slaughter in Egypt**—The campaign in Egypt lasted four months (or seven months according to the "Esarhaddon Chronicle" which has "Tishri" instead of "Tammuz"). Another copy of the present chronicle adds: "Its booty was taken and its gods were carried off."

27 **Its king saved himself; his son and his bro[ther were cap]tured**—The flight of Tirhakah is described in Esarhaddon's inscriptions; see Text nos. 8.03, 8.04, 8.05.

29 **Year 11**—670 BCE.

In Assyria, the king executed a large number of his officers—The reason for the revolt is not noted; some suggest that it was instigated by the issue of succession to the throne.

30 **Year 12**—669 BCE.

30–31 **The king of Assyria marched to Egypt. On the way, he became ill and in the month Marcheshvan, day 10, (went to his) fate**—Esarhaddon's death brought an end to the campaign that sought to quell the rebellion that had broken out in Egypt; it remained for Ashurbanipal to resume his father's operations; see Text no. 9.01, col. i, lines 52–67.

33 **Shamash-shum-ukin in Babylon and Ashurbanipal in Assyria, his two sons, ascended the throne**—Upon Esarhaddon's death while on campaign to Egypt, the arrangements for the succession he had made in 672 BCE were carried out: Ashurbanipal took the throne in Assyria, Shamash-shum-ukin the throne in Babylon.

34 **The accession year. Shamash-shum-ukin**—From the data given here, it is clear that the accession of Shamash-shum-ukin was delayed until the next year for some unexplained reason.

34–36 **In the month Iyyar Bel and the gods of Akkad from the city Ashur went out and in the month Iyyar, day [14/24 ?] entered Babylon**—The images of Babylon's gods had been held in Ashur since their removal by Sennacherib in 689. Their return followed the rehabilitation of the temples of Babylon by Esarhaddon. Another chronicle text notes that the *Akitu*, the Babylonian

New Year festival, had been suspended throughout the twenty years of the gods' sojourn in Assyria (Grayson 1975:131, No. 16, lines 1–4).

37 **(In) the same year, Qirbit was tak[en,] its king captured**—Ashurbanipal inscriptions explain the action against Qirbit, a city in the mountains east of Babylon, as a response to the marauding raids that originated from that direction.

38 **(In) the month Tebeth, day 20, Bel-eṭir, judge of Babylon, was captured and killed**—Nothing else is known of this incident, nor is Bel-eṭir identifiable, as several persons bear this name. But treasonous activity was surely the cause for his execution. See Frame 1992:117–118.

11.02—THE ASCENT OF NABOPOLASSAR—THE REBELLION AGAINST ASSYRIA

The deaths of Ashurbanipal, king of Assyria and Kandalanu, the Assyrian-appointed king of Babylonia, in the same year, 627 BCE, led to instability and fighting in both countries. Rivalry over the succession to the throne in Nineveh between Ashur-etil-ilani and Sin-shar-ishkun, sons of Ashurbanipal, encouraged Nabopolassar, a Babylonian of unknown background, to lead an attack on Assyria and, in the following year, to proclaim himself king. For the next fourteen years, Nabopolassar led his forces, at times associated with the army of the Medes, in an almost continuous war, not only to free Babylon, but to avenge its treatment under Assyrian rule. After the fall of Nineveh in 612 BCE, Babylon continued to pursue its newly embraced imperial goals into the areas of the former Assyrian empire: Egypt, its main rival in the West, was defeated, while areas to the North and East seem to have passed to the control of Media, its former ally.

The events of these years of conflict are recorded in the Babylonian Chronicle, known from a series of tablets of varying sizes, many of them with large gaps. The tablet covering the years 627–623 BCE is shaped like a small Neo-Babylonian business document (52 mm long x 60 mm wide); its upper left-hand corner is broken away.

Text edition: Grayson 1975:89–90, No. 2.
Translations: Glassner 2004:214–219; *TUAT* NF II, 408–410; *HTAT*, 408–410.

1 [*to*] Babylon which he had sent at night

[ ]*x* they did battle within the city all day.
[*the garris*]*on* of Sin-shar-ishkun fled to Assyria.
[with]in the city he appointed. In the month Elul, day 12, the army of Assyria
[*went down*], entered the city of Shaznaku, set fire to the temple,
[*and took its spoil*] and in the month Tishri, the gods of Kish went to Babylon.
[The army of] Assyria marched to Nippur and Nabopolassar retreated before them.
[The army of Ass]yria and the people of Nippur followed him as far as Uruk.
Within Uruk, they did battle against Nabopolassar and retreated before Nabopolassar.
In the month Iyyar, the army of Assyria went down to Akkad. In the month of Tishri, day 12, when the army of Assyria
had marched to Babylon, on that day when the Babylonians
came out of Babylon, they attacked the army of Assyria;
they inflicted a major defeat on the army of Assyria (and) plundered them.
For one year there was no king in the land. The month Marcheshvan, day 26, Nabopolassar
ascended the throne in Babylon.

The accession year of Nabopolassar. In the month Adar,
the gods of Susa that Assyria had carried off and placed in Uruk,
those gods Nabopolassar sent back to Susa.

Year 1. Nabopolassar. The month Nisan, day 17, panic fell on the city (Babylon).
Shamash and the gods of Shapazzu went to Babylon.
The month Iyyar, day 21, the army of Assyria entered Sal[lat] and carried off its property.
‹The month Sivan/Tammuz›, day 20, the gods of Sippar went to Babylon.
The month Ab, day 9, Nabopolassar and his army marched to Sal[lat].
He attacked Sallat, but did not take the city. The army of Assyria arrived, so
he retreated before them and withdrew.

[Year 2]. Nabopolassar. At the beginning of the month of Elul, the army of Assyria
went down [to Akkad] and camped by the Banitu canal.

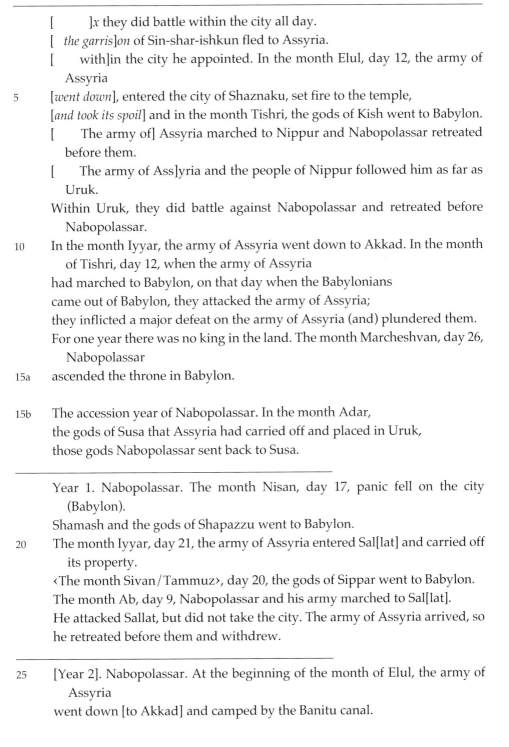

They did [battle against Nab]opolassar, but gained nothing.
[ ] *x x* and they withdrew.

[Year 3. The month *x*, d]ay 8. The city of Der rebelled against Assyria. The month Tishri, day 15
[In that] year, the king of Assyria and his army went down to Akkad and
[ ] *x x* and brought it into Nippur. Afterwards, Itti-ili
[ravag]ed and stationed a garrison in Nippur.
[ ] he went up [from / to] "Beyond-the-River" and against
[ ] he ravaged; he set out for Nineveh.
[ ] who had set out to do battle with him.
[when(?)] they saw him, they bowed down before him.
[ ]

Left edge

The rebel king [ ]
One hundred days [ ]
[ ] when *x* [ ]
[ ] the rebel *x* [ ]

---

1 **[*to*] Babylon which he had sent at night [ ]*x* they did battle within the city all day—**

[*the garris*]*on* of Sin-shar-ishkun fled to Assyria—Son of Ashurbanipal and contender for the throne following his father's death in 627. It is not clear from this line whether he was recognized as king of Assyria or was general of the Assyrian forces.

The army of Assyria [*went down*], entered the city of Shaznaku, set fire to the temple [and took its spoil]—No Assyrian king is referred to as accompanying the army south in its battles with Nabopolassar. This leaves open the question of the recognized successor. The location of Shaznaku is not known; from what follows, it was north of Kish, perhaps on the Diyala River(?) (Wiseman 1961:78).

The gods of Kish went to Babylon—In anticipation of the Assyrian attack, the divine images of Kish were sent to Babylon for safe-keeping; cf. also line 20.

Nabopolassar retreated before them—Nabopolassar lost Nippur, but was able to hold onto Uruk.

Nabopolassar—Little is known of the early history of this future king of Babylon. In a late text Nabopolassar bears the title "king of the Sealand," which may indicate that he had served as an Assyrian appointee in the south prior to his rebellion against Assyria. But this is all that is known of this king who piously speaks of himself as "son of a nobody," that is, without royal pedigree. See the summary of his reign by Brinkman 1998–2001; Beaulieu 2003.

The army of Ass]yria and the people of Nippur followed him as far as Uruk—Nippur had been an important Assyrian stronghold during the years of conflict between Ashurbanipal and the south.

10 **In the month Iyyar**—626 BCE. The royal year, which by Mesopotamian reckoning began in Nisan, had passed.

In the month Tishri, day 12, when the army of Assyria had gone to Babylon . . .—There is a six-month break in the report, but there are other examples of such gaps; see Text no. 11.03, lines 10–11: "In the month Tishri . . . In the month Adar."

For one year there was no king in the land—Following the death of Kandalanu, the Assyrian-appointed king, in 627, Babylon did not recognize the Assyrian pretenders to the throne and so was officially without a king until Nabopolassar proclaimed himself king eight months later.

15b **The accession year of Nabopolassar**—From Fall 626 until Spring 625. Another chronicle text (Grayson 1975:132, lines 24–27 [No. 16]) describes this year as follows:

> After Kandalanu, in the accession year of Nabopolassar, there were uprisings in Assyria and Akkad. There were hostilities (and) battles continued.

The gods of Susa that Assyria had carried off and placed in Uruk, those gods Nabopolassar sent back to Susa—The plundering of the divine images of Susa took place during the last Assyrian campaign against Elam in 645 BCE. Their return by Nabopolassar during the first month of his rule was certainly meant as a gesture of friendship, renewing the political ties between Elam and Babylon severed after the Assyria's wars in both countries.

18 **Year 1. Nabopolassar**—625 BCE.

Shamash and the gods of Shapazzu went to Babylon—A protective measure against the approach of the Assyrians. Shapazzu may have also been in the Diyala region, on the road south to Sippar (Wiseman 1961:78).

The army of Assyria entered Sal[lat] and carried off its property—The Assyrians captured and plundered Sallat, on the Euphrates above Babylon. Nabopolassar failed in his later attempt to retake the city.

25 **[Year 2]. Nabopolassar**—624 BCE.

The army of Assyria went down [to Akkad] and camped by the Banitu canal—The Assyrian army took up a position on the Banitu canal that ran west to east from the Euphrates at Babylon, past Kish to the Tigris. But it was unsuccessful in maintaining its foothold in the heart of Babylonia.

29 **[Year 3]**—623 BCE.

The city of Der rebelled against Assyria—The revolt in Der, north-east of the other Babylonian cities and close to the border of Elam, came on the heels of Nabopolassar's success the previous year.

Afterwards, Itti-ili [ravag]ed and stationed a garrison in Nippur—The Babylonian personage Itti-ili—a general?—is only known from the present text. This line may be evidence for the fall of Nippur to Nabopolassar.

He went up [from/to] "Beyond-the-River"—That is, the territory on the other side (western bank) of the Euphrates, northern Syria. For this Assyrian administrative term, see Text no. 8.02, col. v, 40ff. The subject of this action is unclear; nor is the quarter of the rebel, that is, whether this was a rebellion against Nabopolassar or a report on continuing troubles in Assyria between the contenders to the throne. The "rebel king" headed towards Nineveh and seems to have held out for 100 days.

No. 11.03—THE REIGN OF NABOPOLASSAR—THE MIDDLE YEARS AND THE FALL OF NINEVEH

The tablet covering the years 622–617 is missing. The period 616–610 BCE is preserved on a medium size tablet (132 mm long × 9 mm wide), broken in four parts, with a large hole in the center. These years proved fatal for Assyria's attempt to survive. Despite military support from Egypt, with whom Assyria had contended for many decades over hegemony in the west, Assyria's king Sin-shar-ishkun was unable to prevent the fall of Nineveh

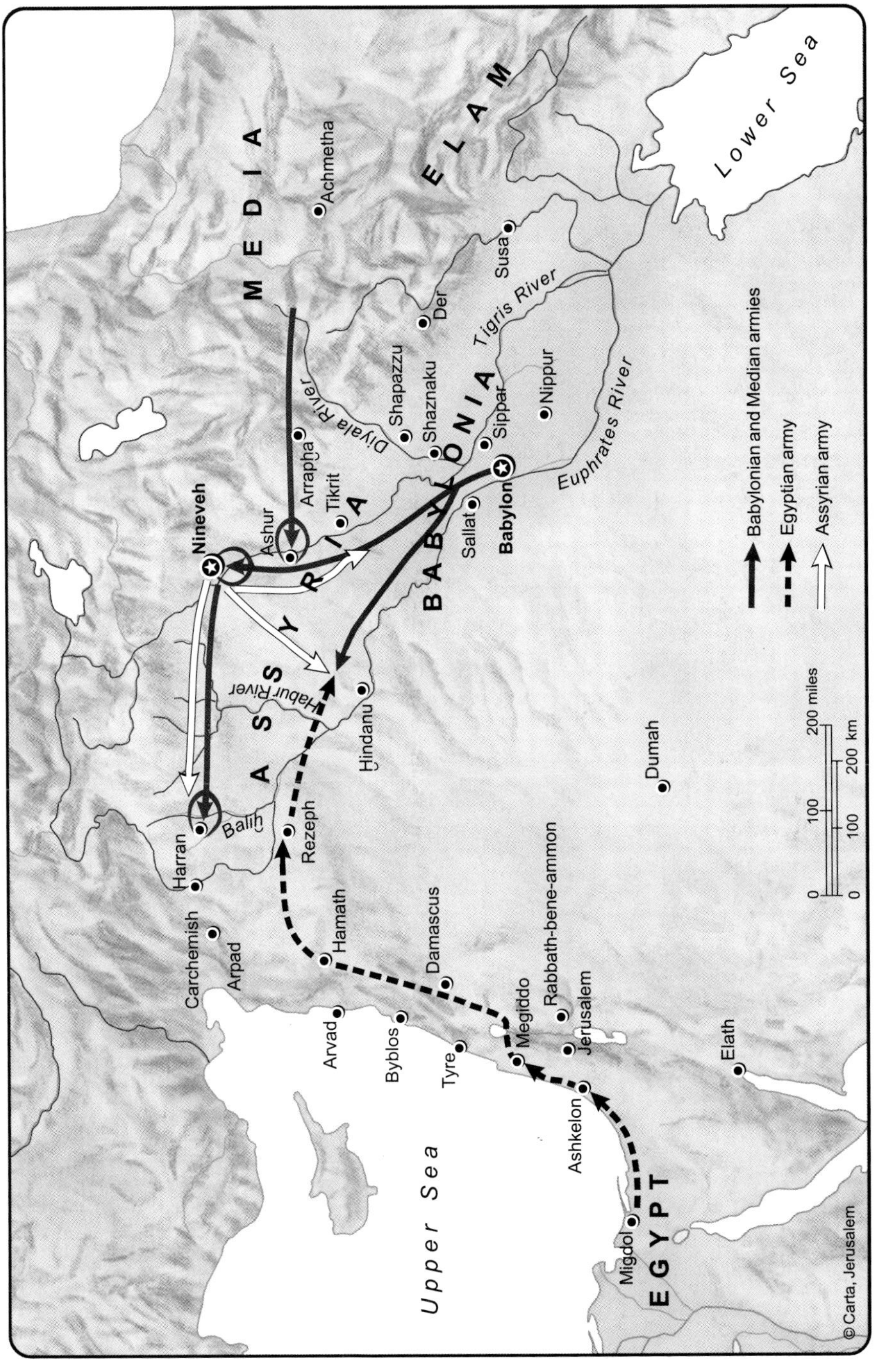

THE LAST YEARS OF ASSYRIA, 616–609 BCE

under the two-pronged assaults of the Babylonians and the Medes. Those who survived regrouped in Harran, but soon faced further attacks from Nabopolassar and his allies.

Text edition: Grayson 1975: 90–96, No. 3.
Translations: *ANET* 303; *TPOA* 136–138; Glassner 2004:218–224; *HTAT* 410–414.

Year 10. In the month Iyyar, Nabopolassar mobilized the troops of Akkad and marched along the bank of the Euphrates.
The Suḫeans and the Ḫindaneans did not attack him; they set their tribute before him.
(In) the month Ab, the army of Assyria arrayed for battle in Gablini. Nabopolassar went up against them.
The month Ab, day 12, he attacked the troops of Assyria and the troops of Assyria retreated before him. He inflicted a major defeat on Assyria
(and) took many of them captive. The Manneans, who had come to their (the Assyrians) aid and the officers of Assyria,
he captured. On that day, he took Gablini. In the month Ab, the king of Akkad (and) his army
went upstream to the cities of Mane, Saḫiri and Baliḫu and took captives from them (and)
took much spoil from them; they carried off their gods. In the month Elul, the king of Akkad and his troops
turned back and on his way, he took (the people of) Ḫindanu and its gods to Babylon.
In the month Tishri, the troops of Egypt and the troops of Assyria marched against the king of Akkad at Gablini, but
they did not overtake the king of Akkad (and) they withdrew. In the month Adar, the troops of Assyria and the troops of Akkad
attacked one another at Madanu of Arrapḫa, and the troops of Assyria
retreated before the troops of Akkad and they (the troops of Akkad) inflicted a great defeat upon them; they pushed them back to the River Zab.
They captured their char[iots] and their horses and took many captives.
They took many of his [ ] with them across the Tigris and brought (them) to Babylon.

[Year 11. The king of] Akkad mobilized his troops and marched along the bank of the Tigris and in the month of Iyyar, he encamped against the city of Ashur.

[On day *x*] of the month of Sivan, he attacked the city, (but) he did not take the city. The king of Assyria mobilized his troops and

pushed the king of Akkad back from Ashur and marched after him as far as Takritain, a [city] on the [bank of the Eu]phrates.

The king of Akkad stationed his troops in the fortress of Takritain. [The king of] Assyria and [his] troops [ ]

encamped against the troops of the king of Akkad that were stationed in Takritain and

for ten days attacked them; but did not capture the city. The troops of the king of Akkad that were stationed in the fortress

inflicted a great defeat on Assyria. The king of Assyria and his troops [ ]*x* and returned to his country.

In the month Marcheshvan, the Medes came down to Arrapḫa and at[tacked the city]

Year 12. In the month Ab, the Medes, when they *x x x* [ ] against Nineveh,

[ ]*x* hurried and they captured Tarbiṣu, a city in the district of Nineveh *x*[ ].

He proceeded along [the Tig]ris and encamped against Ashur. He attacked the city and [ ]

[ ] destroyed. He inflicted a terrible defeat on a large number of people; he took captives (and) [carried off its sp]oil.

[The king of A]kkad and his tr[oops], who had marched to the aid of the Medes, did not reach the battle (in time); the ci[ty *x* [ ]

[The king of Akk]ad and C[yax]eres met one another by the city and concluded a treaty of peace and goodwill between them.

[Cyaxe]res and his troops returned to his(!) country; the king of Akkad and his troops returned to his(!) country.

[Year 13. In the month Iyy]ar, the Suḫeans rebelled against the king of Akkad and became hostile.

[The king of Akkad] mobilized his [tr]oops and marched to Suḫu. In the month Sivan, day 4,

[he attack]ed Raḫilu, a city in the middle of the Euphrates, and on the same day, he took the city.

[ ] its [ ], he built. The people along the banks of the Euphrates came down to him.

[ ] *x x* [agai]nst Anat he encamped. Siege towers [from] the western side
[ ] *x x* He brought the siege towers up to the wall; he atta[cked] the city. *x x x*
[The king of] Assyria and his troops came down and the king of Akkad and his troops [returned to his country].

[Year 14.] The king of Akkad mobilized his troops [*and marched to*].
C[y]axe[res], king of the Umman-manda, towards the king of Akkad
[*marched* ?] *x x* [...] *x x* [...] and they met one another.
The king of Akkad [Cy]axeres [ ] brought across
and they marched along the bank of the Tigris. [They encamp]ed against Nineveh.
From the month Sivan until the month Ab, for three [*months*] *x*
they attacked the city heavily. The month Ab, [*day x*], they inflicted a great [defeat] on a large number of people.
On that day, Sin-shar-ishkun, king of Assy[ria,] *x* [ ] *x*
They carried off the rich spoil of the city and the temple, (and) [turned] the city into a ruin heap. [ ]
of Assyria escaped from the enemy and gr[asped] the feet of the king of Akkad *for his life*.
In the month Elul, day 20, Cyaxeres and his troops returned to his (!) country. Afterwards, the king of Akka[d *and his troops*]
marched to Niṣibin. Spoil and exiles [ ]
and (the people of) Raṣappa were brought before the king of Akkad at Nineveh. In the mon[th *X, day x* *Ashur-uballiṭ*]
in Harran became king of Assyria and ascended the throne. Until the month [*X, day y*]
in Nineveh [ ] From day 20 of the month [X,] the king [ ]
went out and in the city [ ]

Year 15. In the month Tam[muz, the ki]ng of Akkad [mobilized his troops and...]
marched to Assyria. [*From the month X until the month Y he marched about*] victoriously [ ] of the land *x* [*x*] *x x* [ ].
and captured the land Shu[ ]*x x* ; he took cap[tives and carried off] its hea[vy] spoil.
In the month [Marcheshv]an, the king of Akkad t[ook] the lead of his troops and [marched] against Ruggu[*litu*].

He attacked the city and (in) the month Marcheshvan, day 28, he captured the city. [ ] He did not l[eave] a single person (alive). [ ] He returned to h[is country].

Year 16. In the month Iyyar, the king of Akkad mobilized his troops and marched to Assyria. Fr[om the month *X*] *until* the month Marcheshvan

he marched about Assyria victoriously. In the month Marcheshvan, the Umman-manda, [*who*] came to [he]lp the king of Akkad,

they joined their troops; to Harran [against Ashur-uball]iṭ, who had ascended the throne in Assyria,

they marched. Ashur-uballiṭ and the troops of E[gypt] which had come [*to his help* ?],

fear of the enemy overcame them and they aban[doned] the city and crossed [*the Euphrates* ?].

The king of Akkad reached Harran and [ ] he captured the city.

He carried off the rich spoil of the city and temple. In the month Adar, the king of [Akkad] left their [ ]

He returned to his country, and the Umman-manda, who had come to the help of the king of Akkad, withdrew.

‹Year 17.› In the month Tammuz, Ashur-uballiṭ, king of Assyria, a large Egyptian force [ ]

crossed the River (Euphrates) and marched to conquer Harran. [ ]

They defeated the garrison, which the king of Akkad had stationed within it. When they defeated it, they encamped against Harran.

Until the month of Elul, they attacked the city without success. But they did not withdraw.

The king of Akkad marched to the help of his troops *x*[ ]. He went up to Izalla.

Numerous cities in the mountains *x* [ ] he set fire to their [ ]

On that day, the troops [ ] to the district of Urartu

marched. [ ] they took captive their [ ]

The garrison, which the king [*of Akkad* ? had stationed in it we]nt out and

went up to the city [ ] *x*. The king of Akkad returned to his country.

In Ye[ar 18, in the month Elu]l, the king of Akkad mobilized his troops.

...(erasure ?)

Left Edge

May [the one who loves Na]bu and Marduk protect (this tablet) and not let it out to (strange) hands.

---

1 **Year 10**—616 BCE.

Nabopolassar mobilized the troops of Akkad—The chronicler uses the king's name twice at the beginning of the year's report and then "the king of Akkad" from there on until the end of the tablet.

The advance of Nabopolassar along the Euphrates towards the River Baliḫ was unopposed; the local Aramean population submitted and presented tribute to the new overlord. The Assyrian reprisal came only a half-year later, perhaps delayed until the arrival of the Egyptian task force. This move, however, was ill-timed as the Babylonians had already left the area.

10 **In the month Tishri, the army of Egypt and the army of Assyria marched against the king of Akkad at Gablini**—This is the first reference to Egypt in the Babylonian Chronicle. Egyptian participation at the side of Assyria points to its dominant position in the West that may have been attained (and coordinated ?) with Assyria's withdrawal from the region.

11–12 **In the month Adar, the army of Assyria and the army of Akkad attacked one another at Madanu (near) by Arrapḫa**—Later in the same year, the armies of Assyria and Babylon clashed on the eastern front, with the Babylonians gaining the upper hand. The city Arrapḫa is located near modern Kirkuk.

16 **[Year 11]**—615 BCE.

Nabopolassar led an unsuccessful attack on the city of Ashur and was forced to retreat by the Assyrian army that pursued him as far as Takritain—modern Tikrit—where the Babylonians held out for ten days against the counterattack. The Assyrians withdrew, perhaps in order to move their forces to the east in anticipation of a further Median attack.

24 **Year 12**—614 BCE.

The attack on the Assyrian capital by the Medes was broken off for some unexplained reason. The Medes proceeded to take Tarbiṣu, a royal suburb of sorts, just north of Nineveh (modern Sherif Khan); from there, they moved south to the city of Ashur, which was captured and looted.

28 **[The king of A]kkad and his a[rmy], who had marched to the aid of the Medes, did not reach the battle (in time)**—This inexplicable note on the tardiness of the Babylonian army may be the author's way of dissociating Babylon from the havoc and plunder that had befallen the holy city of Ashur at the hands of the Medes.

29 **[The king of Akk]ad and C[yax]eres met one another by the city and concluded a treaty of peace and goodwill between them**—It looks like that until this point in time each had operated independently.

31 **[Year 13]**—613 BCE.

The Arameans along the Euphrates, who just a few years earlier had submitted to Babylon (see above, lines 1–2), revoked their vassalage; they were promptly brought into line. As on previous occasions, Nabopolassar avoided direct encounter with the Assyrian army, perhaps in anticipation of the major attack on Nineveh that was to follow in the next year.

38 **[Year 14]**—612 BCE.

The capture and destruction of Nineveh by the combined Assyrian and Median forces followed a three-month siege, but given the very poor state of preservation of the Chronicle tablet, many of the details are not known. For example, the fate of Sin-shar-ishkun, the last king of Assyria, is irretrievable. One late tradition tells of his having jumped into the flames of his burning palace (so Diodorus, *History*, 2.27, who mistakenly names the king Sardanapalus [i.e., Ashurbanipal]; Eusebius quoting Abydenus correctly identifies him as Sarakos).

C[y]axe[res], king of the Umman-manda—The Akkadian term *Ummān-manda*, "hordes, barbarians," was used in the early 2nd millennium BCE and is applied here to the Median king, probably in order to malign him; assigning the ruin of Nineveh to the uncultured Medes distances Nabopolassar from this scandal. See discussion of Zawadski 1988:127–130. In similar fashion, Nabonidus, the last king of Babylon, disparaged the Medes as sacrilegious barbarians in his reference to their fighting in the war against Assyria; cf. *ANET* 309.

42–43 **From the month Sivan until the month Ab, for three [months] *x* they attacked the city heavily**—The siege lasted three months, during the summer of 612 BCE. According to classical sources, flood waters brought down the city's walls (e.g., Diodorus, *History*, 2.23), but given the low river height at this season of the year, such a scenario is highly unlikely. Late tradition often mixed up stories that had been passed on from the ancient Near East, and perhaps Sennacherib's punitive flooding of Babylon was the kernel of the tale concerning Nineveh's fate; see Baumgarten 1959; Van de Mieroop 2004.

45 **They carried off the rich spoil of the city and the temple, (and) [turned] the city into a ruin heap**—Excavations at the Ḫalzi gate in Nineveh's eastern wall have uncovered the extent of the destruction, as well as the remains of some of the slain defenders; see Stronach 1997.

49–50 **In the mon[th *X, day x* *Ashur-uballiṭ*] in Harran became king of Assyria and ascended the throne**—The remnants of the Assyrian government fled westward to Harran where the unknown Ashur-uballiṭ was declared king of Assyria in exile. Harran, Carrhae, now Altinbasak, 40 km southeast of Urfa, near the headwaters of the River Baliḫ, was a major city on the east-west trade route in northern Mesopotamia, which explains its importance to Assyrian imperial needs, even at this final juncture. On the city Harran and its influential cult of Sin of Harran, see the discussion of Holloway 1995.

53 **Year 15**—611 BCE.

In the month Tam[muz, the ki]ng of Akkad [mobilized his troops and . . .] marched to Assyria—The Babylonian army operated in the area of the upper Euphrates during the four months of the summer, but did not initiate contact with the Assyrian enclave in Harran.

58 **Year 16**—610 BCE.

During the first half of the year, the Babylonians enforced their hold on territories that comprised the former Assyria. With arrival of the Median troops, the united forces attacked Harran. The Assyrians, together with their Egyptian allies, abandoned Harran, which quickly fell to the Babylonians; a Babylonian force was stationed in the city. In texts from the reign of Nabonidus, a half-century later, the destruction of Harran and its temples is assigned to the barbarous Medes (referred by the pejorative term Umman-manda; cf. comment above to line 38); see, e.g., *ANET* 311. But this claim of Median involvement is more likely an attempt to cover up Babylonian embarrassment at the ravaging of the cult sites in Harran than being fact; cf. Rollinger 2003.

66 **‹Year 17›**—609 BCE. The scribe mistakenly omitted the date.

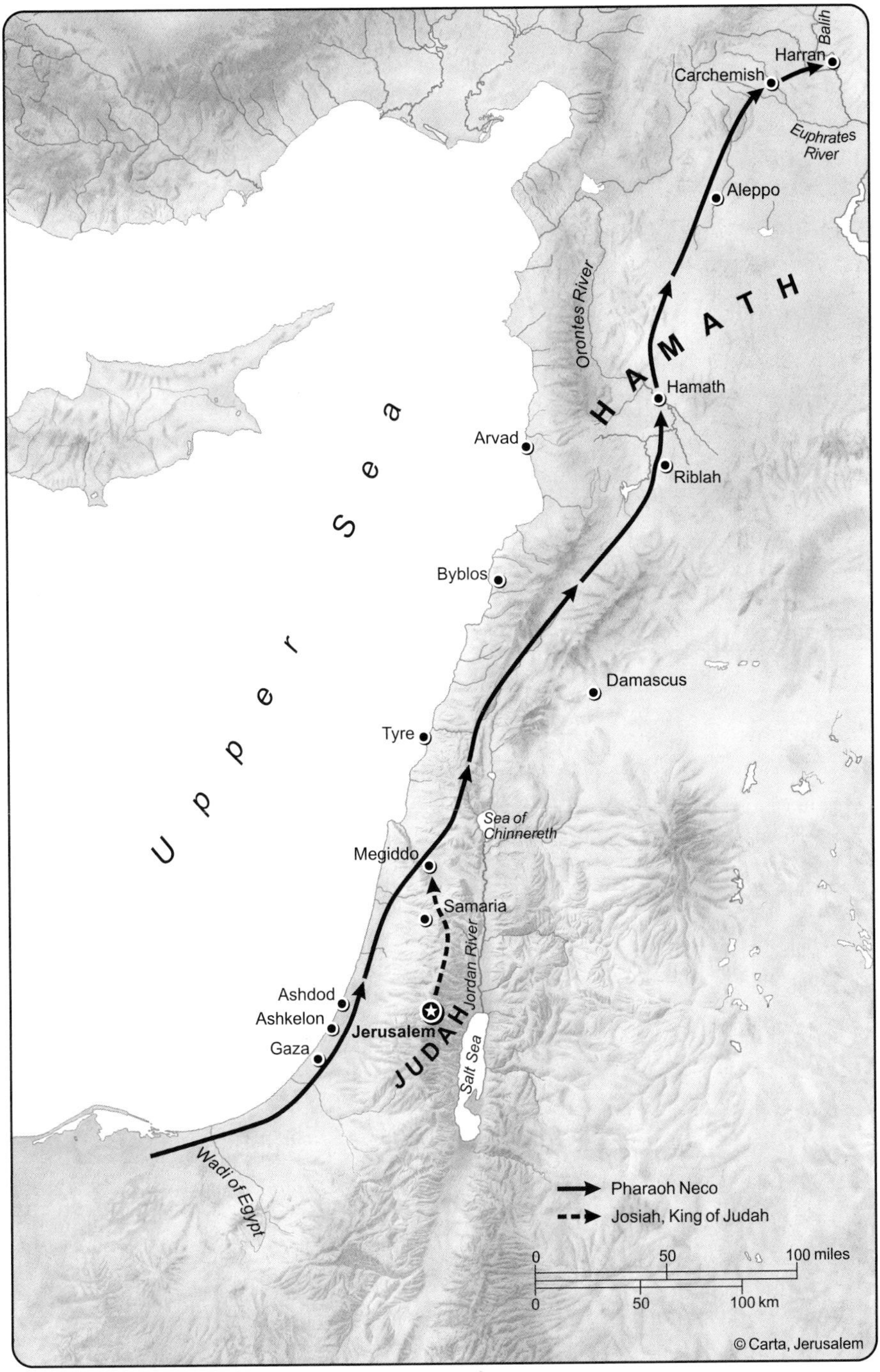

CAMPAIGN OF PHARAOH NECO, 609 BCE

66–67 **Ashur-uballiṭ, king of Assyria, the large Egyptian force [ ] crossed the River (Euphrates) and marched to conquer Harran**—The attempt to retake Harran by the combined Assyrian-Egyptian force was unsuccessful; the Babylonian garrison in the city sustained great losses but held its ground. At the head of the Egyptian troops was Pharaoh Neco, who had come to the throne just a half-year earlier. It was on the way to Harran that Neco encountered Josiah, king of Judah, at Megiddo, at which time Josiah found his death; cf. 2 Kgs 23:29–30; 2 Chr 35:20–25; see Malamat 2001.

76 **In Ye[ar 18, in the month Elu]l, the king of Akkad mobilized his troops**—This is the catch-line, that is, the first line on the next tablet in the series.

No. 11.04—THE REIGN OF NABOPOLASSAR—THE FINAL YEARS

This small tablet, in the shape of an administrative-economic document (45 mm long × 54 mm wide), continues the preceding Chronicle with reports on the next three years. The military action of this period was concentrated in areas to the north and northwest, with the Babylonian army avoiding a head-on encounter with the Egyptian base entrenched in Carchemish.

Text edition: Grayson 1975:97–98, No. 4.
Translations: *TGI* 73; Glassner 2004:224–227; *HTAT* 414–415.

Year 18. Nabopolassar. In the month Elul, the king of Akkad mobilized his troops and
marched along the bank of the Tigris; to the mountain of Bit-Ḫanuniya
in the district of Urartu, he went up. He set the cities on fire;
he took much plunder. In the month Tebeth, the king of Akkad returned to his country.

Year 19. In the month Sivan, the king of Akkad mobilized his troops and
Nebuchadnezzar, his eldest son, the crown prince,
mobilized his troops and they marched to the mountains of Za-*x*-*x*.
The king of Akkad left the crown prince and his troops in the country and he, in the month Tammuz, returned to Babylon.
Afterwards Nebuchadnezzar attacked the mountain fortresses,

he captured the fortresses, [*set* (*them*) *on fire* ?], prisoners of the mountains
in great number he took away. He captured all the mountains as far as the district of [ ].
[In the month] Elul, the crown prince returned to Babylon. In the month Tishri, the king of Akkad mobilized his troops and
marched [to] Kimmuḫu that is on the bank of the Euphrates.
He crossed the river and [att]acked the city, and in the month Kislev, he captured the city.
He carried off its spoil (and) stationed his garrison in it. In the month Shebat, he returned to his country.

[Year 20.] The troops of Egypt, to Kimmuḫu against the garrison
that the king of Akkad had stationed there, marched, and for four months
attacked the city and captured the city; they defeated the garrison of the king of Akkad.
In the month Tishri, the king of Akkad mobilized his troops and marched along the bank of the Euphrates and
pitched his camp in Qurumatu that is on the bank of the Euphrates.
He had his troops cross the Euphrates and Shunadiri, Elammu,
and Daḫammu, cities of "Beyond-the-River," they captured.
They plundered them. In the month Shebat, the king of Akkad returned to his country.
The troops of Egypt that were in Carchemish crossed the Euphrates and
against the troops of Akkad that were camped in Quramatu
marched and they pushed back the troops of Akkad so that they withdrew.

Year 21. The king of Akkad in his country. Nebuchadnezzar, his eldest son
the crown prince mobilized the troops of Akkad and

Year 18—608 BCE.

Babylon's army moved to open a second front in the northeast, against areas in the district of Urartu, perhaps to secure the northern border.

Year 19—607 BCE.

The engagement in Urartu continued and, for the first time, reference is made to the crown prince, Nebuchadrezzar, who accompanied his father on campaign. The note that Nabopolassar left for home may hint at the need to attend to affairs in Babylon; some have even speculated that this return might have been due to the king's ill-health. But the king did take the field again four months later, this time to Kimmuḫu, seemingly the Anatolian country of Kummuḫ (and capital city of the same name?) located at Samsat on the upper Euphrates north of Carchemish. The city was taken and held by a Babylonian garrison.

16 **Year 20**—606 BCE.

The proximity of the Babylonian army to Carchemish, the base of the Egyptian force in northern Syria, instigated Egyptian reaction. Throughout the summer and fall, the two armies engaged one another; each side seemingly could claim some advances. But after Nabopolassar's return home, the Babylonian troops were unable to withstand the Egyptian counterattack and were forced to beat a retreat.

19–22 **The king of Akkad mobilized his troops and marched along the bank of the Euphrates and pitched his camp in Qurumatu that is on the bank of the Euphrates. He had his troops cross the Euphrates and Shunadiri, Elammu, and Daḫammu, cities of "Beyond-the-River," they captured**—These cities have not been identified, but from the description of the advance of the Babylonian army, they lay to the south of Carchemish and their capture was meant to cut the Egyptian force off from the supply routes to the west and south.

27–28 The catch-line quotes the first lines on the next tablet in the series.

No. 11.05—THE REIGN OF NEBUCHADNEZZAR—TO JERUSALEM

This tablet in the Babylonian Chronicle surveys the events from the last year of Nabopolassar, his twenty-first (605 BCE), until the eleventh year of Nebuchadnezzar (595 BCE). The hostilities in northern Syria between the Babylonian forces and the Egyptian army reached their final stage, at the end of which, political control over the entire West passed into Babylonian hands. From the report of the yearly campaigns of Nebuchadnezzar to Syria, it appears that the Syrian kingdoms continued to oppose the replacement of one Mesopotamian empire—Assyria—by another—Babylon. The chronicle entry for the king's seventh year relates the capture of Jerusalem and complements the report of the submission of the kingdom of Judah given in 2 Kgs 24:1–17.

The tablet (59 mm wide × 81 mm long) is poorly preserved and several lines at bottom of the obverse and top of the reverse are entirely missing.

Text edition: Grayson 1975:99–102, No. 5.
Translations: *TGI* 73–74; *ANET* 564; *TPOA* 138–141; *TUAT* 1/4, 402–404; *COS* 1, 467–468; Glassner 2004:226–231; *HTAT* 415–417.
Photograph: Fig. 30.

Obv.

[Year 21.] The king of Akkad in his country. Nebuchadrezzar, his eldest son, [cr]own prince,
[mo]bilized [the troops of Akkad] and took the lead of his troops; he marched to Carchemish that is on the bank of the Euphrates.
[*against the troops of Egypt*] that were encamped within Carchemish, he crossed the river, and
[*attacked them*]. They fought each other and the troops of Egypt retreated before him.
He inflicted a [defeat] upon them and wiped them out of existence. The remainder of the troops of [Egypt]
[that] had escaped [from] the defeat and had not been killed, in the district of Hamath
the troops of Akkad caught up with them and inflicted a defeat upon them; not a single man [returned] to [his] country.
On that day, Nebuchadrezzar conquered Ha[ma]th in its entirety.
Twenty-one years Nabopolassar ruled Babylon.
In the month Ab, day 8, (he went to his) fate. In the month Elul, Nebuchadrezzar returned to Babylon and
in the month Elul, day 1, he ascended the royal throne in Babylon.

Accession year. Nebuchadrezzar returned to Ḫatti and until the month Shebat, in Ḫatti
he marched about victoriously. In the month Shebat, he took the rich tribute of Ḫatti to Babylon.
In the month Nisan, he took the hand of Bel and the son of Bel; he celebrated the *Akitu* festival.

Year 1. Nebuchadrezzar, in the month Sivan, mobilized his troops
and marched to Ḫatti. Until the month Kislev he marched about Ḫatti victoriously.

All the kings of Ḫatti came before him and he received their rich tribute.
He marched to Ash[ke]lon and in the month Kislev, he captured it.
He seized its king, took its prisoners (and) carried off its spoil.
He turned the city into a ruin heap. In the month Shebat, he marched and [returned] to Babylon.

[Year 2.] (In) the month Iyyar, the king of Akkad gathered his considerable troops [*and marched to Ḫatti*]
[ ]*x* He encamped; large siege towers he moved acr[oss ...]
[from the month I]yyar until the month [*X he marched about victoriously in Ḫatti*].

(About four lines missing)

Rev.

[ ] *x x x* [ ]

[Year 3. In the month *X*, day] 13, Nabu-shum-lish[ir]
[In the month ... the king of Akka]d mobilized his troops and [marched] to Ḫatti.
[ ] *x* in great quantity of Ḫatti he brought into Akkad [ ]

Year 4. The king of Akkad mobilized his troops and marched to Ḫatti. In Ḫatti he marched about victoriously.
In the month Kislev, he took the lead of his troops and marched to Egypt. The king of Egypt heard (of it) and mo[bilized his troops.
They fought one another in an open field battle and they inflicted heavy blows on one another. The king of Akkad and his troops turned and [returned] to Babylon.

Year 5. The king of Akkad in his country. He organized his numerous chariots and horses.

Year 6. The month Kislev. The king of Akkad mobilized his troops and marched to Ḫatti. He sent his troops and
they moved into the desert. They plundered in great quantity the property, the flocks and the gods of the many Arabs. In the month Adar, the king returned to his country.

Year 7. The month Kislev. The king of Akkad mobilized his troops and marched to Ḫatti.
He encamped against the city of Judah and in the month Adar, day 2, he captured the city; he seized the king.
He appointed in it a king of his choice; he t[ook] its rich spoil and brought it into Babylon.

Year 8. The month Tebeth. The king of Akkad to Ḫatti as far as Carche[mish marched …]
x x [ ]*x* in the month Shebat [the king to] his country [returned].

Year 9. [The king of Akk]ad and his army [marched] along the ba]nk of the Tigr[is …]
The king of *x*[ ] *x x x x x* [ ]
The king of Ak[kad] *x x x x* [ ] *x x* [ ]
He encamped on the bank of the Tigris. A distance of one day's march between the[m …]
The king of E[lam] became afraid and fear overwhelmed him; he re[turned] to his country.

[Year] 10. [The king of Akk]ad in his country. From the month Kislev until the month Tebeth, a rebellion in Akkad [*x*] *x*
[ ] *x* many of his [troop]s he executed; he himself [caught] his enemy.
[to] Ḫatti he marched and the kings and *x x* [ ] *x*
[came] and their rich tribute [he received.] He re[turned] to B[abylon].

[Year 11.] In the month Kislev, the king of Akkad [mobilized his] troops and [to Ḫat]ti he marched.

Obv.

1 **[Year 21]**—605 BCE.

Nebuchadrezzar attacked the Egyptians entrenched in Carchemish and for the first time since the Egyptians had joined the contest for the hegemony over Syria, they were defeated. Their rout continued as far as Hamath.

The form of the king's name *Nebuchadrezzar* reflects the Babylonian name *Nabû-kudurri-uṣur*, "May the god Nabu protect the eldest son." This is the form that is prevalent in the books of Jeremiah (e.g., Jer 21:2, 7; 29:21; 44:30; 46:2) and Ezekiel (e.g., Ezek 26:7; 29:18; 30:10); the other, more familiar form, Nebuchadnezzar (with the interchange of dental liquids *r* by *n*) is used in other biblical books (e.g., 2 Kgs 24:1, 10, 11; Dan 2:28; Ezra 1:7).

12 **Accession year**—During the remaining part of the year, the months before Nisan when his first regnal year would start, Nebuchadrezzar rejoined the campaign in northern Syria.

14 **In the month Nisan, he took the hand of Bel and the son of Bel; he celebrated the *Akitu* festival**—The Babylonian New Year ritual required the king's participation; he would lead the statutes of Marduk (Bel) and Nabu (son of Bel) in the festal procession. This pair of the major Babylonian deities is referred in Isaiah's diatribe against Babylon: "Bel is bowed, Nebo is cowering; their images are a burden for beasts and cattle" (Isa 46:1).

It is a bit strange that the events of Nisan, the first month of the New Year, are associated with the accession year that had just ended, and not with the king's first year.

15 **Year 1**—604 BCE.

17 **All the kings of Ḫatti came before him and he received their rich tribute**—With the ouster of Egypt from its holdings in Syria, which is summarized in 2 Kgs 24:7: "The king of Egypt did not leave his country anymore, for the king of Babylon seized all that had belonged to the king of Egypt, from the Wadi of Egypt to the River Euphrates," King Jehoiakim of Judah could not but transfer his allegiance from Egypt to Babylon (2 Kgs 24:1). At this same juncture, "in the ninth month of the fifth year of Jehoiakim, son of Josiah, king of Judah," the prophet Jeremiah collected all his words of warning concerning the disaster that he foresaw for Judah (Jer 36:9).

He marched to Ash[ke]llon and in the month Kislev, he captured it. He seized its king, took its prisoners (and) carried off its spoil—Ashkelon seems to have been the sole holdout; the city was attacked and looted, its king and royal household taken off to Babylon. In an administrative tablet from later in the reign of Nebuchadnezzar, "the sons of Agga, king of Ashkelon," are mentioned as residing in Babylon, along with other exiled Ashkelonites, where they received food allotments. (The tablet was partially published in *ANET* 308b; see further below, comment to lines 12–13.) New excavations

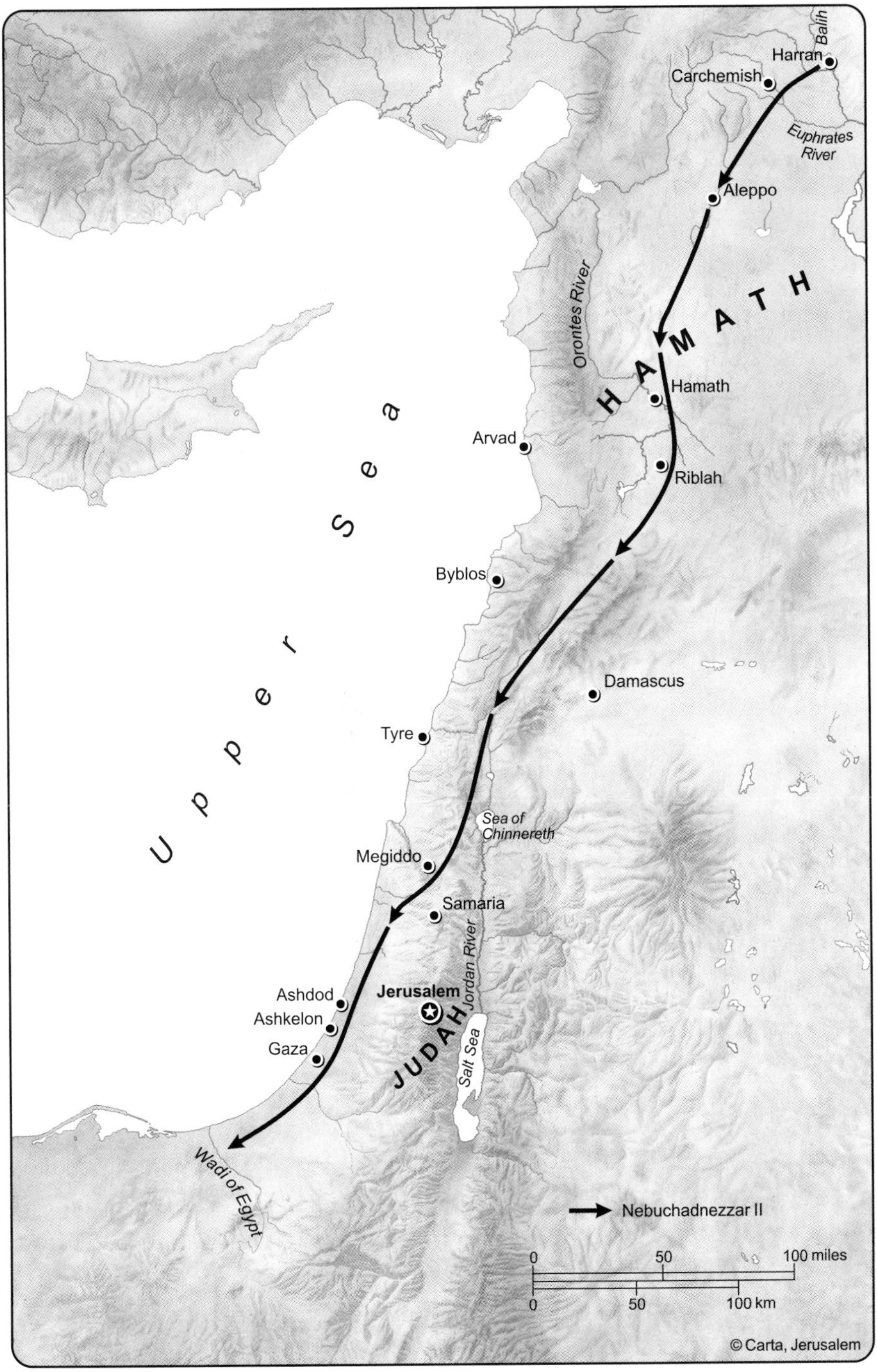

BABYLONIAN CAMPAIGNS, 605–604 BCE

at Ashkelon have uncovered the remains of the massive destruction at the hands of the Babylonian army; see Stager 1996.

It was probably during this same eventful year that Adon, king of Ekron, sent a letter to the Egyptian Pharaoh (Neco II) pleading for prompt military assistance for "the king of Babylon has come (and) reached Aphek" (see *COS* 3, 132–133; Porten 1981).

21 **[Year 2]**—603 BCE.

In the month Iyyar, the king of Akkad gathered his considerable troops—There is much speculation as to the goal of the campaign, but the fragmentariness of the lines prevents knowing the need for the large mobilization of forces.

Rev.

2 **[Year 3]**—602 BCE.

In the month *X*, day] 13, Nabu-shum-lish[ir]—Nabu-shum-lishir was the king's brother, but the report concerning the incident in which he was involved has not survived.

5 **Year 4**—601 BCE.

One suspects that the campaign against Egypt, given its logistic difficulties, was undertaken because of the continued Egyptian support to those in Philistia and other parts of Israel who resisted Babylonian rule. Based on the report in Herodotus (2.159) that Neco defeated the "Syrians" (=Babylonians) at Magdolos and then captured Kadytis (=Gaza), it is often suggested that the decisive battle took place at Migdol in the Delta (see above Text no. 8.05); see Malamat 2001:293–295. The report of the unsuccessful Babylonian thrust into the Delta speaks well for the reliability of the chronicle's data.

The immediate result of Nebuchadnezzar's retreat was the need to refit the army (see Year 5). In political terms, Babylon's loss was interpreted as weakness and seems to have encouraged King Jehoiakim to throw off his vassal status: "In his days, Nebuchadnezzar, king of Babylon, marched forth and Jehoiakim became his vassal for three years. Then he turned and rebelled against him" (2 Kgs 24:1).

8 **Year 5**—600 BCE.

The king of Akkad in his country. He organized the chariots and his many horses—The year was utilized for reorganizing and re-equipping the fighting forces in anticipation of further campaigns.

9 **Year 6**—599 BCE.

Babylon sought to reassert control over the border areas in central Syria by attacking the settlements of the desert nomads. This activity may be reflected in Jeremiah's prophecies "concerning Kedar and the kingdoms of Hazor": "For Nebuchadrezzar, king of Babylon, has devised a plan against you and formed a purpose against you: Rise up, attack a tranquil nation that dwells secure—says the Lord. That has no barred gates, that dwells alone. Their camels shall become booty, and their abundant flocks a spoil; and I will scatter to every quarter those who have their hair clipped; and from every direction I will bring disaster upon them—says the Lord" (Jer 49:28–33). See Eph^{c}al 1982:171–176.

11 **Year 7**—598 BCE.

12–13 **He encamped against the city of Judah and in the month Adar, day 2, he captured the city; he seized the king. He appointed in it a king of his choice; he t[ook] its rich spoil and brought it into Babylon**—The chronicle report complements the one in 2 Kgs 24:8–17. As already noted, following the Babylonian debacle in Egypt in 601 BCE, Jehoiakim rebelled. But as Nebuchadnezzar was unable to suppress the revolt himself, he engaged loyal, local forces against Judah—Chaldeans, Edomites(?), Moabites and Ammonites (2 Kgs 24:2), until he could undertake a march to distant Judah. This he did in his seventh year, when he joined those already besieging Jerusalem (cf. 2 Kgs 24:10–11) and oversaw its surrender.

Jerusalem is named "the city of Judah" (*al Iaḫudu*), a designation also known from 2 Chr 25:28. The date of the city's submission, the 2nd of Adar (= March 16, 597 BCE), important to the Babylonian chronicler, was not preserved in biblical tradition. On the other hand, the Babylonian author dispensed with the name of the Judean kings; Jehoiachin was the king who was exiled; Zedekiah was the king newly crowned. Note, too, that Jehoiachin and his train—"he, his mother, his courtiers, his officers and his officials"—were sent into exile "in the eighth year" of Nebuchadnezzar (2 Kgs 24:12). The difference in dating is explicable; at least a month had passed since the Babylonians' takeover of Jerusalem and the deportation of the royal family. Along with the Judean nobility, "he took into exile . . . all the warriors, seven thousand, and the craftsmen and the smiths, one thousand—all brave men, trained soldiers" (v. 16).

Administrative texts discovered at Babylon from Nebuchadnezzar's thirteenth year (592 BCE) record the distribution of foodstuffs to Jehoiachin (*Yaʾukin*) and his five sons and other Judeans living in Babylon; see *ANET* 308b.

14 **Year 8**—597 BCE.

14–15 **The month Tebeth. The king of Akkad to Ḫatti as far as Carche[mish *marched*] *x x* [ ]*x* in the month Shebat [the king to] his country [*returned*]**— The note records a very brief—just one month—campaign to Syria, likely for the collection of tribute, a reminder to vassals of the loyalty required of them.

16 **Year 9**—596 BCE.

If the reading is correct, this would be the first appearance of the kingdom of Elam as an enemy of Babylon, a far cry from the days when Elam extended help to Babylon in its uprisings against Assyria.

21 **Year 10**—595 BCE.

Nebuchadnezzar suppressed a rebellion in his army, and after restoring control, he marched West to personally collect taxes; this surely was meant as a demonstration that royal power was still intact. The insurrection, however, pointed to internal weakness in his rule, a fact that was not lost on some rulers in the West who thought the time was ripe to free themselves from Babylon; cf. Jer 27–28 and see the discussion of Ephʿal 2003.

25 **[Year 11]**—594 BCE.

Nothing is known about the campaign to Syria in this year.

No. 11.06—THE REIGN OF NABONIDUS—THE FALL OF BABYLON

A fragment of a large tablet (140 × 140 mm) with two columns on each side (see also Text no. 11.01) preserves part of the summary of the reign of Nabonidus, the last king of Babylon (556–539 BCE). Unique to this chronicle is the attention paid to the interruption of the *Akitu* festival due to the king's absence from Babylon. In addition, the author follows the rise of Cyrus, though, at first, this was not directly related to events in Babylon. The report of the taking of Babylon by Cyrus is unexpectedly benign, considering that the city had been conquered by a foreign ruler. Taken together, these perspectives suggest that the author of this chronicle held a negative view of Nabonidus, and in this, he was not unlike other Babylonian writers who criticized the eccentricities of their king (see, e.g., the propagandistic composition "Verse Account of Nabonidus," *ANET* 312–315). For an assessment of the brief statements in the Babylonian Chronicle and their relation to the traditions in the classical sources on the rise of Cyrus, see Briant 2002:31–44.

Text edition: Grayson 1975:104–111, No. 7.
Translations: *TGI* 81–82; *ANET* 305–307; Glassner 2004:232–239; *TUAT* NF II, 40–41; *HTAT* 440–444.

Obv. col. i

[ ] *x x x* [ ]
[ ] *x* he carried. The king
[of] their land they brought to Babylon
[ ] *x*
[ ] *x* they were terrified and he did not lift
[ ] their family, as many as there were,
[ ] *x* the king mobilized his troops and to Que
[marched] *x x*

[*Year 2.*] In the month Tebeth, in Hamath it was cold.
[ ] *x*

[*Year 3.* the mon]th Ab, the mountain Ammananu
[ ] *x* orchards, all of the fruit
[ ] *x* of them into Babylon
[became il]l, but recovered. In the month Kislev, the king his troops
[mobilized] *x x* and to Nabu, Bel-dan, brother
[ ] *x x* of Amurru to
[against E]dom encamped.
[ ] many troops
[the g]ate of Shintini
[he k]illed him

[ ] *x x*

[the tr]oops

col. ii

(Astyages) [mo]bilized (his army) and marched to conquer Cyrus, king of Anshan, [ ]

But the army rebelled against Astyages and he was captured. They ha[*nded him over*] to Cyrus [ ]

Cyrus ‹marched› to Ecbatana, the royal city. Silver, gold, goods, property [ ]

of Ecbatana he carried off as spoil and took to Anshan. The goods (and) property of the troops [of]

Year 7. The king (was) in Tema; the crown prince, his nobles, his troops in Akkad. [The king, in the month Nisan,]

did not come to Babylon. Nabu did not go to Babylon. Bel did not come out. [The *Akitu* festi]val was cancelled.

The offerings in Esagil and Ezida (to) the gods of Babylon and Borsippa a[s in normal times]

were presented. The high priest made a libation and inspected the temple.

Year 8.

Year 9. Nabonidus, the king ‹in› Tema; the crown prince, the nobles and the troops in Akkad. The king, in the month Nisan, to Babylon

did not come. Nabu did not go to Babylon. Bel did not come out. The *Akitu* festival was cancelled.

The offerings in Esagil and Ezida (to) the gods of ‹Babylon› and Borsippa as in normal times were presented.

(In) the month Nisan, day 5, the mother of the king in Dur-karashu, which (is on) the bank of the Euphrates, upstream from Sippar,

died. The crown prince and his army *were in grief* for three days; there was a mourning period. In the month Sivan

there was a mourning period for the king's mother. In the month Nisan, Cyrus, king of Persia, mobilized his army and

crossed the Tigris below Arbaʾil. In the month Iyyar, *x x* [ ]

He killed its king; he took its goods (and) stationed his own garrison (there) [ ]

[Afterwards], his garrison and the king were in it.

Year 10. The king in Tema; the crown prince, the nobles and his troops in Akkad. The king, in [the month Nisan, to Babylon did not come].
Nabu did not go to Babylon. Bel did not come out. The *Akitu* festival was cancelled. The offerings in E[sagil and Ezida]
(to) the gods of Babylon and Borsippa as in normal [times were pre]sented. In the month Sivan, day 21, [ ]
of Elammiya, in Akkad *x x* [ ] the provincial governor in Uruk [ ]

Year 11. The king in Tema; the crown prince, the nobles and the troops in Akka[d. The king, in the month Nisan, to Babylon did not come.]
[Nabu] did not go [to Bab]ylon. Bel did not come out. The *Akitu* festival was cancelled. The offerings in Esagil and Ezida
[(to) the gods of Bab]ylon and Borsippa [as in normal tim]es were presented.

col. iii,
[ ]killed (?) The T[igris . . .]
[ ] of Ishtar of Uruk [ ]
[ ] *x* of Pe[rsia]
[ ] [ ]

[Year 17. N]abu from Borsippa to the procession of Bel [came. Bel went out.]
[in the month] *Nisan* (?), the king entered Eturkalamma; in E[ ]
[ ] *x x x* He made a libation of wine *x x x x* [ ]
[B]el came out. The *Akitu* festival was performed safely. In the month [ ]
[the gods] of Marad, Zababa and the gods of Kish, Ninlil [and the gods
[of] Ḫursagkalamma entered Babylon. Until the end of the month Elul, the gods of Akkad [ ]
which are *upstream* . . . and *downstream* . . . entered Babylon. The gods of Borsippa, Cutha,
and Sippar did not enter (Babylon). In the month Tishri, when Cyrus made an attack at Opis, (which is on) the bank of

the Tigris, against the troops of Akkad, the men of Akkad
retreated; he took spoil (and) killed the men. Day 14, Sippar was taken without a battle.
Nabonidus fled. Day 16, [Ug]baru, governor of Gutium, and the troops of Cyrus without a battle
entered Babylon. Afterwards, after Nabonidus retreated, he was captured in Babylon. Until the end of the month, the shield (-bearers)
of Gutium surrounded the gates of Esagil. There was no interruption of anything in Esagil or (other) temples
and no date was missed. The month Marcheshvan, day 3, Cyrus entered Babylon.
The *wine containers* were filled before him. There was peace in the city; Cyrus proclaimed peace
to Babylon in its totality. He appointed Gubaru as governor of governors in Babylon.
From the month Kislev until the month Adar, the gods of Akkad, which Nabonidus had brought down to Babylon,
returned to their cult centers. The month Marcheshvan, at night, day 11, Ugbaru died. In the mon[th *X*]
the king's wife died. From day 27 of the month Adar until day 3 of the month Nisan, [there was] a mourning period in Akkad.
All the [peo]ple bared their heads. Day 4, Cambyses, son of Cy[rus],
went to E-gidru-kalamma-summu; the official of the E-gidru(-kalamma-summu) of Nabu *x x* [ ]
When he came, because of his Elamite *dress*, the hands of Nabu [ ] *x* [ ]
[sp]ears and quivers from [ ] *x* [ ] for the *wo*[*rk* ?]
[ ] Nabu to Esagil . . . *x x x* before Bel and the son of B[el]

Col. iv Nine lines with single words, no context

---

col. i,

11 **[Year 3.]**—553 BCE. Only the barest outline of the events of this year is retrievable. Activity was centered in the West (Amurru), in the Lebanon (Mount Ammananu) at the outset, and in Transjordan (Edom) towards year's end. In the four months between these two parts of the campaign, it seems that the king fell ill, but successfully recovered. The suggested restoration "[E]dom" and its identification, long the subject of scholarly debate (see

Eph^{c}al 1982:185–188), commends itself with more surety after the recent discovery of a royal inscription on an inaccessible mountain height at Qal^{c}at Sela^{c}, 4 km northwest of Buṣeirah, in southern Jordan (see Fig. 31). Although badly weathered, the iconography and a few readable cuneiform signs on the relief point to Nabonidus as the king responsible for this engraving, most likely in commemoration of his victory in this area of ancient Edom. For the initial publication, see Dalley and Goguel 1997. Only a major victory could have prompted the king to choose this out-of-the-way site for a monumental inscription; see Lemaire 2003. According to 2 Kgs 14:7, the stronghold of Sela was captured by the Judean king Amaziah during his war with the Edomites.

[Year 6.]—550 BCE. The opening lines of this year are no longer preserved, but they no doubt began with the notice that the *Akitu* festival was not observed, as was reported for all the years of Nabonidus's stay in Tema.

Fig. 31. Rock relief at Qal^{c}at Sela^{c} showing king and divine symbols (*photo: A. Izdarechet*).

col. ii, 1 **(Astyages) [mo]bilized (his army) and marched to conquer Cyrus, king of Anshan, [ ]**—Cyrus was vassal of Astyages, king of Media, and the reason for the attack upon him is unclear. This may have been in response to an uprising led by Cyrus that had broken out earlier, and is hinted at in a text of Nabonidus from Sippar.

Anshan—A major Elamite city located at Tell al-Maliyan in southwestern Iran. Elamite kings of the second millennium BCE bore the title "king of Susa and Anshan," which was adopted by Cyrus in legitimizing his dynasty.

5 **Year 7**—549 BCE.

The king (was) in Tema; the crown prince, his nobles, his troops in Akkad—Nabonidus had taken up residence in Tema three years earlier, during his fourth regnal year, and stayed away from Babylon for ten years. During his absence, his son Belshazzar took over the administrative affairs of the realm, but this arrangement did not allow for the celebration of the New Year festival, which required the presence of the king. Late biblical tradition remembered Belshazzar as being the son Nebuchadnezzar and the last king of Babylon, after whom Darius the Mede reigned (Dan 5:11, 29–30). The name of the king (*nbnd mlk bbl*, "Nabonidus, king of Babylon") in the local Temanite dialect has turned up on rock graffiti; see Lemaire 2003:288–289.

Tema—The major oasis in the Arabian desert on the road north to the Fertile Crescent, some 400 km east of the Gulf of Elath; at Tema the road splits, one fork continuing east to Babylon, the other west to Transjordan and the Mediterranean. During the reign of Tiglath-pileser III, the people of Tema had come to an accommodation with Assyria (see Text no. 4.06, lines 27′–29′).

The motive behind Nabonidus's sojourn at Tema is nowhere stated; among the suggestions is the king's desire to control this important north Arabian commercial hub. More to the point may have been his alienation from the religious establishment in Babylon due to the king's support of the cult of the moon god Sin to the disadvantage of the established Marduk priesthood; see discussion in Tadmor 1965; Beaulieu 1989:178–185.

9 **Year 8**—548 BCE. There is a blank space on the tablet after the date. It cannot be known whether the scribe's source text was faulty at this point (so Grayson 1975:107) or if he censored information unfavorable to one of the sides in the developing conflict between the Babylonians and Persians (Beaulieu 1989:199).

10 **Year 9**—547 BCE.

13–14 **In the month Nisan, day 5, the mother of the king in Dur-karashu, which (is on) the bank of the Euphrates, upstream from Sippar, died**—The queen mother, Adda-guppi, died on April 6, 547 BCE. Some details of her life are known from an inscription ascribed to her, wherein she claims to have reached the ripe age of 104; see *ANET* 560–562.

15–16 **In the month Nisan, Cyrus, king of Persia, mobilized his army and crossed the Tigris below Arbaʾil. In the month Iyyar,** *x x* **[ ]**—It has been suggested that this broken passage be read: "[He marched] on *Ly*[*dia*]," and coordinates with the movement of the Persian army and conquest of Lydia reported in Greek sources in 547. But the traces on the tablet do not support this reading (see Grayson 1975:282).

19 **Year 10**—546 BCE.

Elammiya—Perhaps the same town as Elammu, in the vicinity of Carchemish (Text no. 11.04, line 21). This would place the Babylonian army in northern Syria, protecting its northwestern border against possible incursions by the Persian army who were engaged in western Anatolia at the time.

23 **Year 11**—545 BCE. The tablet is broken at this point and the report resumes in the last year of Nabonidus.

col iii,
5 **[Year 17]**—539 BCE. With the return of Nabonidus to Babylon in his thirteenth year, the rites in the temple Esagil were resumed.

9–11 **[the gods] of Marad, Zababa and the gods of Kish, Ninlil [and the gods [of] Ḫursagkalamma entered Babylon. Until the end of the month Elul, the gods of Akkad [ ] which are** ***upstream*** **. . . and** ***downstream*** **. . . entered Babylon**—The gathering of the divine images into Babylon during the summer of 539 was undertaken in anticipation of Cyrus's attack on the southern cities; Babylon was considered a safe haven for these prized statues, and their presence in the capital was intended to guarantee the gods' help and support in the upcoming war; see Cogan 1974:33, n. 67. It is not clear why those cities close to Babylon—Borsippa, Cutha and Sippar—did not follow suit. The care of the gods while in Babylon by their own personnel was studied by Beaulieu 1993.

12–14 **Cyrus made an attack at Opis, (which is on) the bank of the Tigris, against**

the troops of Akkad, the men of Akkad retreated; he took spoil (and) killed the men—Opis lay c. 75 km north of Babylon and was a key point in the defense of the Babylonian heartland. With its capture, no further resistance seems to have been offered. The fall of Babylon was swift. Within a month, Cyrus entered the city that surrendered without a battle. This agrees with the assessment of the Cyrus cylinder, in which the Persian king claims: "I entered Babylon in peaceful manner, I took up my lordly abode in the royal palace amidst rejoicing and happiness" (see Text no. 14.01). In later Greek and Jewish traditions, there are conflicting stories of a siege of Babylon, as well as the city celebrating a feast, unaware of the invading Persians.

15–18 **[Ug]baru, governor of Gutium, and the troops of Cyrus without a battle entered Babylon . . . Until the end of the month, the shield (-bearers) of Gutium surrounded the gates of Esagil. There was no interruption of anything in Esagil or (other) temples and no date was missed**—It is unexpected to find the term "Gutium" used of the Persians as it is a pejorative term referring to the mountain peoples. It looks like the editor of the chronicle juxtaposed the behavior of Nabonidus to that of the army of Cyrus: the Babylonian king had upset tradition, the foreigner respected local custom.

Ugbaru—He is most likely Gobryas, referred to by Xenophon as having switched sides, leaving his post as Babylonian governor of the eastern province of Gutium to join Cyrus. Less than a month after entering Babylon, Ugbaru died (see line 22).

20 **He appointed Gubaru as governor of governors in Babylon**—Not to be confused with Ugbaru who, like Gubaru, bore the same Persian name. It is possible that Gubaru was later promoted, as there is evidence of a Gubaru who held the title "governor of Babylonia and "Beyond-the-River" (*Eber nāri*)." See Briant 2002:64, 71–75.

Another possible translation of this line: "Gubaru, his (Cyrus's) governor, appointed officials in Babylon."

22–23 **In the mon[th *X*], the king's wife died. From day 27 of the month Adar until day 3 of the month Nisan, [there was] a mourning period in Akkad**—Because of the death of Cyrus's wife and the period of mourning, he did not participate in the *Akitu* festival; Cambyses, his son, filled the required role in the ceremonies.

24–26 **Day 4, Cambyses, son of Cy[rus], went to E-gidri-kalamma-summu; the official of the E-gidri-kalamma-summu of Nabu *x x* [ ]. When he came, because of his Elamite *dress*, the hands of Nabu [ ] *x* [ ]**—Cambyses took part in the New Year (*Akitu*) festival but had come attired in foreign garb, and was declared unfit to lead the god in the festal parade. The incident recorded occurred in the temple of Nabu in Babylon.

For another interpretation of the events surrounding the fall of Babylon, see Fried 2004:20–31.

References

Baumgarten, Walter

1959 Herodots babylonische und assyrische Nachrichten. Pp. 281–331 in idem, *Zum Alten Testament und seiner Umwelt*, Leiden.

Beaulieu, Paul-Alain

1989 *The Reign of Nabonidus King of Babylon 556–539 B.C.*, New Haven and London.

1993 An Episode in the Fall of Babylon to the Persians, *JNES* 52:241–261.

2003 Nabopolassar and the Antiquity of Babylon. Pp.1*–9* in *ErIsr* 27.

Becking, Bob

1992 *The Fall of Samaria: An Historical and Archaeological Study*, Leiden.

Borger, Rykle

1965 Der Aufstieg des Neubabylonischen Reiches, *JCS* 19:59–78.

Briant, Pierre

2002 *From Cyrus to Alexander: A History of the Persian Empire*, Winona Lake, IN.

Brinkman, John A.

1964 Merodach-Baladan II. Pp. 6–53 in *Studies Presented to A. Leo Oppenheim*, Chicago.

1984 *Prelude to Empire: Babylonian Society and Politics, 747–626 B.C.*, Philadelphia.

1990 The Babylonian Chronicle Revisited. Pp. 73–104 in T. Abusch, J. Huehnergard, P. Steinkeller (eds.), *Lingering Over Words, Studies in Ancient Near Eastern Literature in Honor of William L. Moran*, Atlanta.

1998–2003 Nabopolassar. Pp. 12–16 in vol. 9 of *RlA*.

Cogan, Mordechai

1974 *Imperialism and Religion: Assyria, Judah and Israel in the Eighth and Seventh Centuries B.C.E.*, SBLMS 19, Missoula, MT.

Dalley, Stephanie and A. Goguel

1997 The Sela^{c} Sculpture: A Neo-Babylonian Rock Relief in Southern Jordan, *ADAJ* 41:169–176.

Eph^cal, Israel

1982 *The Ancient Arabs*, Jerusalem.

2003 Nebuchadnezzar the Warrior: Remarks on His Military Achievements, *IEJ* 53:178–191.

Finkel, I. L. and R. J. van der Spek

2004 Babylonian Chronicles of the Hellenistic Period, http://www.livius.org/cg-cm/chronicles/chron00.html (entered 14 Oct. 2007).

Frame, Grant

1992 *Babylonia 689–627 B.C.: A Political History*, Leiden.

Fried, Lisbeth S.

2004 *The Priest and the Great King: Temple-Palace Relations in the Persian Empire*, Winona Lake, IN.

Glassner, Jean-Jacques

2004 *Mesopotamian Chronicles*, Atlanta.

Grayson, A. Kirk

1975 *Assyrian and Babylonian Chronicles*, Locust Valley.

Hallo, William W.

1988 The Nabonassar Era and Other Epochs in Mesopotamian Chronology and Chronography. Pp. 175–190 in Erle Leichty, Maria deJ. Ellis and Pamela Gerardi (eds.), *A Scientific Humanist: Studies in Memory of Abraham Sachs*, Philadelphia.

Holloway, Steven W.

1995 Harran: Cultic Geography in the Neo-Assyrian Empire and its Implications for Sennacherib's "Letter to Hezekiah" in 2 Kings. Pp. 276–314 in S. W. Holloway and L. K. Handy (eds.), *The Pitcher is Broken: Memorial Essays for Gösta W. Ahlström*, JSOTSup 190.

Kahn, Dan'el

2004 Taharqa, King of Kush and the Assyrians, *JSSEA* 31:109–128.

Lemaire, André

2003 Nabonidus in Arabia and Judah in the Neo-Babylonian Period. Pp. 285–298 in O. Lipschits and J. Blenkinsopp (eds.), *Judah and the Judeans in the Neo-Babylonian Period*, Winona Lake, IN.

Malamat, Abraham

2001 *History of Biblical Israel: Major Problems and Minor Issues*, Leiden.

2001 Josiah's Bid for Armageddon: The Background of the Judean-Egyptian Encounter in 609 B.C. Pp. 282–298 in idem, *History of Biblical Israel: Major Problems and Minor Issues*, Leiden.

Na'aman, Nadav

1990 The Historical Background to the Conquest of Samaria (720 BC), *Bib* 71:210–216.

1991 Chronology and History in the Late Assyrian Empire (631–619 B.C.), *ZA* 81:243–267.

Oates, Joan

1965 Assyrian Chronology, 631–612 B.C., *Iraq* 27:135–159.

Parpola, Simo

1980 The Murderer of Sennacherib. Pp. 171–182 in B. Alster (ed.), *Death in Mesopotamia*, Copenhagen.

Porten, Bezalel

1981 The Identity of King Adon, *BA* 44:36–52.

Rollinger, Robert

2003 The Western Expansion of the Median "Empire": A Re-examination. Pp. 289–320 in G. B. Lafranchi, M. Roaf, and R. Rollinger (eds.), *Continuity of Empire (?): Assyria, Media, Persia*, Padua.

Spalinger, Anthony

1974 Esarhaddon and Egypt: An Analysis of the First Invasion of Egypt, *Or* 43:295–326.

Stager, Lawrence E.

1996 Ashkelon and the Archaeology of Destruction, Pp. 61*–74* in *ErIsr* 25.

Stronach, David

1997 "Notes on the Fall of Nineveh." Pp. 307–324 in S. Parpola and R. M. Whiting (eds.), *ASSYRIA 1995. Proceedings of the 10th Anniversary Symposium of the Neo-Assyrian Text Corpus Project Helsinki, September 7–11, 1995*, Helsinki.

Tadmor, Hayim

1965 The Inscriptions of Nabunaid: Historical Arrangement. Pp. 351–363 in *Studies in Honor of Benno Landsberger on his Seventy-fifth Birthday, April 21, 1965*, Chicago (= Pp. 413–435 in H. Tadmor, *"With my many chariots I have gone up the heights of mountains": Historical and Literary Studies on Ancient Mesopotamia and Israel*, M. Cogan [ed.], Jerusalem 2011).

1966 Philistia under Assyrian Rule, *BA* 29:86–102 (= Pp. 633–651 in H. Tadmor, *"With my many chariots I have gone up the heights of mountains": Historical and Literary Studies on Ancient Mesopotamia and Israel*, M. Cogan [ed.], Jerusalem 2011).

2004 An Assyrian Victory Chant and Related Matters. Pp. 269–276 in G. Frame (ed.), *From the Upper Sea to the Lower Sea: Studies on the History of Assyria and Babylonia in Honor of A. K. Grayson*, Leiden.

Van de Mieroop, Marc

2004 A Tale of Two Cities: Nineveh and Babylon, *Iraq* 66:1–5.

Wiseman, Donald J.

1961 *Chronicles of Chaldaean Kings (626–556 B.C.) in the British Museum*, London.

Zawadzki, Stefan

1988 *The Fall of Assyria and Median-Babylonian Relations in the Light of the Nabopolassar Chronicle*, Poznan-Delft.

Fig. 32. Assyrian King List, Text C, obverse (Gelb, *JNES* 13 [1954], Pl. XVI).

CHAPTER 12

Assyrian and Babylonian King Lists

King lists were composed in ancient Mesopotamia as early as the end of the 3rd millennium BCE, and were compiled down until the Parthian period, two millennia later. Unlike date lists and eponym lists that served calendric purposes, king lists had no practical, everyday use. These lists likely represented the official record of the dynastic lines of rulers and kings. In the Old Babylonian Period, individual city lists were incorporated into a major historiographical work, the Sumerian King List (SKL), that surveyed the passage of kingship from city to city, until reaching the last one over which the legitimate ruler of a united Mesopotamia reigned and under whose aegis the entire list was edited, a process that produced a number of versions of SKL (Edzard 1980–1983; Glassner 2004:55–70; Vincente 1995:267–268). Though similar formulas may appear in the numerical data recorded in king lists and chronicle texts, these genres are to be distinguished; king lists are in essence date lists, in contradistinction to chronicles that, for the most part, summarized the military activity of the king year by year; for another view, see Grayson 1980–1983. Even when a king list, e.g., the Assyrian King List, includes occasional chronicle-like historical notices, these are notes concerning an irregular succession, from which one may deduce that the question of monarchic legitimacy was the goal of the composition of king lists.

Considering the ubiquitousness of King Lists in the ancient Near East—as evidenced in Mesopotamia, Egypt (*COS* 1, 68–73), the Hittite Empire (Otten 1980–1983), Ugarit (*COS* 1, 356–357)—it is reasonable to suggest that king lists were also kept in the kingdoms of Israel and Judah; such lists may have served the author of the Book of Kings in preparing his chronology of the Israelite and Judean monarchies, see Miano 2010:109–119.

No. 12.01—THE ASSYRIAN KING LIST

The Assyrian King List records the history of the Assyrian royal line from its erstwhile beginnings in the distant age of tent dwellers down to the late eighth century BCE. This composition proclaimed the antiquity of the Assyrian monarchy and the trustworthy transfer of rule from generation to generation, even through the occasional dynastic change. In its early sections, only the names of the king are given; later follow names of kings with filiation; and beginning with the reign of Shamshi-Adad I (1813–1781 BCE), fuller data, including the number of regnal years, are given. The list developed over the centuries through a number of editorial stages until it was canonized in the 13th century BCE, after which it was periodically updated; see the thorough discussion of this process by Yamada 1994.

The Assyrian King List is known from five copies (A–E), two of which (D and E) are just small fragments. Text A was written after the reign of Tiglath-pileser II (967–935 BCE), the last king whose reign is recorded. Text C continues down to the reign of Shalmaneser V (727–722). For the absolute dates of each reign, see the chronological table on p. 288.

The following selection presents the kings of the first millennium BCE and is based on a composite of three texts (A, B and C); see the score in Grayson 1980–1983:112–115. The line numbering follows Text C, the youngest exemplar. The lines separating individual reigns are on the tablets. The nub at the top of the tablet and the line of perforations were for a string, indicating that the tablet was hung, available for ready reference (see Fig. 32).

Text edition: Grayson 1980–1983:101–115; earlier Gelb 1954.
Translations: *ANET* 564–566; *COS* 1, 463–465; Glassner 2004:136–145.

col. iii

33–36 Shamshi-Adad (IV), son of Tiglath-pileser (I) came up from Karduniash (i.e., Babylonia) (and) removed Eriba-Adad (II), son of Ashur-bel-kala, from the throne. He took the throne; he ruled as king 4 years.

---

col. iv Ashurnasirpal (I), son of Shamshi-Adad, *ditto* (i.e., ruled as king) 19 years.

Shalmaneser (II), son of Ashurnasirpal (I), ruled as king [x]+2 years.

Ashur-nerari (IV), son of Shalmaneser (II), ruled as king 6 years.

5–6 Ashur-rabi (II), son of Ashurnasirpal (I), ruled as king 41 years.

Ashur-resh-ishi (II), son of Ashur-rabi (II), *ditto* (i.e., ruled as king) 5 years.

Tiglath-pileser (II), son of Ashur-resh-ishi (II), ruled as king 32 years.

10–11 Ashur-dan (II), son of Tiglath-pileser (II), ruled as king 23 years.

Adad-nerari (II), son of Ashur-dan (II), *ditto* (i.e., ruled as king) 21 years.

Tukulti-Ninurta (II), son of Adad-nerari (II), ruled as king 7 years.

Ashurnasirpal (II), son of Tukulti-Ninurta (II), ruled as king 25 years.

16 Shalmaneser (III), son of Ashurnasirpal (II), *ditto* (i.e., ruled as king) 35 years.

Shamshi-Adad (V), son of Shalmaneser (III), ruled as king 13 years.

Adad-nerari (III), son of Shamshi-Adad (V), *ditto* (i.e., ruled as king) 28 years.

20 Shalmaneser (IV), son of Adad-nerari (III), *ditto* (i.e,, ruled as king) 10 years.

Ashur-dan (III), brother of Shalmaneser (IV), ruled as king 18 years.

Ashur-nerari (V), son of Adad-nerari (III), *ditto* (i.e., ruled as king) 10 years.

Tiglath-pileser (III), son of Ashur-nerari (V), ruled as king 18 years.

26–27 Shalmaneser (V), son of Tiglath-pileser (III), ruled as king 5 years.

Colophon of Text B:

Copy (of tablet of) the city of Ashur, by the hand of Kandalanu, the scribe of the temple in the city of Arbela. The month of Lulubu, day 20, the eponym Adad-bela-kaʾin, governor of the city of Ashur, in his second eponymate.

Colophon of Text C:

According to its original, written and checked. The tablet of Bel-shum-iddin, the exorcist, (from) the city of Ashur. May Shamash carry off him (who) carries off (this tablet).

Tiglath-pileser (III), son of Ashur-nerari (V), ruled as king 18 years—This statement is contradicted by contemporary brick inscriptions from Ashur in which Tiglath-pileser is the son of Adad-nerari (III). This means that he was the brother of Ashur-nerari V. The filiation given in Text C could be a scribal error (cf. Yamada 1994:34, n. 78). For this and other copying errors, see Yamada 2003:268*–270*.

The colophon of Text B, discovered at Dur-Sharrukin (Khorsabad), relates that it was a copy of a tablet from Ashur, and that its date is 738 BCE (see the eponym in Text no. 10.01). The last entry of Text B is Ashur-nerari V, which means that the tablet had been in use, most likely at Nineveh, until it was brought, along with other reference works, to the scribes' chambers in the new capital, Dur-Sharrukin.

The provenance of Text C is unknown. Its colophon has no date; its last entry is Shalmaneser V, thus dating this copy of the Assyrian King List to the days of Sargon.

TEXT No. 12.02—BABYLONIAN KING LIST A

This king list records the names of the kings and the length of their reigns from the First Dynasty of Babylon (1894–1595 BCE) down to the beginning of the Chaldean Dynasty (626 BCE). The dynasties are separated by ruling on the tablet and a summation noting the number of kings who held the throne in each dynasty. The writer seems to have overlooked the contemporaneity of certain dynasties—perhaps he was unaware of this fact, and they are presented as successive, so that absolute dates can only be determined by comparison with other sources.

Babylonian King List A is preserved on a large tablet, with two columns on each side, broken at the top and bottom. The following excerpt, rev. col. iv, relates to the 8th–7th centuries BCE.

Text edition: Grayson, 1980–1983:90–96.
Translations: *ANET* 272; *COS* 1, 462.

col. iv

[ ]	Eriba-[Marduk]
[ ]	Nabu-shum-ishkun
[ ]	Nabu-na[ṣir]
2 (years)	[Na]bu-nadin-zeri, his son
1 month, 13 days	Nabu-shum-ukin, his son
	22 (kings), dynasty of Babylon
3 (years)	Mukin-zeri, dynasty of Shapi
2	Pulu
5	Ululaya, dynasty of the city of Ashur
12	Merodach-baladan, dynasty of the Sealand
5	Sargon
2	Sennacherib, dynasty of Habigal
1 month	Marduk-zakir-shumi, son of Arad
9 months	Merodach-baladan, a soldier of Habi
3 (years)	Bel-ibni, dynasty of Babylon
6	Ashur-nadin-shumi, dynasty of Habigal
1	Nergal-ushezib
4 (?)	Mushezib-Marduk, dynasty of Babylon
8 (?)	Sennacherib
[ ]	Esarha
[ ]	Shamash-shum
[ ]	Kandal
[ ]	Sin(?)-shum(?)-lishir (?)

22 (kings), the dynasty of Babylon—Summary of preceding dynasty. The word "kings" appears in all other summaries in this list.

3 (years) Mukin-zeri, dynasty of Shapi—Shapiya, the principal city in southern Babylonia, and goal of the Assyrian campaign in 731 (see Text no. 10.01).

2 Pulu—The shortened nickname by which Tiglath-pileser III was known in Babylonia; it was also in use in the West, cf. פול מלך אשור, "Pul, king of Assyria" in 2 Kgs 15:19 and פאל in a Phoenician inscription from Zenjirli (Kaufman 2007:20). Tiglath-pileser III was recognized as king of Babylonia for two years, from 729–727 BCE.

5 Ululaya—That is "the one born in the month of Elul," Shalmaneser V (727–722 BCE). This byname was in use in common parlance after his death as seen from the seventh-century Aramaic letter from the city of Ashur in the form אללי (*KAI*, no. 233, line 16).

12 Merodach-baladan, dynasty of the Sealand—The Sealand refers to southern marshes of Iraq and likely recalls Merodach-baladan having been a prince of the Yakin tribe settled in that area. The twelve years, 721–710 BCE, cover the period from Sargon's failed attempt to oust him until the second Assyrian campaign; see Text no. 7.01.

5 Sargon—The Assyrian Sargon II was king of Babylon between 709–705, following the ouster of Merodach-baladan.

2 Sennacherib, dynasty of Habigal—The early years (704–703) are assigned to the Assyrian king. Ḫanigalbat is a term known from the mid-2nd millennium BCE designating upper Mesopotamia.

1 month Marduk-zakir-shumi, son of Arad—A Babylonian challenger to Sennacherib. Known only from the King List; the one month falls at the end of 703, before the return of Merodach-baladan. For the suggestion to read his father's name as Arad-Enlil, see Brinkman 1964:24–25, n. 137.

9 months Merodach-baladan, a soldier of Habi—His attempt to return to the throne of Babylon was cut short in quick order by Sennacherib.

3 (years) Bel-ibni, dynasty of Babylon—A Babylonian appointed by Sennacherib, who remained loyal for three years.

6 Ashur-nadin-shumi, dynasty of Habigal—Son of Sennacherib, replaced Bel-ibni.

1 Nergal-ushezib—He, and the next king, are both referred to in the inscriptions of Sennacherib as Shuzubu.

4 (?) Mushezib-Marduk, dynasty of Babylon—The dynastic designation includes both Nergal-ushezib and Mushezib-Marduk; see the notation in Text no. 12.04, col. iv, line 9.

8 (?) Sennacherib—The eight years (689–681) are counted from the conquest of Babylon until his murder.

[ ] Esarha—A short form of the name Esarhaddon.

[ ] Shamash-shum—A short form of the name Shamash-shum-ukin, brother of Ashurbanipal, who ruled Babylon from 668–648; see Text 11.01, iv, 34–38.

[ ] Kandal—A short form of the name Kandalanu, the Assyrian-appointed ruler of Babylon after its reconquest in 648 BCE by Ashurbanipal.

TEXT No. 12.03—URUK KING LIST

The remains of a Babylonian King List, preserved on a small fragment from the middle of a tablet and written in late Babylonian script was recovered at Uruk. From the names on the reverse, it is clear that the list extended down into the Seleucid period.

Text editions: Grayson 1980–1983:97–98; earlier van Dijk;
also www.livius.org/source-content/uruk-king-list/

obv.

21 years	[*Ashurbanipal*]
At the same time	[*Shamash-shum-ukin*]
21 years	K[anda]lanu
1 year	Sin-shum-lishir
and	Sin-shar-ishkun
21 years	Nabopolassar
43 [ye]ars	Nebuchadnezzar (II)
2 [ye]ars	Evil-merodach
3 [years] 8 months	Neriglissar
[ ] 3 months	Labashi-Marduk

17(?) [years]	Nabonidus
[ ]	Cyrus (II)
[ ]	[Cambys]es
[ ]	[Dari]us (I)

rev.

second *name*	Nidin-B[el(?)]
5 [ye[ars]	Darius (III)
7(?) years	Alexander (III)
6 years	Phillip (III)
6 years	Antigonus
31 years	Seleucus (I)
22 years	Antiochus (I)
15 years	Antiochus (II)
20 [years]	Seleucus (II)

rev. 1′ **Nidin-B[el(?)]**—Otherwise unknown. He is not to be confused with the earlier Nidintu-Bel, known from the Behistun monument, who proclaimed himself to be Nebuchadnezzar III, son of Nabonidus, in his rebellion against Darius I. See Briant 2002:122.

TEXT No. 12.04—SYNCHRONISTIC KING LIST

This king list presents the kings of Assyria and Babylonia in synchronistic arrangement. The list begins with the kings of the two kingdoms in the early 2nd millennium BCE and continues down to Ashurbanipal in Assyria and Kandalanu in Babylon in the 7th century BCE. Of note is the inclusion of the names of the chief scribes from the 10th century onward, a clear indication of their privleged high rank within the monarchic administration. The purpose of the list's composition remains unclear. Nor is it is known whether there was a tradition of synchronic study over the millennia; the extant copy is written in Neo-Assyrian script and dates to the mid-7th century BCE. Though Assyria was at its imperial height, this king list text does not express an Assyrian bias, as does the Synchronistic Chronicle (Grayson 1976:157–170).

There are also a number of additional tablet fragments that preserve the names of the kings of the two kingdoms in reverse order, that is, the Babylonian kings are in the left column; in this case, no attempt was made to coordinate them synchronically. There is also a king list that does not follow the columnar fashion, rather lists in linear fashion the kings of Babylon, then Babylonian chief scribes, followed by the kings of Assyria and finally the Assyrian chief scribes. On all these lists; see Grayson 1980–1983:121–125, nos. 15–17.

The only known copy of the Synchronistic King List was discovered at Ashur; it has never been edited properly and its state of preservation is very poor. This large tablet has two sets of parallel columns on its obverse and reverse.

Text edition: Grayson 1980–1983:116–121.
Translation: *ANET* 272–274.

col. iii

1	Eriba-Adad (II), [king of Assyri]a (?)		[	king of Akkad ?]
			x [	]
	Sham‹shi›-Adad (IV)	*ditto*	Ea-[mukin-zeri	*ditto*]
	Ashurnasirpal (I)	*ditto*	Kashu-[nadin-aḫḫe	*ditto*]
5	Shalmaneser (II)	*ditto*	Ulmash-[shakin-shumi	*ditto*]
	Ashur-nerari (IV)	*ditto*	Ninurta-ku[dur-uṣur	*ditto*]
	Ashur-rabi (II)	*ditto*	Shiriktu-[Shuqamuna	*ditto*]
	Ashur-resh-ishi (II)	*ditto*	Mar-biti-[apla-uṣur	*ditto*]
	Tiglath-pileser (II)	*ditto*	[ ]-*x*-[ ]-apli	[*ditto*]
10	*ditto*	[*ditto*	Ninurta-kudurri]-uṣur [II]	[*ditto*]
	ditto	[*ditto*	Mar-biti]-aḫḫe-iddina	[*ditto*]
			[ ] [his] chief scribe	

Ashur-dan (II)	*ditto*	Shamash-mudammiq	[*ditto*]
Adad-nerari (II)	*ditto*	*ditto*	[*ditto*]
		Qaliya, [his chief scri]be	
Tukulti-Ninurta (II)	*ditto*	Nabu-shum-*x*	[*ditto*]
Gabbi-ilani-eresh		[his] chief scribe	
Ashurnasirpal (II)	*ditto*	Nabu-apla-iddina	[*ditto*]
Gabbi-ilani-eresh		[his] chief scribe	
Shalmaneser (III)	*ditto*	[	*ditto*]
[ ]*x*-ḫaya, [his chief scri]be			
[Sham]shi-A[dad (V)	*ditto*		*ditto*]

col. iv

[Senn]acherib, king of Assyria	[and Akkad (?)]
Nabu-apla-iddina, his chief scribe	[ ]
	[ ] *x* [ ] *x*
	king of Akkad. Afterwards
	the people [of Ak]kad
	revolted.
	[As]hur-nadin-shumi took the throne.
Sennacherib	Nergal-shezib, son of [Ga]ḫul
	Mushezib-Marduk, son of D[a]kkuri
	kings of Akkad.
Sennacherib, king of Assyria	and Babylonia
Bel-upaḫḫir (and)	Kalbu, his chief scribes
Esarhaddon, son of Sennacherib, king of	Assyria and Babylonia
Nabu-zeru-lishir (and) Ishtar-shuma-eresh	his chief scribes

Ashurbanipal	*ditto*	Shamash-shum-ukin	*ditto*

Ashurbanipal	*ditto*	Kandalanu	*ditto*

Ishtar-shuma-eresh, his chief scribe

82 kings of Assyria from Erishu, son of Ilushumma,
until Ashurbanipal, son of Esarhaddon.
98 kings of Akkad
from Sumulael until Kandalanu
[*x*] *xx* [*x*] *x x x x x* Nabu-tuklassu.

References

Briant, Pierre
2002 *From Cyrus to Alexander: A History of the Persian Empire*, Winona Lake, IN.

Brinkman, John A.
1964 Merodach-Baladan II. Pp. 6–53 in *Studies Presented to A. Leo Oppenheim*, Chicago.

Edzard, Dietz Otto
1980–83 Königslisten und Chroniken. A. Sumerisch, *RlA* 6:77–86.

Gelb, Ignace J.
1954 Two Assyrian King Lists, *JNES* 13:209–230.

Glassner, Jean-Jacques
2004 *Mesopotamian Chronicles*, Atlanta.

Grayson, A. Kirk
1980–83 Königslisten und Chroniken. B §3, King Lists, *RlA* 6:89–135.

Kaufman, Stephen A.
2007 The Phoenician Inscription of the Incirli Trilingual: A Tentative Reconstruction and Translation, *Ma'arav* 14.2:7–26.

Miano, David
2010 *Shadow on the Steps: Time Measurement in Ancient Israel*, Atlanta.

Otten, Heinrich
1980–83 Königslisten und Chroniken. C. Bei den Hethitern. *RlA* 6:135.

Vincente, Claudine-Adrienne
1995 The Tall Leilan Recension of the Sumerian King List, *ZA* 85:234–270.

Yamada, Shigeo
1994 The Editorial History of the Assyrian King List, *ZA* 84:11–37.
2003 Notes on the Genealogical Data of the Assyrian King List, *ErIsr* 27:265*–275*.

Fig. 33. East India House building inscription of Nebuchadnezzar II (*Courtesy of the Trustees of the British Museum*).

CHAPTER 13

Nebuchadnezzar II

Nebuchadnezzar II ascended the throne of Babylon upon the death of his father Nabopolassar and reigned for forty-two and a half years (605–562 BCE). A partial outline of his first eleven years is recoverable from the Babylonian Chronicles (Text no. 11.05); only spotty information is available for his later years from late sources.

Nebuchadnezzar defeated the remnants of Assyria and their Egyptian ally at Carchemish in 605 BCE after a long four-year struggle. With this victory, the Babylonian king had taken possession of most of the territory formerly under Assyrian control. But the attempt to carry the victory into Egypt itself failed (601 BCE). Nebuchadnezzar's "claim to fame" is his capture and destruction of Jerusalem and the temple of Solomon in 586 (cf. 2 Kgs 25:1–21). Towards the end of his reign, it seems that he undertook military actions against Tyre and Egypt, both of which seem to have ended in Babylonian setbacks; on this evaluation, see Eph^{c}al 2003.

The extant inscriptions of Nebuchadnezzar describe in detail the great efforts expended in strengthening and rebuilding Babylon; see Wiseman 1985:51–80. In contrast to Assyrian royal inscriptions, in which the king's military exploits are the central focus, Neo-Babylonian texts hark back to the rhetoric of Hammurabi and stress the divine designation of the monarch who was to rule all humanity with justice and benevolence, from a resplendent Babylon that was the center of the world; for a discussion of the Babylonian world view, see Vanderhooft 1999:9–59.

No. 13.01—CAMPAIGN TO LEBANON—THE WADI BRISA INSCRIPTION

In Wadi Brisa, north of Hermel, at the end of the Lebanon range, Nebuchadnezzar had his royal image and a lengthy inscription engraved.

The text is inscribed twice, on both sides of the mountain pass—on one side in the archaic Old Babylonian script and on the other side in the contemporary Babylonian script. This usage of the millennium-old script was not mere antiquarianism; rather it was the visible expression of historical continuity with Babylon's venerable past, a sentiment that can also be found in the adoption of Old Babylonian rhetoric in many Neo-Babylonian inscriptions. The first eight columns detail the king's deeds in Babylon and other Babylonian cult centers, and towards the end of the text, in the ninth column, before the closing hymn of praise to the god Marduk, a short historical report is given. The report is couched in the pious rhetoric of the righteous king and the facts of the incident are given in the most general terms. It tells of a successful military action in the Lebanon, undertaken against an unnamed enemy of the local population; and after securing the area, Nebuchadnezzar exported the needed cedar timber for royal construction projects in Babylon. As was the practice with most Babylonian royal inscriptions, the Wadi Brisa inscription does not contain a date. Given the large number of buildings reported to have been built, it probably dates from the later years of Nebuchadnezzar's reign; see Da Riva 2009b:20–21.

The same text as the one at Wadi Brisa was inscribed at Nahr el-Kalb, on the north slope of valley, inland aways from the seaside cliff where other cuneiform and hieroglyphic inscriptions are found and for which Nahr el-Kalb is famous. It, too, was a twin text, with the Old Babylonian copy followed by one in Neo-Babylonian; see Da Riva 2009b.

Text edition: Da Riva 2012:62–63; earlier Langdon 1912:174–175.
Translations: *ANET* 307; *DOTT* 87–88.
Photographs: Da Riva 2012, figs. i–vi.

Col. ix, 13–56

In those days, the Lebanon, [the cedar] mountain, the lush forest of Marduk, whose fragrance is sweet, the mi[ghty] cedars, planted by Anu, another god, which had not been *taken* [*for the palace of*] another king *x* [ ] *x x* . . . *x* . . . *x* My god Marduk, the king, suitable for a king's palace . . . heaven and earth, befitting r[oyalty], (Lebanon) over which a foreign enemy ruled and robbed its riches; its people had scattered and had taken to faraway places. By the strength (given me) by Nabu and Marduk, my lords, I regularly sent (troops) for [battle] to the Lebanon. I wiped out its enemy everywhere (lit., "above and below") and made the land content. I gathered its scattered

Fig. 34. The Wadi Brisa Inscription; text in archaic script (Da Riva 2012:62–63, fig. 66).

population and returned them to their settlements. What no former king had done (I did): I cut through steep mountains and I shattered mountain stone. I opened passes; I made a straight road for (the hauling of) the cedars. By the instance of Marduk, the king, mighty cedars, strong and tall, whose beauty is precious, their fitting appearance, overwhelming, the abundant yield of the Lebanon, like reeds of the river ... I *scented* (*with their aroma*) the Araḫtu canal. In Babylon, (like) poplar wood, I *set them*. I made the people of the Lebanon lie down in safe pastures, and took care that no one would disturb them. In order that no one would harm [*them*] *I set in place* an image of my everlasting kingship [...... *x* ...] I made [ ] and I [ ], I set [ ].

I wiped out its enemy everywhere (lit., "above and below") and made the land content—It is often suggested to identify this "enemy" with Egypt, which despite its rout in 605 BCE at the hands of Nebuchadnezzar at Carchemish (see Text no. 11.05, col. i, 1–8), did not give up its interests in Syria, and especially the Phoenician coast. Egypt's kings continued to instigate uprisings against Babylon; Psammetichus II even penetrated into ostensively Babylonian-held territory in 592; see Kahn 2008.

mighty cedars, strong and tall, whose beauty is precious, their fitting appearance, overwhelming, the abundant yield of the Lebanon, like reeds of the river...I *scented (with their aroma)* the Araḫtu canal—From as early as the days of the Sumerian kings in the third millennium BCE, Mesopotamian rulers boasted of having adorned their palaces and temples with mighty, sweet-smelling cedars from the mountains of Lebanon. Nebuchadnezzar describes their transport down the Euphrates and then to their final destination through the Araḫtu canal within the city of Babylon. The "cedars of Lebanon" were much desired for royal and sacred constructions throughout the Near East as far back as the mid-third millennium BCE in Old Kingdom Egypt (see *ANET* 228) and Sumerian Lagash (*ANET* 269). Assyrian kings boasted of bringing sweet-smelling cedars back from their expeditions to the west; in Israel, King Solomon imported "cedar and cyprus timber" from Tyre for the temple and palace in Jerusalem (cf. 1 Kgs 5:21–25).

I made the people of the Lebanon lie down in safe pastures, and took care that no one would disturb them. In order that no one would harm [*them*] *I set in place* an image of my everlasting kingship ...... *x* ... I made—The presence of the royal image was to serve as a reminder and a warning that the territory was under the protection of the Babylonian hegemon; see Da Riva 2009a.

No. 13.02—THE ETEMENANKI CYLINDER

Among Nebuchadnezzar's projects in restoring the glory of Babylon was the completion of the stepped tower (*ziggurrat*), Etemenanki, which stood alongside Esagil, the temple of the god Marduk (George 2011). The construction of Etemenanki inspired the biblical story of the Tower of Babel. A four-column cylinder inscription, preserved in many copies that were buried as foundation deposits within the structure of the *ziggurrat*, employs the rhetoric typical of Neo-Babylonian royal inscriptions; after the opening praise of the royal sponsor of the project, it provides information on the history of the tower and Nebuchadnezzar's pious efforts on its behalf. And like other inscriptions, it refers to requirement of subject peoples "from the Upper Sea to the Lower Sea" to mobilize workers and supply of materials. Such general statements are all that is available from Babylonian sources on the organization of the territories under its control, as administrative texts that might inform on this issue have yet to be unearthed; Vanderhooft 2003.

Text edition: George 2011:166–167; earlier Langdon 1912:146–149 (Nbk no. 17).
Translation: Da Riva 2008:12.

43–86 Etemenanki, the *ziggurrat* of Babylon, whose site Nabopolassar, king of Babylon, the father, my begetter, purified through the art of exorcism (and) the wisdom of Ea and Marduk, whose foundation he set as deep as (lit., "on the breast of") the netherworld, whose four walls he raised 30 cubits (high), with bitumen and brick on the outside. But he failed to build its top. I set my hands to raise its top (so that) it competed with the heavens. I mobilized the far-flung peoples that Marduk, my lord, had entrusted to me and whose shepherding Shamash, the hero, had given to me. All countries, all the inhabited regions of the world, from the Upper Sea to the Lower Sea, distant countries (and) far-flung peoples of the world, kings of distant mountains and far-away districts in the Upper and Lower Sea(s), whose lead-ropes Marduk, my lord, handed to me so that they pull his chariot pole, I imposed corvée on the troops of Shamash and Marduk to build Etemenanki.

87–132 Ur, Uruk, Larsa, Eridu, Kulla[b], Nemed-[Lagada], Ugar-[Sin], the entire [land of the] Lower [Sea], from its top to its bottom, Nippur, Isin, Larak, [Dilbat, Marad], Puqudu, Bit-[Dakuri], Bit-Amukani, Bit-[Shilani], Biratu, Der (?), Agade, [Dur-Sharrukin], Arrapḫa, Laḫiru, [*xxx*], all the lands of Ak[kad] and [Assyria], the kings of "Beyond-the-Ri[ver]," the provincial governors of Ḫatti, from the Upper Sea to the Lower Sea, the land of Sumer and Akkad, all the land of Subartu (Assyria), the king(s) of the distant districts in the Upper Sea (and) the king(s) of the distant districts of the Lower Sea, the city governors of Ḫatti, on the other side of the Euphrates on the west, who by order of Marduk, my lord, I rule; mighty cedars from Mount Lebanon to my city Babylon they bring. All the far-flung people of the inhabited regions of the world, whom Marduk, my lord, granted me, I set them to work building Etemenanki and imposed corvée on them.

43–86 **whose lead-ropes Marduk, my lord, handed to me**—The figure is that of a driver directing the animals pulling a vehicle by means of a rope through the nose or muzzle.

87–132 **Ur, Uruk, Larsa...**—The list begins with old cities in southern Babylonia, moves to central Babylonia, where tribal units (Puqudu, Bit-[Dakkuri], Bit-

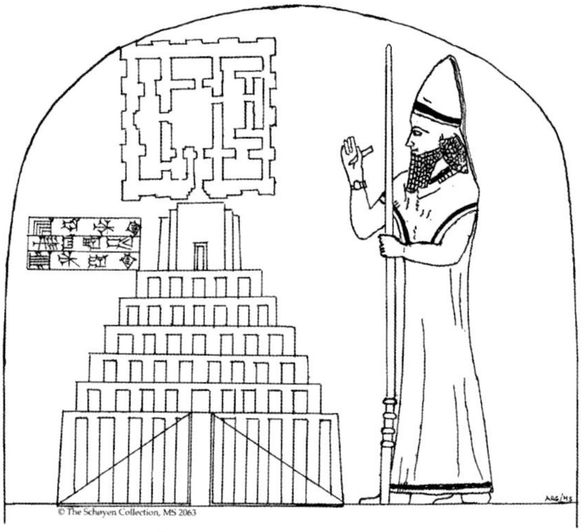

Fig. 35. Plan of Etemenanki on stele of Nebuchadnezzar II. (Reconstruction by Martin Schøyen after an original drawing by Andrew George of MS 2063. *Courtesy of The Schøyen Collection, Oslo and London.*)

Amukanni, Bit-[Shilani]) abound; from there to areas east of the Tigris and south of the Lower Zab.

the kings of "Beyond-the-Ri[ver]," the provincial governors of Ḫatti—In contrast to the detailed list of the homeland areas, two general terms are used in referring to the other territories under Nebuchadnezzar's control. These terms were in use earlier in the Assyrian imperial administration. For "Beyond-the-River," i.e., Trans-Euphrates, see further Text no. 8.02, col. v, line 40–col. vi, line 1. The north Syrian area was also known as Ḫatti. From the statement here, one may deduce that local monarchs ruled the coastal kingdoms alongside state-appointed officials, who governed Upper Syria; whether they were holdovers from the Assyrian period or newly appointed cannot be ascertained. In a roster of officials on a prism from Nebuchadnezzar's 7th year (598 BCE), only part of which is extant, the names of some of the kingdoms are known: Tyre, Gaza, Sidon, Arwad, Ashdod, all coastal maritime cities; see Da Riva 2013:217. The organization of the former kingdom of Judah during the half-century from the destruction of Jerusalem to the Cyrus declaration (586–539 BCE) is essentially undocumented, other than the failed attempt at local rule under the Babylonian-appointed governor (?) Gedaliah (cf. 2 Kgs 24:8–17).

from the Upper Sea to the Lower Sea . . .—A second description of Nebuchadnezzar's realm. This repetitious listing uses a number of traditional formulaic terms that are absent from the one before it, which may explain its inclusion here.

References

Da Riva, Rocío

2008 *The Neo-Babylonian Royal Inscriptions: An Introduction*, Münster.

2009a A note to the Nebuchadnezzar inscription of Brisa (WBC), *N.A.B.U.* 2009, no. 12:15–16.

2009b The Nebuchadnezzar Rock Inscription at Nahr el-Kalb. Pp. 255–301 in A.-M. Afeiche (ed.), *Le Site de Nahr el-Kalb, Bulletin d'Archéologie et d'Architecture Libanaises*, Hors-Série V, Beirut.

2012 *The Twin Inscriptions of Nebuchadnezzar at Brisa (Wadi Esh-Sharbin, Lebanon): A Historical and Philological Study*, AfO Beiheft 32.

2013 Nebuchadnezzar II's Prism (EŞ 7834): A New Edition, *ZA* 103:196–229.

Eph^cal, Israel

2003 Nebuchadnezzar the Warrior: Remarks on His Military Achievements, *IEJ* 2003:178–191.

George, Andrew R.

2011 A Stele of Nebuchadnezzar. Pp. 153–169 in Andrew George (ed.) with contributions by Miguel Civil et al., *Cuneiform Royal Inscriptions and Related Texts in the Schoyen Collection*, CUSAS 17. Manuscripts in the Schøyen Collection, Cuneiform Texts 6, Bethesda.

Kahn, Dan'el

2008 Some Remarks on the Foreign Policy of Psammetichus II in the Levant (595–589 B.C.), *JEH* 1:139–157.

Langdon, Stephen

1912 *Die neubabylonischen Königsinschriften*, VAB 4, Leipzig.

Vanderhooft, David Stephen

1999 *The Neo-Babylonian Empire and Babylon in the Later Prophets*, HSM 59, Atlanta.

2003 Babylonian Strategies of Imperial Control in the West: Royal Practice and Rhetoric. Pp. 235–262 in O. Lipschitz, et al. (eds.), *Judah and the Judeans in the Neo-Babylonian Period*, Winona Lake, IN.

Wiseman, Donald J.

1985 *Nebuchadnezzar and Babylon*, Oxford.

Fig. 36. The Cyrus Cylinder (*Courtesy of the Trustees of the British Museum*).

CHAPTER 14

Cyrus II, King of Persia

Cyrus II, king of Anshan (559–530 BCE), was the founder of the Persian empire. The Babylonian chronicle tablet that surveys the reign of Nabonidus, the last king of Babylon (Text no. 11.06), is largely broken and so only sparse information on the rise of Cyrus is available from cuneiform sources. Much has to be garnered from later classical sources. The key events known: Cyrus overcame the Median king Astyages and captured his capital Ecbatana (Ḥamdan) in 550 BCE; Cyrus undertook a campaign against Lydia and captured Sardis in 546 BCE, during which, according to Herodotus (1.75–84), other cities in western Anatolia were also captured; Babylon fell to the Persians in 539 BCE. Control over Syria and Israel appears to have passed into the hands of Cyrus without the need for military action, and he was recognized as the legitimate heir of the Babylonian empire. From an administrative point of view, all the territories west of the Euphrates, known as *Eber nāri*—"Beyond-the-River," became subject to the governor of Babylon. For a full survey and evaluation of this period, see Dandamaev 1989:1–65; Briant 2002:31–49.

No. 14.01—THE CYLINDER INSCRIPTION

The "Cyrus Cylinder," as it is commonly referred to, was discovered in southern Babylonia, likely at Babylon, in 1879 and is housed today in the British Museum. After the discovery of a small fragment that completed the last broken lines, the dedicatory nature of the text become clear; it was composed as a building inscription to commemorate the strengthening of Babylon's fortifications and was not doubt buried as a foundation deposit in one of the buildings that were reconstructed by Cyrus; Harmatta 1971. Until most recently, the cylinder was the only copy of the inscription known. Its uniqueness was overturned with the identification of two small fragments from a single tablet in the collections of the British Museum identified as containing a duplicate of the Cyrus cylinder; the fragments aid in completing the broken beginning and end of the inscription. It has been suggested that the "excellent script" points to tablet as being "an official copy" from which multiple copies were prepared for burial at various points about the city (Finkel 2013:18–23).

This inscription, though issued at the behest of Cyrus, is in fact a Babylonian text, composed after the conquest of Babylon in 539 BCE, in which the conciliatory policy of Cyrus towards the citizens of Babylon and its temples is affirmed. In modern terms, it might be categorized as "royal propaganda," that depicts the Persian king as the chosen one of the god Marduk, whose purpose was to save his city Babylon, which had come upon bad times under Nabonidus, Babylon's last king. This benign view of the foreign conqueror is surely the expression of the Marduk priesthood towards the "sinful acts" of Nabonidus; it justifies their apparent welcome of Cyrus, who removed the Babylonian king and returned captives to their homelands and restored "abused" cults throughout the land; see the full discussion by Tadmor 1983.

These acts in Babylon have their complement in the permission granted by Cyrus to the exiled Judeans to return to Jerusalem and rebuild their temple (cf. Ezra 1–6); see Kuhrt 1983.

Text edition: Finkel 2013:129–133; Schaudig 2001:550–556.
Translations: *DOTT* 92–94; *TGI* 82–84; *ANET* 315–316; *TPOA* 153–155; *TUAT* 1/4, 407–410; *COS* 2, 314–316; Finkel 2013:4–7; van der Spek 2014:261–263.
Photograph: Fig. 36.

1–8 [When . . . Mar]duk, king of all the heaven and earth, *x* [who] in his [ ] lays waste [*broad*] understanding [the four] quarters[ ] *offspring*, an incompetent person was installed to exercise lordship over his country *and* [. . .] he imposed upon them. An imitation of Esagil he ma[de ?], for Ur and the rest of the sacred centers, improper rituals, [ ] food off[ering *without*] reverence daily he recited. Irreverently, he put an end to the regular offerings; he [ ], he established in the sacred centers. By his own plan, he did away with the worship of Marduk, the king of the gods; he continually did evil against his (Marduk's) city. Daily, [*without interruption* . . .], he [imposed] the corvée upon its inhabitants unrelentingly, ruining them all.

9–19 Upon (hearing) their cries, the lord of the gods became furiously angry [*and he left*] their borders; and the gods who lived among them forsook their dwellings, angry that he had brought (them) into Babylon. Marduk, e[*xalted*] turned back to all the habitations that were abandoned and all the people of Sumer and Akkad who had become corpses; he was recon[ciled] and had mercy (upon them). He surveyed and looked throughout all the lands, searching for a righteous king, his heart's desire, whom he would support. He called out his name: Cyrus, king of Anshan; he pronounced his name to be king over all (the world). He (Marduk) made the land of Gutium and all the Umman-manda bow in submission at his feet. And he (Cyrus) shepherded with justice and righteousness all the black-headed people, over whom he (Marduk) had given him victory. Marduk, the great lord, who nurses his people, looked with gladness upon his good deeds and upright heart. He ordered him to march to his city Babylon. He set him on the road to Babylon and like a companion and friend, he went at his side. His vast army, whose number, like the water of the river, cannot be known, marched at his side fully armed. He made him enter his city Babylon without fighting or battle; he saved Babylon from hardship. He delivered Nabonidus, the king who did not revere him, into his hands. All the people of Babylon, all the land of Sumer and Akkad, princes and governors, bowed to him and kissed his feet. They rejoiced at his kingship and their faces shone. Lord, by whose aid the dead were revived and who had all been redeemed of hardship and difficulty, they greeted him with gladness and praised his name.

20–22a I am Cyrus, king of the world, great king, mighty king, king of Babylon, king of Sumer and Akkad, king of the four quarters, son of Cambyses, great king, king of Anshan, grandson of Cyrus, great king, king of Anshan, descendant of Teispes, great king, king of Anshan, (of an) eternal line of kingship, whose rule Bel and Nabu love, whose kingship they desire for their heart's pleasure.

22b–28 When I entered Babylon in peaceful manner, I took up my lordly abode in the royal palace amidst rejoicing and happiness. Marduk, the great lord, [allotted] me a magnanimous heart as lover of Babylon, (and) I daily attended to his worship. My vast army moved about Babylon in peace; I did not permit anyone to frighten (the people of) [Sumer] and Akkad. I sought the welfare of the city of Babylon and all its sacred centers. As for the citizens of Babylon, [ ] upon whom he imposed corvée, which was not the god's will and not befitting them, I relieved their weariness and freed them from their service (?). Marduk, the great lord, rejoiced over my [good] deeds. He sent gracious blessings upon me, Cyrus, the king who worships him, and upon

Cambyses, the son, [my] offspring, [and upo]n all my army, and in peace, before him, we moved [about].

28–36 [By his] exalted [word], all the kings who sit upon thrones throughout the world, from the Upper Sea to the Lower Sea, who live in the dis[tricts far-off], the kings of the West, who dwell in tents, all of them, brought their heavy tribute before me and in Babylon they kissed my feet. From [*Babylon*] to Ashur and Susa, Agade, Eshnunna, Zamban, Meturnu, Der, as far as the region of Gutium, the sacred centers [on the other] side of the Tigris whose sanctuaries had been abandoned for a long time, I returned the gods to the places where they (once) resided and I had them dwell in eternal abodes. I gathered all their inhabitants and returned (to them) their dwellings; and the gods of Sumer and Akkad, whom Nabonidus, to the anger of the lord of the gods, had brought into Babylon, at the command of Marduk, the great lord, in security I settled in their habitations, in pleasing abodes. May all the gods whom I settled in their sacred centers daily ask of Bel and Nabu that my days be long and may they intercede for my welfare. May they say to Marduk, my lord: "As for Cyrus, the king who reveres you, and Cambyses, his son, [ ] they [ ]." The people of Babylon praise (my) reign. I settled all the lands in peaceful abodes.

37–45 [ ] I increased the offerings [to] geese, two ducks and ten turtledoves above the (former offerings) of geese, ducks, and turtledoves [ ]. I sought to strengthen the [construction (?)] of the wall Dur-Imgur-Enlil, the great wall of Babylo[n]. [ ] The bricks at the bank of the ditch, which a former king had built, but had not completed its construction [ ], on the outside, which no former king had made, a levy of [his land] from Babylon, [with bitumen] and bricks, I built anew and [*completed*] its [*construction*]. [*doors of cedar*] overlaid in bronze, thresholds and pivo[ts *cast in copper I fixed at*] their [doorways]. [An in]scription of Ashurbanipal, a king who had preceded me [I sa]w [*within it*]. [to] its pl[ace]. Marduk, great lord, grant me [long] li[fe, the fullness of old age, a stable throne and long-lasting re]ign. [ ] in your heart for eternity.

Colophon on tablet: [Written, che]cked. Tablet of Qishti-Marduk, son of [ ].

* This translation updates and replaces the one I presented in *COS* 2.

1–8 **An incompetent person was installed to exercise lordship over his country**—This is one of several examples of the vilification of Nabonidus in which he is accused of having appointed an unworthy person to rule (i.e., Belshazzar), and abandoning Esagil, the temple of Marduk in Babylon, in favor of the temple of Sin in Harran; see the satirical poem on this same subject in *ANET* 312–315.

9-19 **Upon (hearing) their cries, the lord of the gods became furiously angry [*and he left*] their borders; and the gods who lived among them forsook their dwellings, angry that he had brought (them) into Babylon**—Divine wrath at man's behavior is a common motif in ancient Near Eastern history writing (Albrektson 1967:98–114), and is invoked here to explain Marduk's actions against Babylon in transferring rule to Cyrus. Among the works employing this rationale are the Sumerian "Lamentation over the Destruction of Sumer and Ur" (*COS* 1, 535–539); the Hittite "Plague Prayers of Murshili" (*COS* 1, 156–160); the stela of Mesha, king of Moab (*COS* 2, 137–138); and numerous instances in the Bible, e.g., "Then the Lord was angry with Israel, and He handed them over to their enemies who plundered them" (Judg 2:14); "The Lord was angry with Israel and He handed them over to Hazael, king of Aram and Ben-hadad, son of Hazael, for many years" (2 Kgs 13:3); "The Lord vented all His fury, poured out His blazing wrath; He kindled a fire in Zion which consumed its foundations" (Lam 4:11); see also Text 6.05.

He surveyed and looked throughout all the lands, searching for a righteous king, his heart's desire. . . And he (Cyrus) shepherded with justice and righteousness all the black-headed people—Other non-Babylonians saw themselves as having been chosen by Marduk to treat the people of Babylonia with justness, e.g., the Chaldean Merodach-baladan (Text no. 7.01) and the Assyrian Sargon (*ARAB* 2, § 31).

He called out his name: Cyrus, king of Anshan—For this title, see Nabonidus Chronicle (Text no. 11.06, col. ii, line 1).

He pronounced his name to be king over all (the world)—The selection of Cyrus by Marduk may be compared to the declaration of the Israelite prophet living in Babylonian exile, who said of Cyrus: "Thus said the Lord to Cyrus, His anointed one—whose right hand he has grasped, treading down nations before him, ungirding the loins of kings, opening doors before him and letting no gate stay shut" (Isa 45:1; also 44:28).

He (Marduk) made the land of Gutium and all the Umman-manda bow in submission at his feet—The reference is to the Medes. Gutium and Umman-manda were traditional literary designations for the mountain peoples; see Text no. 11.03, line 38.

28–36 **[By] his exalted [word], all the kings who sit upon thrones throughout the world, from the Upper Sea to the Lower Sea**—From the Mediterranean to the Persian Gulf.

Who live in the dis[tricts far-off], the kings of the West, who dwell in tents, all of them brought their heavy tribute before me and in Babylon they kissed my feet—Indeed, Cyrus had won recognition of his rule in a decade of military engagements in all the territories to the north and west of Babylonia.

From [Babylon], Ashur and Susa, Agade, Eshnunna, Zamban, Meturnu, Der, as far as the region of Gutium—All the major cities and holy centers to the north and northeast of Babylon were to be restored.

I returned the gods to the places where they (once) resided and I had them dwell in eternal abodes—This is a succinct statement of the Persian policy of toleration of the varied cultic expressions within its empire. A further example of this is the permission granted the exiled Judeans living in Babylon to rebuild the temple in Jerusalem. Biblical tradition records that Cyrus proclaimed: "The Lord God of Heaven has given me all the kingdoms of the earth and has charged me with building Him a house in Jerusalem which is in Judah. Anyone of you of all his people—may his God be with him, and let him go up to Jerusalem that is in Judah and build the House of the Lord God of Israel, the God that is in Jerusalem" (Ezra 1:2–4; cf. 2 Chr 36:22–23); and see the discussions of Tadmor 1983; Kuhrt 1983.

37–44 **[An in]scription of Ashurbanipal, a king who had preceded me [I sa]w**—During the construction work, an inscription of the Assyrian king Ashurbanipal was discovered, apparently buried in the wall at the time of its earlier repair. One often finds, as the concluding statement in a royal inscription, the request that a future ruler, who may come upon the inscription, respect it and return it to its site, for which the gods will reward him.

References

Albrektson, Bertil
1967 *History and the Gods*, Lund.

Berger, Paul-Richard
1975 Der Kyros Zylinder mit Zusatzfragment BIN II Nr. 32 und der akkadischen Personennamen in Danielbuch, *ZA* 64:192–234.

Briant, Pierre
2002 *From Cyrus to Alexander: A History of the Persian Empire*, Winona Lake, IN.

Dandamaev, M. A.
1989 *A Political History of the Achaemenid Empire*, Leiden.

Finkel, Irving (ed.)
2013 *The Cyrus Cylinder*, London.

Harmatta, J.
1971 The Literary Pattern of the Babylonian Edict of Cyrus, Acta Antiqua Academiae Scientiarum Hungaricae 19:217–231.

Kuhrt, Amélie
1983 The Cyrus Cylinder and Achaemenid Imperial Policy, *JSOT* 25:83–97.

Schaudig, Hanspeter
2001 *Die Inschriften Nabonids von Babylon und Kyros' des Grossen*, AOAT 256, Münster.

Tadmor, Hayim
1983 The Rise of Cyrus and the Historical Background of His Declaration. Pp. 5–16, 253–255 in *The Restoration—The Persian Period. World History of the Jewish People*, Tel-Aviv (Hebrew). (English translation: pp. 835–859 in H. Tadmor, *"With my many chariots I have gone up the heights of mountains": Historical and Literary Studies on Ancient Mesopotamia and Israel*, M. Cogan [ed.], Jerusalem.)

van der Spek, R. J.
2014 Cyrus the Great, Exiles, and Foreign Gods: A Comparison of Assyrian and Persian Policies on Subject Nations. Pp. 233–264 in M. Kozuh, et al. (eds.), *Extraction and Control: Studies in Honor of Matthew W. Stolper*, Chicago.

Fig. 37. Stelae fragments from Ashdod (left) and Samaria (*Israel Antiquities Authority*).

APPENDIX

Royal Inscriptions from the Land of Israel

The expansion of the Assyrian empire was marked by the concomitant spread of the royal stelae, the visible symbol of Assyrian rule, to conquered territories throughout the ancient Near East. Whether free-standing or engraved on mountainsides, these monuments were more than expressions of self-aggrandizement by the Assyrian monarch; they served as ever-present reminders for the local populations of the hegemon who resided in distant Nineveh to whom fealty was due.

The Land of Israel came under direct Assyrian control in the late 8th century BCE, and like other lands, it became the home for royal stelae. The earliest reference to this practice is reported in inscriptions of Tiglath-pileser III who erected a stela at the border of Philistia: "My royal stela in the city of the Wadi of Egypt, a river[-bed without water...I set up"] (Text no. 4.07, line 18). This stela of Tiglath-pileser has not been found, but fragments of other stelae have been recovered, mostly in archaeological excavations; a few have come to light as chance surface finds. In all cases, the majestic form of the monuments did not protect them from the elements and the passage of time, for all of them were most certainly torn down and demolished with the retreat of the empire.

The following survey of the remains of royal stelae according to find site draws upon the comprehensive collection of all cuneiform finds from Israel by Horowitz and Oshima 2006.

1. SAMARIA. Samaria was conquered by Sargon II in 720 BCE and resettled in the following years with deportees from various lands (see Text nos. 5.01–5.03). A single fragment of a stela was discovered at Samaria. The remains of eight lines, with only single words on six of them (e.g., "] locusts [ ] dust-storm ["), are insufficient for identifying the text. But it stands to reason that the stela was set up after the fall of the city to the Assyrians. See Horowitz and Oshima 2006:115 (Samaria 4).

2. ASHDOD. Three fragments were discovered in two separate locations at the site of ancient Ashdod. From the measurement of the height of the letters and the variations in script, it appears that they are all that remains of two different stelae. Ashdod 2 and 3, from Area A, are too fragmentary for identification; Ashdod 4, from Area G, preserves the remains of five lines that belong to the description of Sargon II's eastern campaigns. These stelae were likely erected sometime during the years that the Assyrian army was engaged in restoring order in Ashdod. See Horowitz and Oshima 2006:40–41 (Ashdod 2–4).

3. QAQUN. This fragment of a royal stela was found out of context in a pile of rubble and is still unpublished. From the contents of the lines, it can be identified as coming from a stela erected by Esarhaddon on his return from his conquest of Egypt. See Horowitz and Oshima 2006:111 (Qaqun 1) and above, Text no. 8.05, note to rev. 1–19.

4. BEN SHEMEN. A small fragment of a stela, found out of context by a hiker in the Ben Shemen forest. It may be part of the stela of Esarhaddon found at Qaqun. The few remaining words, "Egypt," "governors," "Ashur and the [great g]ods," seem to have been part of the description of the reorganization of Egypt after its conquest. See Horowitz and Oshima 2006:45 (Ben Shemen 1); Cogan 2008.

Photographs: Fig. 37.

References

Cogan, Mordechai

2008 The Assyrian Stela Fragment from Ben Shemen. Pp. 66–69 in M. Cogan and D. Kahn (eds.), *Treasures on Camels' Humps. Historical and Literary Studies from the Ancient Near East Presented to Israel Ephᶜal.*

Horowitz, Wayne and Takayoshi Oshima

2006 *Cuneiform in Canaan: Cuneiform Sources from the Land of Israel in Ancient Times*, Jerusalem.

Glossary

Frequently Used Terms and Titles

Accession Year—Akkadian *rēš šarrūti,* "beginning of reign." The period of time from the king's ascending the throne until the next New Year celebrated in the month of Nisan. This period is not counted in the total number of regnal years of the king.

Akitu—The Babylonian New Year's festival celebrated in the spring (Nisan) with a procession of the gods to the *Akitu* temple. The Babylonian Epic of Creation (*Enuma Eliš*) was read and the god Marduk proclaimed king of the gods. During the ceremonies, the earthly king was reinstalled for another year. See *ANET* 331–334.

Eponym—Akkadian *limmu,* "circle, turn." The person by whose name the Assyrian year was counted. Persons of rank, including the king and provincial governors, served as eponyms in more or less a fixed order for a single year. Similar systems were in use in some Greek city-states and in Rome (the consular calendar). See further in chapter 10.

Rabshakeh—Akkadian *rab šāqê,* "the chief cupbearer." The royal cupbearer, one of the senior Assyrian courtiers, was sometimes sent on military missions; cf. 2 Kgs 18:17.

Tartan—Akkadian *turtānu,* "deputy, second-in command." The commander-in-chief of the Assyrian army. His high rank at court earned him the eponymate immediately following the king. Cf. 2 Kgs 18:17; Isa 20:1.

The offices of Assyrian court officials are discussed by R. Matilla, *The King's Magnates: A Study of the Highest Officials of the Neo-Assyrian Empire,* SAAS 11, Helsinki 2000.

Ceremonial Names of Mesopotamian Temples

Ebabbar—Sumerian é.babbar, "Shining House." The temple of Shamash and Aya in Sippar.

Egidrukalammasummu—Sumerian é.gidar.kalam.ma.sum.ma, "House which Bestows the Scepter of the Land." The temple of Nabu of the *ḫarû* in east Babylon.

Ekur—Sumerian é.kur, " House, Mountain." The temple of Ninlil at Nippur.

Esagil—Sumerian é.sag.íl, "The house whose Top is High." The temple of Marduk in Babylon, destroyed by Sennacherib and restored by his son Esarhaddon.

Esharra—Sumerian é.šár.ra, "House of the Universe." The temple complex of the god Ashur in the city of Ashur.

Eturkalamma—Sumerian é.tùr.kalam.ma, "House, Cattle-Pen of the Land." The temple of Belet-Babili (Ishtar of Babylon) in Babylon.

Ezida—Sumerian é.zi.da, "True House." The temple of Marduk, later of Nabu, at Borsippa.

Ḫursagkalamma—Sumerian (é).ḫur.sag.kalam.ma, "(House), Mountain of the Land." The temple of Ishtar at Kish.

Concerning Mesopotamian temples, their location and histories, see A. R. George, *House Most High: The Temples of Ancient Mesopotamia,* Winona Lake, IL 1993.

Chronological Tables (9th–6th Centuries BCE)

1. Kings of Assyria

Ashurnasirpal II	884–859
Shalmaneser III	859–824
Shamshi-Adad V	824–811
Adad-nerari III	811–783
Shalmaneser IV	783-773
Ashur-dan III	773–755
Ashur-nerari V	755–745
Tiglath-pileser III	745–727
Shalmaneser V	727–722
Sargon II	722–705
Sennacherib	705–681
Esarhaddon	681–669
Ashurbanipal	669–627
Ashur-etil-ilani	627–623 ?
Sin-shum-lishir	?
Sin-shar-ishkun	623 ?–612
Ashur-uballiṭ II	612–609

2. Kings of Babylonia: The Chaldean Dynasty

Nabopolassar	626–605
Nebuchadnezzar II	605–562
Evil-merodach	562–560
Neriglissar	560–556
Labashi-Marduk	556
Nabonidus	556–539

The dates of the kings of Assyria and Babylonia are reckoned from their accession year. The native Mesopotamian practice was to count the king's first year of reign from his first full year following the accession, which began in Nisan (= March/April). John A. Brinkman in A. Leo Oppenheim, *Ancient Mesopotamia* (rev. ed.; Chicago 1977), Appendix, Mesopotamian Chronology of the Historical Period, 335–348, follows the Mesopotamian practice.

3. Kings of Egypt

25th (Cushite) Dynasty

Alara	?
Kashta	?–753
Pi(ᶜankh)y	753–721
Shabaka	721–707
Shabatka	707–690
Tirhakah	690–664
Tanatamon	664–656

26th (Saitic) Dynasty

Psammetichus I	656–610
Neco II	610–595
Psammetichus II	595–589
Apries	589–570
Amasis II	570–526
Psammetichus III	526–525

4. Kings of Judah and Israel

Judah		**Israel**	
Asa	908-867	Baasha	906–883
		Elah	883–882
		Zimri	882
		Tibni	882–878**
		Omri	882–871
Jehoshaphat	870–846*	Ahab	873–852*
Jehoram	851–843*	Ahaziah	852–851
		Jehoram	851–842
Ahaziah	843–842		
Athaliah	842–836	Jehu	842–814
Joash	836–798		
		Jehoahaz	817–800*
		Jehoash	800–784
Amaziah	798–769		
Azariah	785–733*	Jeroboam II	788–747*
Jotham	759–743*	Zechariah	747
		Shallum	747
Ahaz	743–727*	Menahem	747–737
		Pekahiah	737–735
		Pekah	735–732
Hezekiah	727–698	Hoshea	732–724
Manasseh	698–642		
Amon	642–640		
Josiah	640–609		
Jehoahaz	609		
Jehoiakim	609–598		
Jehoiachin	597		
Zedekiah	597–586		

* Includes years as co-regent

** Rival rule

INDICES

A. INDEX TO CITATIONS FROM THE HEBREW BIBLE, CLASSICAL SOURCES, AND THE MISHNAH

B. INDEX TO DIVINE NAMES

C. INDEX TO PERSONS

A

O

P

Q

R

S

D. INDEX TO GEOGRAPHICAL AND ETHNIC NAMES

A

B

C

D

L

M

T